6, 12, 1,
Placidus

Essence and Application: **A View from Chiron**

T. ♀ is ⚹ my 10 ☿   1 ½° no more
⤳ feel it!

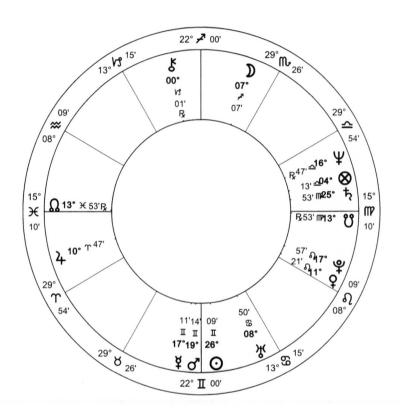

ZANE B. STEIN
born 17 June 1951, 11:43:17 PM EST, 75 W 09' 31", 40 N 02' 43"

This book is published by

Centaurean Astrology
Zane B. Stein, 16 Bottrill St, Hamilton Hill 6163
Western Australia

On line at
http://www.zanestein.com/chiron.htm

ISBN 978-1-933303-44-4

Distributed by
Astrology Classics
The publication division of
The Astrology Center of America
207 Victory Lane, Bel Air, MD 21014
On line at http://www. **AstroAmerica**.com

Essence and Application:
A VIEW FROM CHIRON

by

Zane B. Stein

Expanded to include the text of Zane B. Stein's
historic lecture to the Guild [1979]
and his pamphlet
Interpreting Chiron [2nd Edition 1985.]

Astrology Classics
Bel Air, Maryland

TABLE OF CONTENTS

Section Two: The Application

THANK YOU (1995)

This book has gone through a number of printings (incarnations) since it was first published ten years ago. In that first edition I gave thanks to a long list of people who had, in one way or another, been of assistance in my research and/or my writing.

In May of this year, my publisher and friend, Al H. Morrison, passed away. Without his being there, this book never would have gotten off the ground, nor would it have been published in the second, and third editions. So, more than anyone else, I want to thank Al for everything. (This volume should properly be labeled the Fourth Edition, but Al had several covers left in his apartment for the third edition, and it seemed a shame to waste them.)

I also want to dedicate this book to him. Al, I miss you every day.

I also want to thank all the members of the A.S.C., and to everyone through the years who has sent in observations and research on Chiron. Next, another big 'Thanks!' to all my friends who have given me their support and encouragement. I especially want to thank all of the astrologers I have met over the Internet; if not for their encouragement, this volume would not have been printed.

Here is a list of some other people I wish to thank:

LYNETTE MALONE STEIN

VINCE YOUNG

DEBBI KEMPTON-SMITH

NEIL MICHELSEN

JIM LEWIS

SANDY BENNETT

And, most important, I want to thank God for being there to answer my prayers, and for giving me the strength to finish this book.

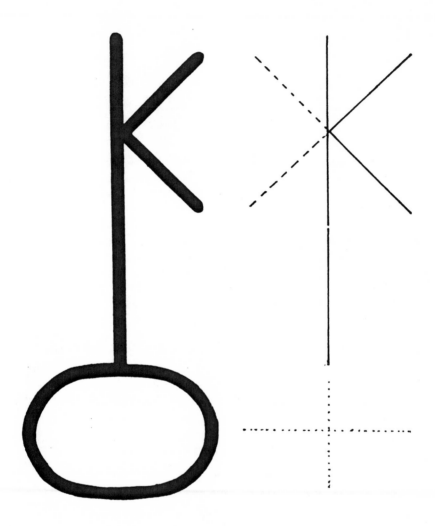

This is a facsimile of the original Chiron glyph, reduced in size.

Note the half-hidden perfect X cross pierced by the vertical staff. The sections of the staff are in subtle proportional sequences with the arms of the crosses, and with each other. The width and length of the horizontal loop (variant of orb) are in Golden Section relation, and in sequential proportions with the other elements of the glyph.

An Appreciation
by Debbi Kempton-Smith

This is a marvelous book — fun, sparkling, seriously useful, absolutely necessary, and wholly original.

But *Essence and Application: A View From Chiron* turns out to be more than that. Its author, Zane Stein, has produced an historic, breakthrough book of heroic scholarship. It has changed the game, blown the field wide open, and forever altered the ways we look at the wondrous art/science/ language we call astrology.

How Zane conducted his research, and *what* he decided to study — a weird, just-discovered, hard-to-classify celestial body — has launched us, via his hard work and a disturbing surprise, through the gateway into a hugely expanded world of modern astrology.

What makes Zane's book so bracing is his method, or, as he puts it, 'How I learned to stop assuming and start searching.'

The story of Chiron is well known: in the autumn of 1977, at Palomar observatory in California, an astronomer, Charles Kowal, discovered a new celestial body in our solar system. What is not so well known is what happened next: Zane Stein speedily produced an ephemeris for this new celestial discovery, with encouragement and help from his (and my) great friend and mentor, the astrologer and publisher Al H. Morrison.

What followed was a brilliant bit of scholarship and high-speed derring-do: Zane and Al carefully designed and carelessly (on purpose) distributed hundreds of copies of a Chiron survey to astrologers and their clients. The objective was to gain as much insight into the workings of Chiron in horoscopes in as little time as possible.

Astrologers around the globe pitched in. They interviewed clients, friends, family and strangers to complete as many Chiron surveys as possible. Subjects were asked to report events that correlated with transits of Chiron to their natal Suns, Moons, Venuses, Ascendants, etc. Other questions asked people to recall significant experiences first, and then to check to see if Chiron was making angles, and if so, which ones, at significant times. Progressions and solar arc directions were also included.

These first-hand testimonies and reports, along with decades of new

Chiron observations, give Zane's book a richness and texture rarely found in astrological work. There is subtlety here, a cornucopia of impressions and perceptions, that rub along nicely with Chiron's tendency to produce real events and life-altering decisions.

Back in the Eighties, behind the scenes, a bitterly contested race to form the symbol ended when *The American Ephemeris'* publisher, Neil F. Michelsen, added Chiron and its key-like (or Kowal-like) symbol to all new editions. Chiron would now be on the map.

Meantime, many moons waxed and waned, and in the long, awful, historic tradition of genius unappreciated, Zane's book remained self-published. I trotted this masterpiece around Manhattan — in the snow! — to mainstream publishing houses. The bigs do not like to take chances on astrology beyond Sun-Signs for pets or sex, it seems. And the little guys rarely have the brains or vision to back a virtuoso, or, perhaps, to even recognise one.

Then, on 9 May 1990, astronomers at Kitt Peak observatory in Arizona confirmed that Chiron was, in fact, a 'dirty snowball' — astronomers' slang for comets. Chiron was — and is — not a planet. Not. A. Planet. Not even close. All that work - on a comet!

Oops.

Yet meticulous research had revealed Chiron as an influencer of the first order in horoscopes and the art of forecasting. The evidence was irrefutable. Planet, schmanet, gasball, dustball, iceball — every orbiting object asks to be studied.

That's Chiron for you. 'An inconvenient benefic'— Al called it. Lucky for us it kicked us in the head in 1990. Five years later, the first exoplanets, planets orbiting other suns, showed up.

Now we have 700-odd exoplanets and counting, and asteroids, plutinos, cubewanos, Oort objects, IMPS (icy Mini Planets), SDOs (Scattered Disc Objects) and our new pals Eris, Sedna, Pholus, Makemake, Chaos, Quaoar, and more. The implications for astrological research are immense.

Zane and a handful of pioneering astrologers are looking at them, too.

In the past, ideas about new planets were a matter of wishful thinking, if not outright fantasy. A planet's name and its creaking mythological legend were all astrologers needed to start spinning theories. No serious, *immediate,* methodical attempts were made to understand planetary influences. Watching and observing a new celestial body takes years. For 21st century astrologers, this isn't good enough. .

I once wrote that 'Zane Stein is a national treasure', and I meant it. But Zane has since moved to Australia. Now he is an international treasure, and perhaps, by rights, an intergalactic treasure. You may never have had the pleasure of knowing or meeting Zane. Perhaps you never even heard of him until you learned about this book. But he is, and has been, more than any living astrologer I know, a towering intellectual force in shaping modern astrology.

Now, at last, Zane Stein's masterwork is published well, by a visionary publisher, our good friend Dave Roell. The long years — too many! — of intellectual injustice are over. His new publisher calls Zane's book 'the best writing on aspects I've ever come across', and he should know.

You hold in your hands a book of breath-catching scholarship, a ground-breaking part of history. You will not find a book like it anywhere, before or later, in this, or in any other galaxy. Thank you, Zane Stein. Thank you, Dave Roell.

Debbi Kempton-Smith
Islamorada, Florida
11 November 2011

Debbi Kempton-Smith is the author of *Secrets From A Stargazer's Notebook: Making Astrology Work For You* (Topquark Press, 1999)

Note to the Third Editon of 1988
by Al H. Morrison, *the first publisher of this book:*

Zane B. Stein is the Bobby Fischer of astrology. About the time of his clear and dramatic victory as world's champion in Chess, Bobby Fischer enjoyed a religious re-birth. After that he retired from all participation in chess, never defended his title.

Just as the second edition of this book, *Essence and Application — A View from Chiron* was coming onto the market, Zane Stein withdrew from all astrology, in his on-going religious rebirth.

Since all copyrights to all his astrological works have been formally assigned to CAO TIMES, the happy thought has occurred to us that the thing to do is gather all of his public presentations within a single cover, this Third Edition.

It should be noted that Zane Stein responded within hours of the discovery announcement, and achieved a fluent cooperative exchange of information, data, and suggestions with Dr. Brian C. Marsden at the Minor Planet Center, Smithsonian Institution Astrophysical Observatory. All of the fees paid to Minor Planet center for computation were paid by Al H. Morrison, from his own resources. An example of the correspondence is presented here (page A-13) in reduced facsimile.

Beginning with the generous encouragement from Dr. Marsden, going on with Maria Bianco's conversion of his RA/decl. ephemerides into long./lat. values, the distribution of the world's first information on Chiron by the Guild, CAO, and CAO TIMES, the recognition of Chiron as an astrologically major planet is just now beginning.

We now have extremely accurate ephemerides computed from the most recent high-tech astrophysical observations by Dr. Green at Minor Planet Center [10-day positions], Eve Gregory, [daily positions], for the present century, plus the Early Chiron Ephemeris beginning in 1490 by Mark Pottenger.

This Third Edition of Zane B. Stein's formal writings on Chiron, subsumed under his final title, is a sort of crystal, completed, finally edited, the first of its kind, a base for more study of Chiron.

Al H. Morrison

SMITHSONIAN INSTITUTION
ASTROPHYSICAL OBSERVATORY
60 GARDEN STREET   CAMBRIDGE, MASSACHUSETTS   02138
TELEPHONE 617 495-7000

1978 July 28

Mr. Zane B. Stein
~~201 W. Maple Street~~
Ambler PA 19002

Dear Mr. Stein,

Thankyou for your letter of July 25 and money order. I enclose
ephemerides of (2060) Chiron back to 1890, which is about as far as I
can reasonably go. There are slight discontinuities at the ends of
each ephemeris, but I think these can be smoothed out without too
much trouble.

The discovery of the Plutonian satellite must, I think, still be
regarded as tentative, but if the satellite should be confirmed, Pluto
is indeed less massive than almost any astronomer has previously
surmised. It is of course possible that further more distant planets
exist, but I doubt that any are particularly massive, and I do not think
one need postulate their existence in order to explain any possible
irregularities in the orbits of Uranus and Neptune.

I noted the remarks about Chiron in Newsletter 8 of the Congress
of Astrological Organizations. You are of course at liberty to choose
a symbol for Chiron if you wish, but I wonder why astrologers should
be interested in Chiron when they ignore the much larger (and closer)
minor planets. We have classed Chiron as a minor planet, giving it the
number 2060 in the series in which 1 refers to the largest minor planet,
Ceres.

Yours sincerely,

Brian G. Marsden

BGM/cv

INTRODUCTION to the First Edition

I am both a Christian and an astrologer. Long before I discovered that my Sun-Sign is Gemini, I had a deep faith in God. So whatever insight I receive from astrology, I believe comes from The Creator, who put the planets in the heavens.

When I first began to research Chiron, it rapidly became clear to me that this little body was His Hand at work. Many of the myths about Chiron parallel the life of Christ. Chiron people are searching for universal truths that last long after Saturnian rules decay with age. Chiron is related to the concept of 'first cause.' And, it is a major factor in healing the sick.

Data on Chiron have been arriving in massive doses, from all over the world, ever since I formed the Association for Studying Chiron in 1978. And every new piece seems to support the premise that God revealed Chiron to us at the present time, to heal mankind, before we push ourselves to annihilation. But, as I said, the data are massive. In 1983, I published a pamphlet entitled INTERPRETING CHIRON, in which I attempted to give the reader a handle on how to utilize this new little planet. [That pamphlet should be used as a companion to this book.] While this pamphlet was well received, [the second edition has now been translated into German and French], I was not content, for there were so many things left unsaid.

In January, 1984, there was a Jupiter-Neptune conjunction at 0° Capricorn—right on my natal Chiron. I came to the realization that what I really wanted was to unify the various themes that had been surfacing into one holistic view of Chiron. But, how ?

Through the next several months, the answer slowly came to me. In November, 1984, when my natal Chiron was again being transited by Neptune, I began seriously organizing my data, my ideas, and getting one book after another out of the library—books on astrology, the immune system, health, psychology, and every other subject I could think of. I went on an intensive read- in. And, on the Winter Solstice, when the Sun was $0^\circ 01'$ Capricorn, I began to write this book.

With full awareness that Neptune was pushing me to describe the whole picture, I decided to try and tie all the pieces together by approaching Chiron from all different directions. This became SECTION ONE: THE ESSENCE.

Then, a good friend and excellent astrologer from Philadelphia, Zulma

Gonzalez, asked me to write a thorough analysis of Chiron and the aspects. This became the core of the second section, THE APPLICATION, and the rest just seemed to write itself.

I am a Chironic astrologer. You won't find that word in the dictionary, but there are quite a few of us, and our number is increasing day by day. We are astrologers who believe that discovering the truth is more important than personal theories, and also that we should always keep our minds open to the ideas of others.

Therefore, please do not take this book as the final word on Chiron. After all, the little body was only discovered in 1977—and we have so much more to learn. In fact, you are welcome to disagree with things on these pages. I only ask, if you do, that you back it up with data, or at least with logic. Since I am more interested in discovering Chiron's true nature than in my words being taken as gospel—I welcome any insights that you may have, no matter how different they may be from mine.

By the time you finish reading this book you will know even more about what a Chironic astrologer is. Perhaps you, too, may like to become one. Who knows, perhaps you already are.

Zane Stein

INTRODUCTION to the 1995 edition:

Many things have been discovered about the solar system in the ten years since the first edition was published. Some of these discoveries include:

Chiron is now viewed by most astronomers as the largest periodic comet in the solar system, 10,000 times the mass of Halley's Comet. In 1992, a body similar in many respects to Chiron was discovered, and was named Pholus, after another Centaur. These two bodies have since been linked with a few other recently discovered bodies, (at this writing it includes 1993 HA2, 1994 TA, 1995 DW2 & 1995 GO), and the category is listed as the Centaurean objects (although Chiron is still the most significant one). The same year that Pholus was discovered, an asteroid was found that was soon named Heracles. (Heracles was the demi-god responsible indirectly for Chiron's famed wound, and Pholus' accidental death). And of course, there have been a multitude of bodies discovered out past Neptune and Pluto, with many scientists theorizing that this is where the Centaurean bodies came from.

We are now approaching Chiron's Perihelion (closest approach to the Sun) and Perigee (closest approach to the Earth) in 1996. So I wanted to include the exact data on these events for you. Plot the charts for your location, and see how they relate to you. How did Chiron's 1945 close approach interact with your chart — even if your were born afterwards. How will you be Chironized by the next one?

According to Dave Tholen, the exact times (Eastern Standard Time) of these close approaches in 1945 & 1996 are:

Year	Perihelion	Perigee
1945	Aug. 29, 7:57 am	Mar. 22, 5:19 pm
1996	Feb. 14, 1:35 pm	Apr. 1, 2:38 am

On another subject, I need to respond to those who are curious why I dropped out of astrology in the 1980's, and why I returned in 1992.

In the 80's, I was dating a girl who's brother was a very devoted Christian. The longer I was with her, the more involved I became, and soon found myself totally immersed in the study of Christ. At this point, my perception of astrology was, not that it was evil, but that it was unnecessary because one could commune with God without it.

In 1992, I met and fell in love with a remarkable woman who soon made me realize how empty my life was without astrology to study. While still a Christian, I realized that astrology was a way to better understand God's handiwork, including the purpose he has in mind for each one of us.

The woman's name is Sandra, and her Venus is less than half a degree away from exact conjunction with my Chiron. And when I met and fell in love with her, transiting Chiron was conjunct my natal 6th house Venus (of course, we met at work.)

This book, with some minor changes, is essentially the same as the previous edition. The most significant changes are: More noted people have been added to the Chiron aspect section; the EPHEMERIS of Chiron in the back has been updated; the text is now spiral bound with a new cover.

I am working on a new book on Chiron, which will, I hope, continue where this one left off. Don't ask me for an estimated date when it will be finished; I guarantee you that it won't be until after Chiron's perihelion. But it WILL explore Chiron's relationship with Pholus, and the other Centaurean bodies.

While there is no longer an A.S.C., I still welcome your Chiron discoveries. Drop me a note, and tell me how Chiron has influenced your life. I'll try to answer every letter.

Chronically,

Zane B. Stein

INTERPRETING CHIRON

Copyright 1983 by Zane Stein   2nd Edition 1985

Chiron was discovered in 1977, and already we know a great deal about it — more, in fact, than we knew about Pluto only a few years after its discovery. But in order to really understand Chiron's nature it must be viewed in relation to what other discoveries were made around the same general period of time. For, while Chiron definitely has a unique meaning, it is also part of a large picture of changes which are occurring in mankind's awareness.

In March of 1977 the world was astonished by a new discovery about the planet Uranus. Now Uranus has always been a shocker. In 1781 it startled the world simply by being discovered. For thousands of years Saturn was viewed as the final body — the absolute limit. Its rings were viewed as representing the limitations that Saturn stood for. So, when Uranus was found, it totally destroyed the existing pictures of the solar system. Upon further research its very motion proved unconventional, for it was found to revolve in reverse motion in comparison to the other planets, and also to have its axis inclined at an angle almost ninety degrees from the angle of the axes of the other planets. Even its moons were named unconventionally — after Shakespearean characters instead of after mythological beings. It was thought to have absolutely nothing in common with the planet Saturn.

But in that fateful March, RINGS WERE DISCOVERED AROUND URANUS! Saturn no longer had a monopoly on them, and now, the two planets had something very definite in common. Thus Uranus shocks again. What do they have in common? They both teach lessons of responsibility and concern for the future; they are both concerned with time (Saturn with bringing the past into the present, Uranus with bringing the present into the future); and they both have to do with self-definition (Saturn defining one's limits, and Uranus pointing the way to one's individuality). The fact that we now know that both have rings indicates that we now realize (or should realize) that the principles of both are inter-connected; that too much of one is just as bad as too much of the other; that when we go too far into Saturn, Uranus must come and bring about a balance (and visa versa); and that they are both necessary steps in the

1

process of one's evolution.

Once the rings were discovered, the way was paved to discover Chiron, and this was done by astronomer Charles Kowal on November 1, 1977. Chiron was found to orbit between Saturn and Uranus!!! Its orbit was also found to be highly elliptical, even more so than Pluto. At aphelion (that is, when furthest from the Sun), Chiron actually reaches the orbit of Uranus. Even more interesting is the fact that at perihelion (closest to the Sun) Chiron crosses Saturn's orbit and thus comes closer to us than Saturn ever does! Thus Chiron is found to act as a link or bridge between the two major planets, swinging back and forth between them once every cycle (which varies from 49 to 51 years, by the way). Now we can see why it was necessary for the rings of Uranus to be found first, so that we could appreciate the linking process that Chiron represents.

The third major piece of the puzzle was discovered in the following year. Pluto, which previous to Chiron had held the distinction of having the most elliptical orbit of all the major planets, was suddenly found to have a moon. This did drastic things to our perception of the size of Pluto: Pluto was suddenly MUCH smaller than previously thought! Some astronomers were beginning to wonder if it should be demoted in status from major planet to planetoid! In fact, had its actual size been known in the 1930's when it was discovered, it is possible that astrologers would have ignored it totally, considering that anything that small, so far out, could not possibly have an influence.

But we all know just how powerful Pluto is. It would be difficult to imagine not including it in charts today. Thus Pluto's moon (called Charon, by the way), was verification that even a small body has powerful influences. And thus it made it much more plausible for Chiron, which is the size of a large asteroid, to have the influence of a major planet.

One more thing about Pluto. Dr. Brian G. Marsden, of the Smithsonian Institution's Astrophysical Observatory, has suggested that a special category be devised and a new name invented for the Orbit-crossers. They would not be classed as planets, or asteroids, or comets, but would be unique with this class. The members of said class would be Pluto (which crosses the orbit of Neptune), Chiron (which crosses the orbit of Saturn), and Hidalgo (previously called an asteroid, but which crosses the orbit of Jupiter). Hidalgo, incidentally, is also being studied. It has a 14 year-year orbit so ties into Saturn (7 x 4), Chiron (7 x 7) and Uranus (7 x 12).

So, with the above frame of reference related to you, I now want to begin describing Chiron's specific meanings as they have surfaced so far. Obviously we are only beginning to understand Chiron since it was discovered so recently. But the results of current research suggest certain themes repeatedly. I will, repeatedly, refer to Chiron's relationship to Saturn and Uranus as described above, and to its relationship to Pluto and Hidalgo.

KEYWORDS

The most potent keyword representing Chiron is MAVERICK. This word came from Samuel A. Maverick, an American pioneer and rancher, who did not brand his cattle (unlike the other ranchers around him). The word came to mean one who takes a stand apart from his associates; an independent individual who refuses to conform to his own group; one who does not align himself with any party, faction or particular stand; one without the mark of the herd branded into his side as it is in his contemporaries. Mavericks may make enemies among those who do belong to some particular group, for those people may feel, "If you are not with us, you are against us." Yet as far as the Maverick is concerned he is neither for or against their principles. This is where Chiron differs from both Saturn and Uranus. Saturn wants to uphold tradition, and defend traditional beliefs. Saturn creates an "us-or-them" division. Uranus wants to break down the old, often to the point of being an iconoclast. Uranus can easily get the urge to "blow up" the very structure of the group. But Chiron, the MAVERICK, neither defends nor overthrows the establishment. Rather, it is apart from it.

HEALING and WHOLEMAKING are Chiron words. When one has an imbalance (too much or too little of something), one needs to rectify the situation as soon as possible. If not it can lead to health problems, either physical, emotional or even spiritual. If one is closed off one may be keeping oneself from becoming whole by not even being aware of whole other worlds out there to explore and make one complete. Saturn can be a wall which keeps us protected from whatever is outside yet also isolated from new experiences and necessary growth. Saturn can produce stagnation or an impasse. On the other hand, Uranus can represent a new world waiting on the other side of the wall, but if the person refused to open to it Uranus can become a devastating force destroying the wall and really wrecking havoc with one's health. Then one must rebuild, if one can, and it can be slow and painful. But Chiron is a KEY, opening a door in Saturn's wall, allowing us to enter through the doorway into Uranus' world so that we can discover what we need to heal us or make us whole without abruptly removing all of Saturn's protection. It may be that it removes something from our lives so that the impasse no longer exists. It is almost always a time which we look back on and say, "It was a real turning point." The Chiron wholemaking can bring experiences and trials which enable

3

us to counsel others when we have been through them. One can say that, due to Chiron's tendency to emphasize either Saturn or Uranus (whichever is under emphasized), its healing brings change when there is too much stability and stability when there is too much change. When Chiron comes, new world open up or old doors close forever.

Chiron represents COMMON GROUND. Let us view the walls of a house as Saturn and everything outside as Uranus. With the doors and windows shut tight someone in the house can have no knowledge of what is going on outside the walls. And someone who is outside not only has no knowledge of what is inside, but unless he can find a key to the door, the only we he can get into the house is to break in. However, if the door is unlocked and opened, someone from within can get out and explore, while someone outside can come in, without in any way damaging the walls of the structure. Thus if you think about it, the DOORWAY itself is common ground. Once the door is opened, it allows access in both directions, so you can say that the doorway itself belongs to both Saturn and Uranus, or to neither.

When one is born, one's parents are preoccupied by certain problems that they feel *must* be solved, difficulties and obstacles that *must* be overcome, and these problems are made quite clear to the child as it grows up. The sign in which Chiron falls at any given time represents what the current preoccupation of the parents is, and thus, it shifts whenever Chiron enters a new sign. However, for the child who was born while the parents worried over the obstacles produced by a particular Chiron transit, the desire to overcome these obstacles does not fade when Chiron changes signs. Instead, it has become a PERSONAL IMPERATIVE, staying with the child all his life. He grows up feeling that these problems are always high priority, that nothing must stand in the way of resolving any difficulties which arise in these areas, and that the difficulties represented by Chiron's sign are those that everyone should consider important as well. Within the area (by sign and house) that is influenced by Chiron, the person believes that no wall, obstacle, rule or regulation is truly important enough to stop him from resolving a problem, thus in these areas he will be most likely to go beyond Saturn if necessary, or ignore Saturn if he has to.

Through time and experience Chiron soon becomes the need to search for a meaning to life that is deeper than that represented by Jupiter, more durable than Saturn, and that will last in spite of the changes brought about by Uranus. It can become a personal QUEST, as a person searches everywhere for something that will be meaningful throughout all time and in every place. It thus represents NOW, the link between the past and the future, and will show a concern to bridge any gap that exists between these two. And, as the person

4

begins to discover life's deeper meanings, Chiron represents the TEACHER who desires to pen new worlds for others and instill in others the same spark to want to learn, and to want to begin their own quests. It can also be expressed as the desire of the parent to open worlds for the child, or as any person who acts to prepare a child to face the world, thus any foster parents.

It is time beyond chronological time. Chiron = CHIROS, timeless time, when ordinary clock time ceases to have meaning. It is in these moments when major decisions are made and when some of the most creative work is done. There appears to be a connection between Chiron and the period of time known as Void-Of-Course-Moon, as well.

And Chiron represents a TURNING POINT, which can seem either good or bad at the time, but is definitely remembered as a period when one's life changed direction in some way, or had to adjust to some new circumstances. Usually one remembers this as a time when a new world opened, or when some door closed which forced one to look in a new direction and thus avoid stagnation in some way.

Some things are kept in line by a system of checks and balances. This system keeps things from growing too fast, or too large, or possibly it keeps things working together so that they do not fall apart. If one part of the system goes bad or is found to have been bad all along, the whole system may be looked upon as suspect. Temporarily the checks and balances may break down, resulting in uncontrollable growth or expansion, or breaking apart. Chiron can be this PULLING THE PLUG or REMOVING THE DAM, and initially it can seem that there is no way to put a brake on whatever was unleashed. But Chiron has a specific purpose in removing the restraint. As human beings we tend to rely too heavily upon a system once we find that it works. Chiron comes along and reminds us that no system is perfect. But unlike the planet Uranus, Chiron does not destroy the whole system. It calls our attention to some weak spot, or to the way in which we are relying too heavily upon it. By correcting this we soon find that we can return to the system of checks and balances again, although (hopefully) we will be much wiser this time.

What is more, when the plug was pulled we had the opportunity to learn a great deal more about the true nature of whatever was unleashed. Thus we now have the knowledge to make much better use of it, and to TAP its power. This period is a great teacher. If we are good students, we find we have a great deal more power in our own life now which we can turn on and use, almost like turning on a faucet.

And Chiron represents LOOPHOLES, enabling one to get around the system, instead of being imprisoned by it.

RULERSHIP

This has not been decided. In fact there seem to be several different views on this, each with its own group of 'believers.' But much research has yet to be done to establish this with any degree of certainty. The views so far: Libra; the whole region of Scorpio-Sagittarius; Sagittarius; Gemini; Virgo; the Libra decanate of Aquarius; and of course, no sign at all. Personally, I feel (from the evidence so far) that Chiron has the most in common with the higher side of Libra, but I will reserve any final judgement. Oh, one other view was submitted: that in the age of Aquarius, Chiron will rule *Tropical* Sagittarius but *Sidereal* Libra, for those two will coincide!

TRANSITS

A good idea of Chiron-transits can be achieved by reading the Keyword section. However, a few points must be discussed here. Chiron seems to bring both difficult AND easy situations by transit, whether the aspect is a conjunction, trine, square or other. It will, more often, bring a door-opening to a person, unless in aspect to Mars or Saturn. Then it seems to more often bring a door-closing and the need to look beyond one's present environment. Although it is possible that it has an influence a few degrees away, I have not noticed any manner of influence from its transits when they were more than 3° away, and clear, distinct events only when within 1½° orb.

To me the most interesting Chiron transits are the aspects it makes to its own natal place. First of all, Chiron has a *very* eccentric orbit. It is in Libra for only about 1¾ years, yet it stays in Aries for over 8¼ years. This process produces drastic differences, depending on Chiron's sign, as to when it makes its first aspect to the natal position.

Now with Saturn the astrological literature is filled with articles about how Saturn-to-Saturn aspects divide mankind's life into regular sections of about seven years each (Saturn being so regular in its orbit that you can tell without an ephemeris approximately what part of its cycle someone is in simply by asking his or her age.) For example, first transit of Saturn square natal Saturn happens to *everyone* at about 7 years of age, and first opposition around age 14. Thus you can define what stage mankind is in at any time by Saturn's aspects. You could use them to describe the archetypal human life.

But with Chiron the story is different, drastically different. A person with Chiron in early Virgo will have the first square (with Chiron in early Sagittarius) when he is only about 5½ years of age. Yet a person who was born when Chiron was in early Pisces will not experience the first square (when Chiron transits early Gemini) until he is past 23 years old! What a drastic difference. And with the other Chiron signs, the square occurs at various ages between these two extremes. Think of the ramifications and permutations. A 5½ year old is still a child, his personality is still being formed (most scientists say that the personality is formed by about age 7, in other words, by the time of the first Saturn square), he is still living totally under the influence of his parents or other adults, he has seen almost nothing of the world, and has not even seen one whole Jupiter cycle yet! On the other hand, a person past the age of 23 is an adult and has been considered so by society for a few years already, his personality has been long formed, in most cases he no longer lives with his parents, is probably self-supporting, possibly married for a few years already. He has already seen transit Saturn square, opposition and again square his natal Saturn, is soon to see his second Jupiter return, and has already experienced transit Uranus square natal Uranus! What a drastic difference. How differently must one be influenced by the first Chiron square depending on what age one is when it occurs.

To give you a clearer picture of how drastic the age difference is, look at the chart. Across the bottom you will find each sign. Find the sign your own Chiron is in, for example. Then up and down the left of the graph are the ages for the first Chiron square. So after you have found the column for your sign, run your finger up until you find the graph line, then look for the age to the left of that point. If you know whether your Chiron was early or late in its sign you can be more specific as to age. For example, I have Chiron at 0°01' Capricorn, which means the first square occurred at a little past 17 years of age. My wife has Chiron at 18°51' Capricorn, so the first square for her was about 19½ years of age. My sister has it at 13°37' Leo, so she was only 5½ when Chiron made its first square.

What does all this mean? Well the first square is a major lesson which brings the turning point, a new world opens up to you, or something new will come into your world. The exact nature of the event depends on the natal house, the house the transiting Chiron is in, and of course, other planets which are involved at that time. A few examples may help to shed light on this.

THE VERTICAL COLUMN ON THE LEFT REPRESENTS THE AGE WHEN CHIRON MAKES ITS FIRST SQUARE TO ITS NATAL PLACE

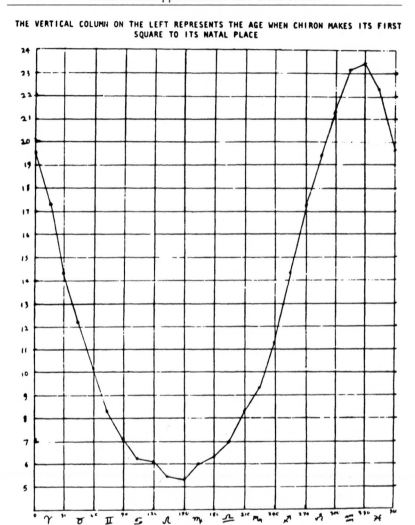

CHIRON'S SIGN POSITION

1. A very shy introverted person with difficulty communicating with others (yours truly as a child) had Chiron in Capricorn in the tenth house. At the time of my first square I was informed that since I was #3 in my graduating class in high school, and therefore Salutatorian, I had to give a speech at graduation. I had never talked to a large group before, and never had given any kind of speech. I was terrified, but went ahead, and got through it. My self-confidence grew. My ability to communicate grew with it.

Due to retrograde the square happened twice more. The second time I suddenly found myself, for the first time, living away from home at a college, making my own hours, meeting people, cultures and philosophies I had never dreamed of. The final time I changed my major from botany to psychology. This was major because I had wanted to be a botanist since age 7!

II. One person with Chiron in Leo in the fifth found that, at the time of her first square at age 5½, her parents moved her to a new neighborhood. In her old neighborhood she had been an ordinary person but now she was made fun of and 'picked on'. She began to make friends with others who were also 'underdogs', and feels that it was for this reason that she has always felt that she has more in common with the underdogs in life.

III. A person with Chiron in Capricorn in the fourth met her fiancee when Chiron in her seventh made its first square. At the retrograde square they discovered that he had terminal cancer, but married anyway. At the third square his sickness became very severe and he died shortly thereafter.

IV. A person with Chiron in Libra in the second received a present from her parents at age 7 when Chiron made its first square: a piano. She later became a music teacher.

Also, the exact nature of the Chiron turning point depends upon one's age. For those Chiron-signs who make a first square before the first Saturn square, the Chiron lesson must be learned first, in order that the Saturn lesson be truly understood. This is a small group, as you can see by the graph, from Cancer to mid-Libra. However you define the first Saturn square, it IS the first real test to one's reality structure; it marks the first real awareness of the concept of time. Since Chiron denotes non-chronological time, perhaps people with these Chiron positions must discover "Chiros" before Chronos so that the latter does not fit them into too tight a mold.

From age 7 to 14, and thus AFTER the first square of Saturn but prior to the first opposition, we have a large segment of the population: Chiron in Taurus and Gemini, and then also mid-Libra to mid-Sagittarius. All of the people born with these positions need a basic ground in Saturn's view of reality and time before they can take a look at Chiron's Chiros, yet they must get a glimpse of Chiron's doorway into another world before the Saturn opposition Saturn brings their first confrontation with the reality structures of their peers. Perhaps without the Chiron square these people would be unable to get truly beyond their own world enough to deal with other people at age 14.

9

From age 14 to 21, and thus between the opposition and second square of Saturn, we have Chiron in Aries, and then mid-Sagittarius through Capricorn. These people need the confrontation with the reality of others before they can begin to appreciate that any other world exists beyond their own.

Finally we have the age 21 to 23½ group; past the second Saturn square, with only the Saturn return awaiting them before they have experienced the entire Saturn cycle. These people need as much Saturn influence as possible before they are ready to look through the doorway into another world, or to experience another kind of time. Perhaps because the rulers of Aquarius (Saturn/Uranus) and Pisces (Jupiter/Neptune) are on either side of Chiron, or perhaps because Uranus and Neptune teach of things that are way beyond Saturn's earthly structure and material viewpoint, these positions for Chiron need an extremely thorough, extensive grounding in Saturn before the Chiron square so that the people don't get carried away into totally irrelevant directions.

Anyway, it is important to note that ALL Chiron positions have their first square BEFORE the Saturn return, and thus all people need to understand that there are things beyond their own reality before they can begin to build their own reality, separately from the past, at the Saturn return.

And of course transit of planets to one's natal Chiron are also quite significant. They are times when you can use the energy of the transiting body to cross over into uncharted areas, or accomplish something you have wanted to do for a long time, or when unusual circumstance arise giving you an opportunity to do something outside the normal routine. Sometimes a transit of a planet to your Chiron coincides with an event that brings a major change in areas of life that are ruled by the house Chiron occupies.

A few examples of transits to natal Chiron's:

Mars - an individual won an argument with someone for the first time — someone to whom he had lost arguments for years Mercury — when it passed over my tenth house Chiron I received a letter from my father from California (he lived in Pennsylvania so the postmark surprised me). Inside was the news that my father's mother had died and my parents had flown to California for the funeral, but they did not have the time to let me know before they could catch the plane. Also inside was a note that they had made me the beneficiary of the flight insurance, which made me a bit nervous.
Venus - an individual begins to teach astrology to a girl. What is so unusual is the fact that, a few years earlier, she had been more knowledgeable about the subject than he, and was the person who had gotten him involved in

the first place.

Jupiter - an individual with Chiron in the tenth decided to search all around his neighborhood for the best prices on food and found that they existed in a store he had totally avoided before because he had not liked the outer appearance of the store.

Jupiter - when Jupiter crossed my tenth house Chiron my first set of business cards arrived from a mail-order printer. Also on that day I was called upon to help calm down an individual by explaining to him that he should not feel guilty for becoming paralysed with fear while being a witness to a crime; I was truly able to help him get back to everyday life.

HOUSE POSITIONS

The house position of Chiron denotes a number of things. It points to major lessons one must learn after one has learned the lessons of Saturn. It points to an area where one can best focus the energy of the Saturn/Uranus midpoint, even if it makes no aspect to this midpoint. The affairs of this house have a element of "NOW!" to them; when a problem arises here you cannot wait until later to resolve it and nothing must stand in your way when you are trying to overcome obstacles here. This house is where the greatest focus for healing and wholemaking lies. By using the positive energy of this house once can help heal problems arising in the whole being. The people represented by this house are of a special import to you; you feel that, at least in the areas and affairs represented by this house, you have something in common with everyone. And therefore you find it easiest, in this house, to relate to the common man as opposed to some "special interest group." In this house one is most likely to hold a maverick viewpoint, to believe in ideas which do not fit in with the accepted view, yet not be interested in tearing down the accepted view either. AND, Chiron can act like a doorway to the basic energy force of the house itself, enabling you to tap the particular power inherent in the house, and use it almost without limit or restriction (if you have first learned the lessons of Saturn which relate to that house). Finally, events in this house often do not fit any previously described set of conditions or rules; often they have a nature totally unrelated to any previous experiences which their associates may have had.

Some possibilities should be considered, but have not been researched as yet:

The specific meaning of Chiron in a house may be altered depending upon what part of its orbit Chiron is in. For example when Chiron is in Libra, it is at its closes point to the Sun, and can actually cross Saturn's orbit. Does its

11

proximity to Saturn give it a different meaning in a house than when it is in, say, Aries, which is the sign Chiron occupies when it is closest to the orbit of Uranus? It has already been observed that world events are colored by Saturn or Uranus, whichever planet Chiron is moving closer to. For example, from 1920-1945, and currently since 1970 (until 1996), Chiron has been moving closer and closer to Saturn. We have seen the current cry for a return to traditional values, the reversal of a number of decisions made in the liberal '60s, the increasing demand for law and order. In the first period we had the rise of men like Hitler, and recently the rise of those like the Ayatollah Khomeini. On the other hand, look at 1945-1970 with Chiron moving gradually toward Uranus.

CHIRON IN HOUSES

First House: This person orients himself to the universe in a way that goes beyond any particular path, established viewpoint or structured life-style. The first impression this person gives is that he cannot be categorized. He looks familiar sometimes, but you cannot put your finger on the reason. The eyes have a look about them as if the person were from another dimension, a stranger in a strange land. There is a refusal to let any obstacle interfere with the pursuit of his personal growth. If some such obstacle exists, he goes through it as if it did not, or tries to. Overcoming obstacles and resolving problems, in fact, is one way this person discovers himself. He believes he has something in common with everyone he meets and that all people should also have that belief. In the developed type there is a special knack for opening doors for others and a desire for all people to exist on the same level, thus a hatred of inequality. Unless there are serious aspects to the contrary, these people are dynamic, radiating energy, and tend to be quite disarming. Their integrity is usually beyond question (unless the rest of the chart drastically disagrees). There is a strong "loner" quality to their personal lives, even though they may deal with people all the time. They often have the ability to get around the system, the unique ability to see beyond what others see, and often have a "wild" look in their eyes which makes them quite attractive.

Norman Mailer, Rollo May, Mercedes McCambridge, Dan Rather, John Scali, Mike Schmidt, Anne Tyler, Archie Griffin, John DeLorean, Uri Geller, Rex Harrison, R.D. Laing, Vincent Price, Burt Reynolds, Rennie Davis, Kareem Abdul-Jabbar, Gregg Allman, Vida Blue, James Arness, Steve McQueen, Wilt Chamberlain, Huey P. Long, James Stewart, Marshall Tito, Adelle Davis, Joseph Alioto, Rosie Greer, Pete Townshend, Sally Fields

Second House: Once these people become aware of what direction they are going in life they have the ability to draw upon unimaginable resources.

Their desires are extremely powerful and they truly feel that nothing should stand in the way of the gratification of those desires. On a lower level there is a desire to control friendships and relationships. There is an ongoing search for people whose personal values are the same as theirs, and their attitude toward money and possessions is quite unique. There are lessons to be learned about money, possessions, values, and other forms of personal resources, but once they have learned these there is often a need to help others who are poor or needy in some way. They are capable of total immersion in their work to the point where they become extremely skilled in one specific field. This position also gives them inventiveness, often a good deal of technical skill, and an increase in management ability. Once they have found something they truly value, or something they feel is truly worthwhile, they take it quite seriously and it provides them with a great sense of personal power and an air of authority. Usually they are quite observant. There also seems to be a great attraction for all eighth house affairs such as power, sex and the occult. Unless other things point to the contrary they are usually "cool and calm".

William Lipscomb, Marsha Mason, Kate Millett, Walter Mondale, Jack Paar, James Wyeth, Marjoe Gortner, Mick Jagger, Mike Love, Cat Stevens, Alice Cooper, David Bowie, Johnny Weissmuller, Bobby Fischer, Malcolm Dean, Benjamin Disraeli, Anthony Armstrong Jones, Jean Claude Killy, Sandy Koufax, Bela Lugosi, Henri Petain, Max Schmeling, Leopold Stokowski, Arturo Toscanini, Pearl S. Buck, Barry Goldwater, Eva Braun, Don Ameche, Kenneth Berquist, Karen Black, Craig Breedlove, Garth Allen, "Mean" Joe Greene, John Updike, James Daly, Diane Feinstein, Lauren Hutton, Sally Struthers, Sharon Tate

Third House: Unless other things point to the contrary, there is an innate belief (which goes back to childhood) that all things are possible. Relationships of all kinds are always on these people's minds. In the lower type the sense of humor is very "pornographic" (dirty-minded), which stems from the importance of relationships. No matter what social level they are on they have an ability to think like, and communicate with, the common man. Even the people who have elevated their minds are usually noted for their good sense of humor. Basically they are of a liberal bent, often libertarians. They allow no limitations to stand in the way of their mental processes, and they let their thoughts roam everywhere, even to the taboo. In fact their logical minds are not confined to logic; they are very closely linked to their emotions, their instincts, and other areas; and their emotions are very easily aroused. Usually mental experimenters with fast minds, they tend to be mentally versatile, often controversial in thought and word, usually straightforward, possessed of a unique writing style, and often talkative.

13

Xaviera Hollander, Hugh Hefner, Larry Flynt, Gypsy Rose Lee, Jean Cocteau, Beverly Sills, Paul Newman, Robert Redford, O.J. Simpson, Clarence Lillehei, Roger Morton, George Steinbrenner, Casper Weinberger, Steve Cauthen, Phil Donahue, James Taylor, Arlo Guthrie, Algernon Swinburne, Joan Crawford, Betty Davis, Arthur Rimbaud, Ethel Merman, Dr. F. Regarde, Jean Paul Sarte, Robert Cummings, Betty Friedan, Erma Bombeck, Steve Allen, Ray Bradbury, Sigmund Freud, Alan Watts, Fritz Perls, Edgar Degas

Fourth House: These people feel a very strong tie to humanity. They feel deeply inside that they share common roots with all mankind and therefore have something in common with all people. There is usually a powerful desire to uplift others either mentally, emotionally or spiritually, and there is a powerful sympathy with the "little man", the common man, who can be victimized by larger groups and corporations. These people don't want to start anything they feel might fail, for to them failure is failing mankind, not just themselves. The want to enlighten others, to build a world where everyone is treated equally, to bring joy to everyone they meet. But their powerful insecurity surfaces if they feel they have failed — they "can't fail!" If other things in the chart are unstable, this is a prime position for suicide when they feel they have failed. Also these people are extremely upset when things are going on without their knowledge, or when things are going on which exclude them, or exclude someone they know. Theirs is a deep feeling that the whole world is a family; this gives them a strong community spirit. There are two basic types: the extremely undervalued type, often shy, tense and nervous, whose fear of failure has kept him back somewhat; and the "tough under fire" type who receives great respect, is quite popular, and is comfortable being controversial. Both types like to work!

Ken Kesey, Henry Lewis, Mickey Lolich, James Lovell, Marie McCarthy, Patricia Neal, William Rehnquist, Donna Summer, Helen Hayes, John Lindsay, Joan Baez, Carmen Delavallade, Bradford Dillman, David Carradine, Arthur Godfrey, Ernest Hemingway, Lenny Bruce, Herman Hesse, Oscar Wilde, Dr. Sam Sheppard, Albert Speer, Vincent Van Gogh, Paul Goebbels, Hal Holbrook, Elton John, Karl Krafft, Troy Perry, Clifford Odets, Zubin Mehta, Mark Goodson, Walt Disney, John Denver, Ralph Nader, Jerry Reed, Robert Kastenmeier, Toulouse-Lautrec, Bonnie Franklin, Red Skelton, John Voight

Fifth House: These people want to be exclusively what they are; they don't want their creativity to be influenced by anyone else. They tend to be uninhibited and temperamental, and there is frequently an "anything goes" attitude in the way they express themselves. The less evolved types have

14

reputations for loose morals or as playboy types. No rules govern their creativity, and their style is totally their own. These people have a certain something that lives on after they die. There is something so totally unique about them that people know who you are talking about when you mention this quality, mannerism or creation. These people have major lessons to learn through children and/or lovers, and these lessons will change their whole lifestyle, once learned. They often add a whole new career after pursuing one career for many years, yet frequently keep the old one as well. They have a strong competitive streak, lots of enthusiasm for their field, and if they need to train for something they train hard. Many are known for their sharp or caustic wit. There is often a strong bent toward trying to create a totally realistic style. They are true defenders of self-expression and freedom of thought, unless other things point to the contrary.

Eartha Kitt, George Lucas, Ross McDonald, Burgess Meredith, Kenneth Patchen, Valerie Perrine, Richard Pryor, Philip Roth, Shirley Temple-Black, Sarah Vaughan, Merle Haggard, Jules Lenier, Oscar Levant, Henry Miller, Chris Reeves, Arnold Schwarzenegger, Phoebe Snow, Ringo Starr, Simon Wiesenthal, Jacques Cousteau, John Derek, Barbara Streisand, Pierre Renoir, Bertrand Russell, Jean Harlow, Frank Sinatra, Melina Mercouri, Maria Callas, Tyrone Power, Rock Hudson, Robert Goulet, Art Arfons, Groucho Marx, Ruth Buzzi

Sixth House: These people have unique health problems. Often what seems to help others does nothing for them, or does the opposite of what it was meant to do. But health is a dominant concern for them. If these people come to terms with their own health problems there is often a strong desire to help others in the medical field. They are hard-working people, determined, with a sense of duty and self-responsibility. They pay a lot of attention to detail and often develop unique skills at some craft or handicraft. Whatever they decide is the best avenue for their skills, they want to be as expert and perfect as possible, and hate being restricted to any category within their field. They want freedom to try any and all techniques that may perfect their skills and enable them to best do the job. Most of these people are shy and introverted as children. Often they are poor or indifferent students in spite of the fact that they have high intelligence. As adults they are often brooding, withdrawn, and leaning toward pessimism or realism; very few optimists have this position. They often appear as cold, aloof and into their own private worlds. Unevolved types consider everyone as either inferior or superior to themselves. Two reasons for the previous two sentences are: they fear the ending of any relationship because it is extremely painful to them so they are afraid of getting too closely involved with anyone; and they have great lessons to learn in the way of service, and until these are learned, they fear not knowing how much of themselves to give (the fear of being used), so they may appear to be selfish. But when they overcome these fears they can be the most giving, helpful and healing types.

Mia Farrow, James Goddard, Joel Grey, Alan Leo (opposition Asc.), Janet Leigh, Daniel Nathans, Robert Wagner, Jackie Onassis, Bob Hope, Ingrid Bergman, Gwendolyn Brooks, Geraldine Chaplin, Francis Ford Coppola, Jimmy Carter, A. E. Housman, Lous Pasteur, Maurice Ravel, Auguste Rodin, Joanne Woodward, Rita Hayworth, Lana Turner, Errol Flynn, Katherine Hepburn, Eleanor Bach, Stephen Crane, Sir William Crookes, Dr. Tom Dooley, Dennis Weaver, Clint Eastwood, Dustin Hoffman, Billy Rose, Martin Sheen, Cathy Rigby, John Knowles, Paul McCloskey, Liza Minelli, Pierre Salinger, Bruce Springsteen.

Seventh House: These people don't like having to deal with people in any set pattern or order; theirs is, typically, a non-discriminatory approach dealing with others. But their need for contact with people is powerful, and especially contact with the opposite sex. Co-operation, however is difficult, and competitiveness is strong, especially with members of the same sex. They need to be seen as "just as good as" anyone else, and especially as good as anyone else in their own fields. Often high-strung, but almost always good in a debate, they are unyielding in their arguments. Many are strongly opinionated, and most have a crusading "urge". They are controversial, aggressive, often sharp tongued, usually loquacious and candid. The ability to improvise is strong. They are often flamboyant and have skill at clowning around. The family is usually very important. If they marry, it always opens up new worlds for them. Their enemies are always of a unique type and they find it hard not to have at least a few. They hate to get involved in any kind of party machinations, if they are in politics, and usually end up going against the machine or totally destroying it, thus becoming THE power.

Adlai Stevenson, Wendell Wilkie, John Anderson, Earl Warren, Richard Nixon, Fidel Castro, Benito Mussolini, Arthur Schlessinger, John Mitchell, Hamilton Jordan, Upton Sinclair, Redd Foxx, Brian Keith, Dennis Hopper, Kurt Russell, Yvette Mimieux, Susan St. James, John Cage, Eleanor Clark, Woody Herman, Ray Davies, John Entwhistle, Richard Basehart, John Barrymore, George Moscone, Carl Sandburg, Albert Schweitzer, Princess Grace of Monaco, William Blake, Rudolph Valentino, Mary Pickford, Rossano Brazzi, John Wayne, Gary Cooper, Charlton Heston, Sidney Poitier, Erwin Rommel, Bette Midler, Eleanor Smeal, Gloria Steinem, Gale Sayers, William Holden, Carol Channing.

Eighth House: These people usually have very strong instincts and often have to work hard to re-channel a basic animal or "killer" instinct into something constructive. There is usually a basic "coolness" or sophistication, yet you can sense that, beneath it, they are quite volatile. These are people who, if they work on themselves, develop great self-discipline, control and "toughness", yet there is still the "killer" instinct there. Often as children they are in trouble due to lack of self-control. These people try to concern themselves with simplicity, to get the basic "flavor" of something, or to get to the real roots of a situation. There is a desire for precision and often a love and desire for research, with a knack for quickly penetrating a problem. They want to develop and sharpen their power and skills and are quite capable of controlling others if they choose to do so. You can usually recognize them by their calm self-assurance, animal magnetism and sense of utter conviction. They have the potential to tap and channel vast energies and life forces, and to open doors to other worlds. Their sexual desires are often unique but they are capable of transcending them in ways others would not even think of. Their greatest lessons concern sex, power and death.

Omar Sharif, Yul Brynner, Henry Winkler, James Dean, Stacy Keach, Richard Chamberlain, Robert Mitchum, Montgomery Clift, Robert Blake, Ryan O'Neal, Karl Malden, Bruce Lee, Joe Frazier, Jackie Robinson, Jack Nicklaus, Eddie Arcaro, Indira Gandhi, Mao Tse Tung, Dr. Louis Berman, C. C. Zain, William Masters, Bishop James Pike, Komar, F. Scott Fitzgerald, Christopher Isherwood, Jack Kerouac, John Steinbeck, Yoko Ono, Leonard Bernstein, Jimi Hendrix, Raquel Welch, Elizabeth Montgomery, Deobrah Kerr, Christine Jorgensen, John Dunlop, Shirley Hufstedler, Lawton Chiles, Baudelaire

Ninth House: In their direction of interest these people have a talent for finding and understanding basic laws, general principles and the underlying significance of a situation; the root, basic meanings which are often hidden from others. They also can work with these in ways that are quite unbelievable, synthesizing them into more complex patterns, or finding ways to explain them to others in words that an ordinary person can understand. Or they may not use words as their medium but find some other way of communicating their in-depth understanding of symbols. It often comes out as a talent for simplifying technical explanations, an ability to "tune-in" on the current of today, a talent for really identifying with the audience, a desire to teach, or a fantastic ability to persuade (or mold public opinion.) They love challenges, are usually perceptive observers, good at ad-libbing, and outspoken with pronounced opinions. They have a powerful need to seek others with the same philosophies and beliefs, and usually, an equally powerful need to convince nonbelievers to believe in them. In its most negative expression this produces a VERY narrow philosophy, a dislike or hatred of those who don't fit into this philosophy, and an almost "police mentality." Whether positively or negatively, they search for verification and clarification of what they believe in, in all areas of life.

Gay Talese, Paul Theroux, Tom Wicker, George Bernard Shaw, Andre Malraux, Alfred Hitchcock, Dane Rudhyar, John Addey, Marc Edmund Jones, Edgar Cayce, Nietzsche, David St. Clair, Judy Blume, John Clifford, Graham Nash, Jack Sheldon, Dolly Parton, Eric Satie, Edouard Manet, Andy Warhol, Howard Cosell, Julie Andrews, Goldie Hawn, Greta Garbo, Jim Bailey, Roddy McDowell, Candice Bergen, Ava Gardner, Shelley Fabares, Robert Stack, Ronald Reagan (if you use the Cancer-rising chart), William Colby, J. Edgar Hoover, Richard Daley (Sr.), George Wallace, Ayatollah Khomeini, Adolf Hitler, Herman Goering, Everett LeRoy Jones, James Earl Ray, John W. Gacy, Enrico Fermi, Lotte Strahl, Stanley Hiller, Mary Wells, Arthur Okun.

Tenth House: These people drive themselves hard in their own field, often keeping gruelling schedules, yet they are usually known for being vital, alive and hardworking with a single-mindedness of purpose and a hatred of inactivity. When they talk about their purpose they tend to lecture like a preacher. It is not unusual for them to reach a high position in some field without many of the requirements which are normally necessary to do so, such as a high school graduate working at a job usually filled by a college graduate. In any event, they are usually in a position where they just don't seem to fit in with their co-workers, such as the only non-family member in a family-run business. Even if they chose a field where it is normal to be "different", they still seem to just not be like anyone else in the field. Thus they are definitely conspicuous and capable of making quite an impact on their profession. They are known for having a "something extra" which makes them stand out as mavericks, or for NOT having something which others in their field have which also makes them stand out. The public knows these people for their willingness to go beyond conventional methods in their careers, even if there is opposition from others, and they often disdain critics. Many have a great charisma. They usually have a fast wit and tend to be known for their self-deprecating humor . They always feel they must have an immediate goal, and if they don't have one they invent one. Often they find it difficult to concern themselves with long-range goals. They make good crusaders.

Jerry Lewis, Paul Lynde, Tom Poston, Jonathan Winters, Tom Smothers, Peter Ustinov, Flip Wilson, Tom Bosley, Dick Cavett, Truman Capote, Gale Storm, Loretta Young, Shirley MacLaine, Marilyn Monroe, Judy Garland, Joan Caufield, Diana Ross, Orson Welles, Willie Nelson, Sam Peckinpah, William Saroyan, Alfred Tennyson, Paul Verlaine, Giuseppe Verdi, Jack Anderson, Thomas Huxley, Isabelle Pagan, Alan Oken, Alice Anne Bailey, Nikola Tesla, Michel Gauquelin, Georg Moore, Milton Shapp, Thomas Eagleton, Robert McNamara, Jerry Rubin, F. Lee Bailey, Leon Trotsky.

Eleventh House: Major lessons for these people include choosing friends and associates wisely, learning how to deal with the ways in which other people express their own unique abilities and talents, understanding children other than their own, and fitting versus non-fitting into society. One's Chiron can become submerged in this house, never seeming to surface, unless one finds a unique role in society. Then one becomes very much the maverick. The urge to participate in society is unusually strong, and this group is quite aware of the needs and desires of their peers. In fact, once they find their own unique niche, they often become the hub or center for a whole group of people, leading the way down a different path, or bringing together people with a common goal. But for those who cannot find a totally unique role there is an overpowering need to "fit", to be part of society, and this usually comes out in one of two ways: either a VERY marked conservative streak, or a total disillusionment with society leading to a revolutionary tendency. In the former, there is a tendency to seem "solid" or "dull", and to appeal to a conservative crowd. Often one has a "loser" image, even if in no way a loser, and a tendency to be modest about one's achievements and, in general, to have a low-key or understated manner and a tendency toward self-deprecation. It is quite common for someone to start off as one of the above types and then switch to another. One thing everyone in this position wants to be is a problem-solver, so many become interested in science. Their hopes and wishes are very powerful. They have strong ideals, and once they have a specific picture of the world they want to live in they will let no closed doors keep them from getting there. In most, loyalty, team spirit and sportsmanship are very strong.

Edith Custer, Herman Melville, William F. Buckley, Dr. Benjamin Spock, Robin Moore, O. Henry, Vance Packard, John Gardner, William Lamb, Robert Good, Luis Alvarez, Dr. Brian Marsden, Albert Einstein, Allard Lowenstein, Charles Duncan, Henry Kissinger, Gamal Abdul Nassar, Governor Jerry Brown, Yvonne Burke, Richard Alpert (Ram Dass), Anita Bryant, Jane Fonda, Diane Baker, Peter Graves, Phyllis Diller, Bob Crane, Linda Blair, Viven Leigh, Jack Nicholson, Merv Griffin, Diane Keaton, Gregory Peck, Lawrence Welk, Tom Jones, B. J. Thomas, Jose Feliciano, Judy Collins.

Twelfth House: These people are experimenters and are multi-talented. They always have at least one goal to work on and an unlimited desire to learn and to increase the foundation of knowledge. Most especially, they want to learn of the hidden truths behind the apparent reality, to the point where they have a fear that some door will open to them when they are unprepared, so they feel that they must always try to learn as much as they can on every subject (to prepare them for anything they may uncover.) They have an interest in the past, and usually a talent for bringing things from the past into the present to make them once again serve a useful purpose. Almost always they have many projects going on at the same time so they are frequently in danger of overextending themselves. They usually have a very strong awareness of the unrealized potentials in both situations and people. Quite frequently they are known for their intellectual arrogance, and for the fact that they enjoy the role of dissenter. Yet it is quite common for them to not realize how they hinder themselves by holding maverick views. One of the most frequently experienced traits of this position is a tendency to not receive credit for things they have done, but at the same time they lack concern when this happens. There also exists a talent for "do-it-yourself" because often they cannot find anyone else to do what they want done. Most are moody. And most have a very strong awareness that the universe is filled with greater laws than those which are visible only through the five senses, and greater power than any which humans are capable of completely understanding.

Francoise Gauquelin, Neil Armstrong, Arthur Janov, Frank James Dixon, Pierre Teilhard de Chardin, Grigori Rasputin, Charles Richter, Al H. Morrison, Neil F. Michelsen, Noel Tyl, Richard Nolle, Kirk Oakes, Billy Graham, Toni Morrison, Jean Stafford, Joan Didion, Leo Guild, Marcel Proust, James Blish, Walt Whitman, Robert Smithson, George Gershwin, Harry Belafonte, Harry Bertoia, Rockwell Kent, Ottorino Respighi, Miles Davis, Ron Ely, Robert Culp, Richard Crenna, Jim Backus, Sally Kellerman, Elizabeth Ashley, George Peppard, Jackie Gleason, Barbara Stanwyck, Audrey Hepburn, Dean Martin, Robert Taft, Jack Valenti, Patricia Harris, Francisco Franco, Jack Kemp, Brendan Byrne, Robert Kennedy, Willy Brandt, Linda Lovelace.

ASPECTS

It would take a whole book to go into Chiron's every aspect with every planet, but I would like to discuss several points.

Orbs: For the purpose of research I only used a one-degree orb for all Chiron aspects, except three degrees for the Sun and Moon. The only real exception to this was when Chiron was intimately involved in some aspect pattern, such as a grand square. But, from my own observations, I feel that the following is a good picture of true Chiron orbs in natal charts: Conjunction = $3°$; square = $3°$; opposition = $3°$; trine = $3°$; sextile = $1\frac{1}{2}°$; semisquare = $1\frac{1}{2}°$;

sesquiquadrate = 1½°; quincunx = 1½°; semi-sextile, septile and quintile, 1°
each. I would add 2° for aspects to Sun or Moon if conjunction, square,
opposition or trine; 1½° if sextile, semisquare or sesquiquadrate; and 1° if one
of the others. I also give the extra orb to the ascendant, but I am not yet sure
about the MC. As for Chiron's aspects to any of the asteroids, I cut all of the
above orbs in half. Finally, for a major aspect of Chiron to a point, such as the
Ascendant/MC midpoint (a very sensitive point, by the way, along with its
opposition and square points), I only allow a 1° orb.

Now I would like to discuss a few of Chiron's aspects that I find particularly interesting.

Chiron conjunct Sun: Three actresses who have this position are Gale
Storm, Shirley Temple, and Doris Day. Except for Shirley (now Shirley Temple-
Black), who went from show-business to being an ambassador, I do not know
too much about the life-styles of these people, but all three presented in their
movies the image of a wholesome, yet somewhat mischievous female who was
always getting into some type of trouble. From my personal research, as well
as the list of other famous individuals with this aspect, I have concluded that
this combination gives the following traits: a disregard for what others say
can't be done, a need to express oneself in a way that separates one from his
peers, an ability to see beyond the limits others may not even have considered,
a concern for people's problems, and a tendency to divide people into two
distinct groups: those that really like one, and those that dislike one (i.e. either
you like this person with the conjunction, or you don't; no indifference.) A few
other examples: Neil F. Michelsen, Jean Claude Killy, Huey P. Long, Vance
Brand, Howard Cosell, Jean Cocteau, Jeff Bridges.

Chiron opposition Sun: These people are competitive and quite full of
spirit. They hate to be inactive and are fighters at heart. In fact, once they
discover a goal that is important to them, they become extremely active in the
fight to obtain that goal. They have very definite viewpoints, and most of them
are very people conscious, even humanity-conscious. They seem to be unable to avoid making enemies in life and are very much interested in change.
They have definite ideas of the way things could change for the better and
have no reservations about trying to make the ideas into reality. Some examples: Jane Fonda, Leon Trotsky, Melina Mercouri, George Bernard Shaw,
Henry Cabot Lodge, Leon Spinks, John Koch, Roger Daltry.

Chiron quincunx Sun: Aloofness? Or at least it seems that way. These
people are in their own world, seeing things from their own perspective, and it
never quite matches the views of their associates. They may be liked, even

loved, but a distance between them and others is nevertheless noticeable; it is quite difficult to get really close to them. This also often gives a coolness, especially if Chiron is in an eighth house position to the Sun. This coolness can make them seem even more attractive to others; they can represent the unattainable. Behind the aloofness, however, is a definite insecurity, especially in those with Chiron in a sixth house position to the Sun. It makes these people a bit nervous, or hyperactive, or jumpy, and gives them a very strong need to try to emphasize their sense of self — to emphasize whatever they identify as themselves. This can mean a need to emphasize the masculinity or femininity, if that is what they identify with. I suspect, deep down inside, that they have a large fear of being forced to change in some way, and a fear of not controlling their own lives. Some examples: George Peppard, Charles Bronson, James Daly, Tom Bosley, Bela Lugosi, Jack Valenti, Paul McClosky, Leonard Bernstein, Candice Bergen, Bonnie Franklin.

Chiron sextile Moon: These people tend to view others differently than the average person — they have a strong awareness of the needs, wants and desires of others and usually also of their weaknesses. There is, naturally, a temptation to use others with this aspect, but the more evolved souls resist it. Nevertheless, they are usually able to give people what they want. They have an instinct for giving things a unique, personal "twist" which makes them one-of-a-kind. They seem to have very strong survival instincts and an absolute hatred for anything they perceive as unfair or unjust. They are perfectly willing to push against seemingly insurmountable odds if they feel there is something they need to do. Some examples: Billy Rose, Arnold Schwarzenegger, Luciano Pavarotti, Malcolm Dean, O. Henry, Betty Friedan, Mark Goodson, Nina Simone, Jane Fonda, Mickey Rooney, Henry Perot

Chiron conjunct Mercury: Here are the innovators, the inventors, and those with a particularly unique way of communicating. If they write, or are in show business, they succeed in communicating far beyond simple words; they reach others on many other levels beyond just the verbal. Admittedly, they can be quite controversial, but they have an understanding of the common man's mind and know how to reach it. Often there is a desire to open doors, previously closed to all but a very select few, for everyone; there is also a hatred of injustice and imbalance, and often of anything that restricts or limits others in any way, or that keeps people on a particular path. Some examples: Troy Perry, Clive Sinclair (inventor of the ZX81 and Timex/Sinclair 1000 computers), Ted Mack, Eugene McCarthy, B. J. Thomas, Benjamin Disraeli, Martin Sheen, Dwayne Hickman, Roman Gabriel, Yogi Berra.

Chiron square Venus: An extremely unique taste in art fits this aspect; if the person goes into the arts in any way, he often covers subjects that may be taboo, or that others simply have not considered. There is almost always an unusual sense of humor as well, and an appreciation for beauty where others do not perceive it. Their value system does not fit with society's, and many eventually develop the desire either to leave society or to ignore it. Others make the decision to try to change society's values. They have a very highly developed aesthetic sense, and a soft side — the males often will go overboard in asserting their masculinity, putting on a shell to protect themselves from being considered soft. Or, if they are not worried about being hurt, they may flaunt their soft, romantic side. Some examples: George Steinbrenner, Bruce Lee, Marjoe Gortner, Peter Fonda, Liberace, Adlai Stevenson, Charles Addams, Edgar Degas, Judy Collins, Brook Shields, Sophia Loren, Le Petomane (known in Europe for "passing wind" in ways that imitated other sounds.)

Chiron semi-square Mars: These people cannot stand the thought of being stopped if there is something they are trying to find out, or some task they are trying to accomplish. It seems that here, Chiron constantly eggs Mars on to go a little further, try a little more, try a different method, ignore this obstacle — and Mars seems unable to refuse. These people have a strong sense of self-assertiveness and usually have quite a temper, unless they are channelling it for some "cause." They also have very definite likes and dislikes and are usually quite frank in letting you know about them. Unless other things in the chart point to the contrary, they usually have a good deal of sex appeal. Some examples: Omar Sharif, Keith Emerson, Dr. Martin Luther King Jr., Wilt Chamberlain, Bertrand Russell, Greta Garbo, Bishop James Pike, Redd Foxx, Madeline Kahn, Bette Midler.

Chiron square Jupiter: One thing that sets these people apart is their unique or unusual interpretations of situations or ideas. They are capable of perceiving meanings that are hidden from others, and of interpreting the most complex things so that even the common man can understand them, but this latter talent comes through experience. They go through continual upheaval in what they believe in and how they perceive life until they learn to accept change. At this point, they make the best teachers, interpreters, legislators, and excel in any position where they deal with basic meanings and symbols. However, if they refuse to accept the idea that all things change — if they refuse to integrate the concept of change into their belief system — the continual upheaval eventually can disrupt the very fabric of their lifestyle. Some examples: Rosalind Russell, Marcel Proust, Percy Bysshe Shelley, Rudolph Valentino, John Cage, Henry (Scoop) Jackson, Dan Rather

Chiron sesquiquadrate Saturn: To these people, tradition, rules and structures are all well and good, but are meant to be changed or gone beyond whenever the need arises. They always feel compelled to test the facts as they stand, and to go past them without much hesitation if necessary. They never see any structure or rule as always valid or always binding. There is a tendency to have a good bit of difficulty with authority, unless the authority gives them much freedom to forge ahead into the future. These people don't believe in the phrase, "You can't." Some examples: Francoise Gauquelin, Toulouse-Lautrec, Princess Grace of Monaco, Frank Borman, James Lovell, James Earl Ray.

Chiron opposition Uranus: I feel it is still too soon to arrive at a clear idea of the meaning of this aspect, as many people have it and some are still quite young. The one thing I can say is that these people have real spirit, and a very strong need to feel that their independence and individuality are not threatened. Some examples: Leon Spinks, Tracey Austin, Archie Griffin, Tatum O'Neal.

Chiron conjunct Neptune: While this intrigues me, I do not have enough cases to identify its meaning. It is interesting that two important figures in Communism, Joseph Stalin and Leon Trotsky, had this, as well as the blind singer Jose Feliciano, whose songs are full of emotion.

Chiron conjunct Pluto: Again, this intrigues me, but I have not enough examples. Karl Marx and Benito Mussolini had it, but so did Walt Whitman, and so does actor Michael Moriarity.

Chiron conjunct South Lunar Node: There seem to be two types: the unevolved type who is always getting in trouble for his eccentric or erratic behavior; and the evolved type who gets much pleasure out of sharing his unique insights and unusual life experiences with others. The former tend to fall back on Chiron's maverick nature whenever anything goes wrong in life, or whenever they are under stress, and thus express it negatively. The latter type has integrated Chiron and thus instinctively knows how to use Chiron as part of the larger picture. Some examples: Craig Breedlove, Clifford Odets, Arturo Toscanini, John Anderson, Merle Haggard, Dick Martin, Billy Carter.

Here are a few guidelines as to how
Chiron acts in aspect to various planets:

CONJUNCTION: Unlike a regular conjunction, when Chiron is in conjunction with a planet a fusion of the two bodies does not occur. Chiron does bring out the maverick nature of the other planet and seems to shape it so that it won't fit into any mold. Yet the planet appears to have very little effect on shaping Chiron. Could that be because Chiron refuses to align itself with anything? There is a desire to equalize extremes, an ability to find something in common with everyone, and the ability to either open doors or go beyond obstacles for other people.

SEMI-SEXTILE (30°): It seems to be more powerful than other planets in semi-sextile. While the person is not necessarily unconventional, he does seem to have an innate talent or knack for getting around obstacles without putting forth much effort.

SEMI-SQUARE (45°): The person feels compelled to use the planet that Chiron is aspecting; he cannot let it be idle. What is more, he feels the need to shape the planet, to control it, and accomplish things with it.

SEPTILE (51°): Great potential to change society. The person seems to have Chiron activate automatically, the moment the other planet is activated, yet the two bodies may act independently of each other. It is just that he cannot use one without the other becoming active.

SEXTILE: Chiron refuses to remain still and refuses to allow the other planet to be still as well. Chiron is always encouraging the other planet to go out, to solve problems, to be active. Chiron encourages the person to use the other planet as a tool to go beyond the ordinary. There is a definite understanding of people and things that are not in the "norm."

QUINTILE (72°): An ability to use the aspected planet to go way beyond one's present reality, to alternate realities, and then to bring back what one finds there into one's own world....and then to interrelate seemingly unrelated things.

SQUARE: This never produces stagnation, like other squares. On the contrary: ordinarily a planet tends to get into a rut, get set in its ways, but Chiron only lets this go on so long. Then it "pulls the rug out from under you," and you are thrown off balance. You may end up falling down, but if you do, you will find that you have stumbled upon something really valuable that had been hidden from you before. (Perhaps there were diamonds under that rug, but you did not find them until the rug was removed and you fell upon them.) Anyway, when Chiron throws you of balance, you have to learn to adapt, must learn to change. Until one learns this, it seems that the planet goes back and forth to extremes, as the person must balance and rebalance. Once he learns that change is necessary for the growth of this planet, he welcomes change. In some people, a danger surfaces at this point: some people begin to thrill in change and new experiences so much that they live for them. These people must learn a new lesson: to welcome change, but it is not the end, only one part of the path.

TRINE: Untypical of a trine. Normally we expect a trine to be easy and flowing, something we can take for granted. We do not expect any lessons to come from the areas 120 degrees away from a planet. But Chiron brings unexpected lessons from an area we thought we could feel quite comfortable with. It opens doors to worlds in areas we thought we knew quite well. Chiron in trine teaches us not to take anything for granted. Once we have learned this, we can now purposely use the aspected planet as a key to explore new worlds. We can express our own unique style with ease, and take for granted this part of ourselves. Of all Chiron aspects, the trine is least likely to get us into trouble for being different.

SESQUIQUADRATE (135°): The planet in aspect to Chiron is quite often restless. It often finds itself in some situation where things suddenly come to a halt, and the person has to realign his energies. This aspect produces a resiliency, a spirited nature, and increases one's sense of humor.

QUINCUNX (150°): There is an ability to observe the subtle forces behind things, the undercurrents, the twists and turns of life that others do not see. The person can use the aspected planet to draw other people out, and, to some extent, to control others.

OPPOSITION: A need to go beyond ordinary methods of doing things because the person cannot help perceiving alternate methods. However, there is often difficulty working within any structures, because the person sees so many alternatives. (One lesson here is: just because the alternatives exist doesn't mean one has to choose them.) This is an aspect that brings challenges from Chiron's house to the planet which said planet cannot ignore. It brings out the "fighting spirit" in the planet, or at least, a constant need to keep that planet active.

CHIRON'S SIGNS

Figuring out the meanings of Chiron in each sign is a complicated affair. For one thing, Chiron has such an eccentric orbit that it stays in some signs a great deal longer than in others. Thus we have had a much larger section of humanity to study with Chiron in Aries, for example (where it stayed for over eight years) than with Chiron in Libra (where it stayed less than two years.)

For another thing, there is an increasing evidence that it is not just Chiron's sign that is significant but also where Chiron is in relation to Saturn and Uranus. This factor can actually divide signs into two categories. For example, Chiron reaches perihelion in Libra. When it first enters that sign it is moving away from Uranus. But after perihelion, it is still in Libra for awhile yet now moving toward Uranus.

Nevertheless certain definite traits are appearing for each Chiron sign position, and so here follows a brief description of Chiron through the signs.

ARIES: The best way to understand these people is to look at the two most recent periods with Chiron in Aries. The 1920's (The Roaring Twenties) with their "flappers", self-expression and uninhibitedness, and the 1970's, often termed the "Me Generation", were both very Arien times. Theirs is a personal imperative to push their potentials to the maximum, and a belief that everyone should express himself. There is a strong need to overcome any obstacles that may stand in the way of exploring new areas, especially if these areas lead to greater self-understanding. They have a strong need to make their point of view understood, and believe the rights of the individual are paramount. They want to be first at *something.* Major lesson: controlling their aggressiveness and coping with the aggressiveness of other people.

TAURUS: Values change through time and cultures, but these people have a personal imperative to search for values that will remain when everything around them changes. All typical Taurean things, such as possessions and security, are important, but they have unique viewpoints on them. They feel that nothing must stop them from acquiring what they feel they need to survive, and this includes material security. Many lessons come to them from this area of life, and as they evolve they develop a great deal of concern for the needy. They feel that no one should be deprived of the necessities of life, and no one should become wealthy at the expense of others. The less elevated types may not feel this way, but they are working out problems that will eventually lead them to this attitude. These people often are quite innovative in

27

solving problems in the material world.

GEMINI: High on the list of priorities with these people is, as you might suspect, communication. It is especially important for them to understand why there is a communication breakdown, or why there is an obstacle to communication, and to do everything to resolve the situation. Therefore these are the best people to have around as non-biased third parties in a dispute. The want very much to contact as many people as possible, and it hurts them if they are misunderstood. If they take up a cause, they can be quite fiery advocates. Learning is paramount to them, and they love to learn new ways of thinking, new ways of problem solving. They are always testing, testing, to see just what limitations their immediate environment puts on them, and on others.

CANCER: "Security!" Nothing must stand in their way as they work to achieve this. Their family is paramount, and in the evolved types the family is viewed as all of humanity. Thus nothing must threaten whatever they define as family and it is a personal imperative to protect the self and family at all costs. They have a hatred of aggression and animosity as a rule, although a severely afflicted chart may counteract this trait. They are usually more in tune with their emotions than is the average person, and tuning in more all the time. One of their major lessons to learn is to control their emotions, not to let them run haywire or to become lost in them. They have a knack of taking things from the past and bringing them into the present and future in a way that they become useful again, bridging the generations.

LEO: One thing almost everyone with this position has experienced are circumstances where they have had to take control because everyone else around was unable to cope with what was going on. One major lesson for these people is self-reliance. They have a personal imperative to be individualists so it is very difficult for them to take advice. They have a unique sense of pride — they need to be called upon to do something "only you can do." They also must maintain their self-respect at all costs and nothing must stand in the way of their doing this. They cannot stand any restrictions on self-expression, not only for themselves but also for others. They usually have a strong affection for children and for adults who still keep a childlike quality about them.

VIRGO: Many of these people have the soul of Don Quixote. They have a personal imperative to right wrongs, correct errors, and will not let anything stand in their way of doing so once the errors are found. They are very much aware of all that is wrong in the world. One thing that irks these people more than anything else is to find that something has again gone wrong once it has

28

been corrected. There is a deep belief that no one should control another, and no one should keep anyone from being himself and discovering his skills and abilities. They seem to have a knack for figuring out new ways of doing things, although in unevolved types these "new ways" may not be socially acceptable.

LIBRA: One major lesson these people must learn is how to really tell when something is fair or just. They have a personal imperative to discover which side is correct, and a hatred of injustice — it must end NOW, not later. People are extremely important to them and they feel that nothing must stand in the way of their trying to understand the viewpoints of others. They also feel the reverse, that no one should close their mind to his views. So they hate close-minded people, or people who shelter themselves from the views of others. Relationships all produce major lessons for them. Art, in some form, is a necessity; if they do not have a talent they must have art or music or some aesthetic pleasure as an integral part of their life....they must nourish their souls.

SCORPIO: The unevolved types feel that nothing must stand in the way of gratification of their desires. The evolved types feel that nothing must be in the way of understanding their desires and working toward perfecting their higher selves. All types have a personal imperative to control their own lives at any cost. They have the ability to tune in to the universal energy and power, and use it for themselves. That is why many are involved in the occult, Eastern religions and such. They have a powerful awareness of sex and sexual energy, which the higher types transmute to more powerful forces. The lower types tend to make enemies easily for they feel that their own value system is easily superior to that of other people. The higher types search for common values that they can share with all mankind.

SAGITTARIUS: Want to get these people angry? Tell them something is "Off limits!" They cannot stand the thought that anything should be forbidden, especially if they feel it is something from which they can learn. They have a strong adventurous streak and are always searching for something to believe in that will hold up when everything else changes. They need to feel that they thoroughly understand the philosophy or religion in which they were brought up, and also what others believe in. When they find something to believe in they have a strong need to let no obstacles stand in the way of their sharing it with others.

CAPRICORN: These people need to create some type of order or structure that will not fall apart when other things do and which, it is hoped, will function after they are gone. They need to feel that they are on THE right path for them, and they deeply believe there is one specific path they must find for themselves. They also believe this is true for others, that each person has a correct path for himself. The more evolved types believe that each person's path is totally his own; the lesser types believe, once they find a path, that it is for everyone to follow. They hate anything that can sway them from their course and feel the same is true for others. They have a strong need to succeed at their unique path and they can't stand failure.

AQUARIUS: The personal imperative for these people can be summed up in two words: THE FUTURE. they can't tolerate people who refuse to move forward and they feel nothing must stop them from evolving, from discovering the new and the different. They have the souls of the Bohemians (free souls) and have a great deal of sympathy for those who stand out. They need people and want to solve problems for others, as well as to bring people together. They cannot stand closed doors — they want (to steal a line from Star Trek) "to boldly go where no one has gone before."

PISCES: They have a personal imperative to feel that whatever they are involved in is THE truth, the important cause. They want to avoid involving themselves in anything that is not important, or not possible to achieve. In this last point, what qualifies "possible" is their evolutionary state for the evolved ones believe that nothing is impossible. They want to be truly universal in lifestyle, and so will go beyond their world to become more whole. They have a deep optimism that they can make the world a better place, although this can be curtailed severely by heavy Saturn aspects. They are almost all quite psychic, and full of dreams. But one of the major lessons they have to learn is to avoid falling for wrong causes. They have an overpowering need to express love.

Progressions

So far, I have only studied the progressions of Chiron in the 'day-for-a-year' method. Obviously Chiron itself does not progress very much this way no matter how old someone gets. When Chiron does progress into a more exact aspect than at birth the individual's Maverick qualities definitely become more prominent. When it becomes exact the person can definitely expect some major crisis which results in his becoming much more aware of his potentials and his limitations.

But the more common event is a progression of another planet to one's natal Chiron. This always brings new experiences to the person in the area of life represented by the progressing planet. And everyone who makes it to his first lunar return has had the Moon over his Chiron, as well as the square, opposition and other aspects. So the progressed Moon-to-Chiron aspects are important to everyone.

My first experience with such an aspect was naturally in my own life. I wanted to be with my wife in the delivery room for the birth of our second child. So, I had to take special classes to make me eligible for such an honor. I finished the classes as the Moon progressed to less than one degree from my Chiron; my wife started her contractions when the Moon was on my Chiron; and I helped in the delivery while the Moon was separating but still in orb.

Since then I have seen many cases of progressed Moon to natal Chiron and the one common thread they all share is an experience that opens up another area of life in a way that changes their opinion or image of themselves, and relates in some way to something connected with the Moon. This could be a birth, or security, or food, or any of the many other lunar related things.

All progressed aspects to Chiron appear to be significant. Sometimes one may happen at quite an early age. One mother told me that she was having trouble with her 2½ year old son. She couldn't seem to toilet train him nor break him of his bottle-drinking. Then she decided to try a new tactic: she told him he was getting to be a young man and young man did not have "accidents" in their pants, and that they drank from cups not bottles. Overnight he was completely toilet-trained and never used a bottle again. His progressed Sun was closely opposition his natal Chiron.

A young man was shy and always getting "picked on" by his classmates. Finally his parents took him to see a psychologist as his progressed Mars came within 30' of opposition to his natal Chiron. The therapy was quite successful and he began to make friends (and stopped getting picked on) at the time the opposition was exact. His grades improved, he began to be able to defend himself if necessary, and he got his first real girlfriend, all before the progressed Mars moved more than 30' past the opposition.

Saturn and Uranus

Due to Chiron's special relationship with Saturn and Uranus, the aspects that Chiron makes with these two bodies are of particular importance. In light of this I am including a special aspectarian for this century of the conjunctions, squares and oppositions Chiron makes with Saturn and with Uranus. The dates of the aspects are based on ephemeris time. The exact aspect may be a day earlier or later in your time zone.

As you can see this not a typical pattern of aspects. For example from 1935 to 1952 Chiron squares Saturn twenty-one times before the distance between them begins to shrink significantly. Then in 1966 these two bodies are conjunct for the only time this century. Uranus has just as unusual a relationship. In 1943 these two were square one time. Then between 1952 and 1989 Chiron opposes Uranus forty-one times. Finally, these two square each other once, in 1997. One of the things this means is that we have very few examples of individuals with certain Chiron aspects to study and an overabundance of others. (NO ONE born this century has Chiron in conjunction with Uranus.) Another thing it means is that whole generations of individuals can have certain Chiron/Saturn or Chiron/Uranus aspects — a good portion of the first half of this century has Chiron square Saturn while the second half is almost all Chiron opposition Uranus. And another thing: the aspect seems to set the tone of the times. The Chiron/Uranus oppositions began in 1952 and seem to tie into the accelerated pace of scientific advancement during the second half of this century.

Jul	26 1913	Chiron 90° Saturn	Jan	17 1946	Chiron 90° Saturn
Jan	14 1914	Chiron 90° Saturn	Apr	7 1946	Chiron 90° Saturn
May	19 1914	Chiron 90° Saturn	Jan	8 1947	Chiron 90° Saturn
			May	20 1947	Chiron 90° Saturn
Nov	2 1922	Chiron 180° Saturn	Jan	8 1948	Chiron 90° Saturn
			Jun	19 1948	Chiron 90° Saturn
Apr	15 1935	Chiron 90° Saturn	Jan	13 1949	Chiron 90° Saturn
May	22 1935	Chiron 90° Saturn	Jul	11 1949	Chiron 90° Saturn
Feb	16 1936	Chiron 90° Saturn			
Aug	7 1936	Chiron 90° Saturn	Jan	28 1950	Chiron 90° Saturn
Jan	16 1937	Chiron 90° Saturn	Jul	21 1950	Chiron 90° Saturn
Oct	2 1937	Chiron 90° Saturn	Feb	21 1951	Chiron 90° Saturn
Dec	17 1937	Chiron 90° Saturn	Jul	22 1951	Chiron 90° Saturn
			Feb	22 1952	Chiron 180° Uranus
Sep	29 1943	Chiron 90° Uranus	Mar	26 1952	Chiron 90° Saturn

May 23 1952	Chiron 180° Uranus	Aug 27 1975	Chiron 90° Saturn
Jul 10 1952	Chiron 90° Saturn	Mar 21 1976	Chiron 90° Saturn
Jan 23 1953	Chiron 180° Uranus	Jun 11 1976	Chiron 90° Saturn
Jul 5 1953	Chiron 180° Uranus		
Jan 4 1954	Chiron 180° Uranus	Aug 17 1985	Chiron 180° Uranus
Aug 7 1954	Chiron 180° Uranus	Oct 1 1985	Chiron 180° Uranus
Dec 20 1954	Chiron 180° Uranus	Feb 25 1986	Chiron 180° Saturn
Sep 6 1955	Chiron 180° Uranus	Mar 4 1986	Chiron 180° Saturn
Dec 5 1955	Chiron 180° Uranus	Jul 23 1986	Chiron 180° Uranus
Oct 8 1956	Chiron 180° Uranus	Nov 8 1986	Chiron 180° Uranus
Nov 15 1956	Chiron 180° Uranus	Jan 13 1987	Chiron 180° Saturn
		May 14 1987	Chiron 180° Saturn
Nov 13 1964	Chiron 180° Uranus	Jul 4 1987	Chiron 180° Uranus
Dec 31 1964	Chiron 180° Uranus	Dec 11 1987	Chiron 180° Uranus
Nov 1 1965	Chiron 180° Uranus	Dec 30 1987	Chiron 180° Saturn
Jan 22 1966	Chiron 180° Uranus	Jun 14 1988	Chiron 180° Uranus
Apr 13 1966	**Chiron 0° Saturn**	Jun 16 1988	Chiron 180° Saturn
Oct 23 1966	Chiron 180° Uranus	Dec 22 1988	Chiron 180° Saturn
Feb 9 1967	Chiron 180° Uranus	Jan 18 1989	Chiron 180° Uranus
Oct 15 1967	Chiron 180° Uranus	May 18 1989	Chiron 180° Uranus
Feb 27 1968	Chiron 180° Uranus	Jul 12 1989	Chiron 180° Saturn
Oct 6 1968	Chiron 180° Uranus	Dec 22 1989	Chiron 180° Saturn
Mar 15 1969	Chiron 180° Uranus		
Sep 29 1969	Chiron 180° Uranus	Jul 30 1990	Chiron 180° Saturn
		Dec 29 1990	Chiron 180° Saturn
Apr 1 1970	Chiron 180° Uranus	Aug 11 1991	Chiron 180° Saturn
Sep 22 1970	Chiron 180° Uranus	Jan 14 1992	Chiron 180° Saturn
Apr 18 1971	Chiron 180° Uranus	Aug 15 1992	Chiron 180° Saturn
Sep 14 1971	Chiron 180° Uranus	Feb 7 1993	Chiron 180° Saturn
May 5 1972	Chiron 180° Uranus	Aug 14 1993	Chiron 180° Saturn
Sep 4 1972	Chiron 180° Uranus	Mar 11 1994	Chiron 180° Saturn
May 24 1973	Chiron 180° Uranus	Aug 9 1994	Chiron 180° Saturn
Aug 26 1973	Chiron 180° Uranus	Apr 23 1995	Chiron 180° Saturn
Jun 16 1974	Chiron 180° Uranus	Jul 28 1995	Chiron 180° Saturn
Aug 12 1974	Chiron 180° Uranus	Oct 10 1997	Chiron 90° Uranus

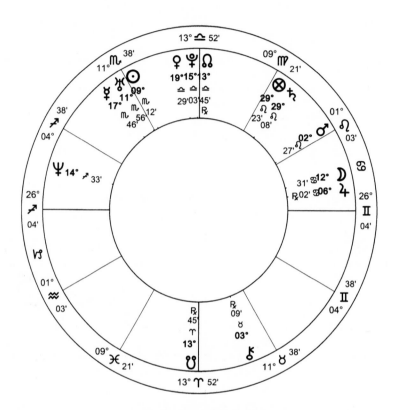

Chiron Discovery Chart
November 1, 1977, 10:00 am
Pasadena, CA

NOTE: This chart should be rectified. What Charles Koval said in answer to the question was **"<u>about</u>"** ten o'clock. Four clock minutes earlier gives a chart which fits events since then much better, and also relates more exactly to the charts of those who are concerned with the astrology of Chiron.

Essence and Application
A View From Chiron

Section One: The Essence

Chapter I: Keywords

Ever since 1975, when research on Chiron began in earnest, keywords for Chiron have been coming in from all parts of the world. The spectrum of different aspects of Chiron has been wide; each researcher seemingly caught up in his or her own personal view of the new planet. There IS a common thread running through these seemingly unrelated words and phrases, but it may not be easily discernible to you.

Here follows a list of the many keys for Chiron that have been found so far, with a brief definition for each one. In subsequent chapters, you will be shown how all these ideas tie together, to suggest the main Chironic theme. If you have been working with Chiron, you may want to skip this chapter, and refer back to it from time to time, as you read the rest of the book.

KEYWORDS

MAVERICK: This was one of the earliest keys suggested for Chiron, and was originally derived from a statement from Dr. Brian G. Marsden, of the Smithsonian Institution Astrophysical Observatory. Dr. Marsden mentioned the fact that Chiron most-likely originated from outside our solar system and would one day leave us again, and is, therefore, a Maverick. Many people do not really understand the meaning of this word and tend to confuse it with words like rebel, and even revolutionary. When they do this, naturally they assume that Chiron is just a smaller version of Uranus. But Maverick does not mean rebel. Maverick is one who takes a stand apart from other members of his group, yet does not necessarily try to get others to change to his views. He is not for, nor against, any group, in whatever area the Maverick side shows. A rebel, on the other hand, directly opposes some group or authority, even to the point of open disobedience—usually with the intention of causing some type of major change in the group structure. The easiest way to understand the term Maverick is to think of Chiron's placement—in between Saturn [the authority, the established group and its rules], and Uranus [the rebel, the revolutionary, the individualist who openly breaks away from the system]. So Maverick does not wear any brand to say he can be labeled as following the group ideology—yet at the same time, he does not carry the banner of protest against said ideology. Maverick follows his own course—although he soon may discover that he attracts followers along the way.

QUEST: This is an important key. It is the root from which we get the word question, and has as its essence a seeking after truth. Along with this come romantic images conjured up from great, oft-told myths and tales. Thus the word also has come to connote a transformation that occurs in the Questor as a result of pursuing his quest.

GUIDE: This is someone, or something, which helps to lead or direct someone on a course they are taking, or in the proper direction to reach their goal. It is important to realize that a guide need not be a living being. It can be a spirit, or even some inanimate object, or the words of someone coming to one from a book.

KEY: This is something that enables one to gain access to someplace, or to something, but it is also a means of preventing such access. It can be that one small piece of information, that enables one to understand the solution to a problem.

What is most important about a Key is the recognition of its existence. Before one realizes a Key exists one may not believe there is any solution to a problem—or, one may not even recognize that a problem exists. But once the Key is discovered the first step in the solution has been taken. One who has the Key actually also has control. He can keep others from opening a door, and therefore keep them from solving their problem. Thus a Key is necessary to both open—and close—a door [or even an electric circuit—Key is used to denote a small electric switch].

DOORWAY: A doorway is, in effect, not belonging to either world. Take the doorway of a house. If you are outside, you cross through to go in, while if inside, you cross through to go out. While the door may be part of the house, and block entrance or exit when closed—the doorway itself is totally neutral. It belongs to both worlds—or neither, depending on your point of view. If you think of the walls of the house as being Saturn, the insides of the house as being the inner planets, and the outside of the house represented by Uranus, Neptune and Pluto—then the doorway itself can be seen as Chiron.

NOW: Chiron is a very small body. It is only with us and our solar system for a short time, as far as the universe is concerned—only the briefest moment of universal time. The present is the moment we live in, right Now. But any present event immediately becomes a past event. Even future ones soon pass into the past. Chiron represents this brief present moment—this fleeting event that we are paying attention to right Now, before it goes into a 'was'. To put it in another way—we are always living only in the present, and Chiron represents the awareness of this. Saturn represents events once they become past, while Uranus are those yet to come. We can turn our attention toward Saturn or Uranus, but never live in either. It could be that this is part of the lesson to be learned from the knowledge that both Saturn AND Uranus are surrounded [imprisoned ?] by rings.

LEARNING: This word means the gaining of knowledge, and possibly skill, and often implies that this takes place through some type of instruction or study. Learning may have the effect of modifying, or even drastically altering one's behavior or lifestyle. The brain acquires a new furrow when one learns something new. Thus, any learning produces a change in someone, even if only a new furrow.

HEALING: There are differences in opinion over exactly what constitutes a healing, but I use it to describe both the restoration of balance, and the process leading to make one whole. Thus, it is not just the removal of some undesirable condition, but a much deeper, more involved process. A healing can also take place on a larger scale, such as healing a rupture that has occurred in a relationship, or a division that has taken place in a group or organization. And thus healing need not be thought of only in medical terms, but on any level.

LOOPHOLE: This is a very special means of escape. In a legal document, if there is some ambiguity in the text, or the omission of some important point, one can use this Loophole to get out of the contract, or evade the obligation. Taking this a bit further, a loophole is any small opening that may permit air, or light to come in—or permit what is in to come out—without destroying the document, wall, or division which contains the loophole.

QUALIFIER: Each category [ruled by Saturn] has very specific requirements or standards that describes all members of the category. Those not in the category may be in other categories, but that is unimportant for this discussion. What is important is that there must be members that are near the edge of the line—that are just barely a part of the category, and if changed a bit, would no longer be a part of it. Take for example the concept of elements, such as Gold, Silver or Nitrogen. An ounce of Gold is Gold, and so is a pound of Gold. Even a molecule of Gold is still the same element. An atom represents the smallest piece of matter which can still retain the name Gold. Break it into smaller pieces—such as electrons, and you no longer have Gold. Thus, an atom is a qualifier of the category 'element'.

CHIROS: Time has usually been considered the realm of the planet Saturn, but in actuality, Saturn only rules one type of time—chronological time [duration]. Chiros represents time that is outside that realm—time that obeys an entirely different set of laws [if it does, indeed, obey any laws at all]. It is this

39

time that Einstein referred to in his explanation of relativity: "When a man sits with a pretty girl for an hour, it seems like a minute. But let him sit on a hot stove for a minute—and its longer than any hour. That's relativity. And it is also this concept that Robert Heinlein focuses on, when [in his book, **Stranger in a Strange Land**] he has his character Michael Valentine Smith talk about a 'cusp'—a time when all else fades away, and all attention is turned to the making of a crucial decision. Chiros has even been called 'timeless time'. Many people have been able to enter this type of time through deep meditation. Remember that Chiron's orbit is, for the most part, beyond Saturn, and that will assist you in contemplating a time which is not ruled by the clock or the calendar.

TAP: A tap is a device used to let out, or cause to flow, the liquid that is contained within some container—without altering the structure of the container. Taking the concept a step further, the tap could open to let out other things that are contained, such as energy, power, healing forces. The important point to remember is— the tap allows the structure to keep its basic integrity.

MENTOR: This is someone you trust, and tend to look up to, who can counsel you, guide you, possibly teach you. Many people need to find a mentor at some stage of their evolution—although one frequently outgrows this need after one has evolved a bit more. The most crucial thing about a mentor, I feel, is the timing. When one is in need, a mentor shows up.

Here are some other words and phrases for Chiron, most of which can be related to the words already mentioned. Of course, the reader will be able to add others to this list. For that reason, a blank page has been included at the end of this chapter. The author invites all readers to send in their words for possible inclusion in the next edition.

OTHER WORDS AND PHRASES:

Teacher, Guru, Foster parent, Turning Point, Catalyst, Self-Transformation, Bridge, Link, Stepping stone, Passageway, Common Ground, Union of Opposites, Wholemaking, Holistic, Personal Imperative, Pulling the Plug, Balance, Mediator, The Passage from Dependence to Independence, Turning the Corner, Therapy, a Koan [in Zen Buddhism], A Wound that will not Heal, a way to break free of a matrix.

In closing, I would like to define just one more word, in Chiron's list: SYNERGISM. This is defined in Webster's New World Dictionary as "The simultaneous action of separate agencies which, together, have greater total effect than the sum of their individual effects." I hope this will emerge, by the end of this book, as one of the primary Chiron keys.

This page has been left blank so that you can write in additional KEY-
WORDS for Chiron.

142 ♀ ⚷ ☊ No. Node

paradox, duality, polarity
Self centered vs centered in Self
we are here to become whole not wholly
Here & now reality, balance ⚷ ♅ v ♆
wholistic understanding, experience is the grand teacher
always support family - A⚷ & B⚷ are my mirror

⚷ physical - ♆ metaphysical

Chapter II: What Is Reality?

The ancients had it easy. They perceived Saturn as the final planet, and so Saturn became the definer of reality. It represented every measure by which they judged what was real—structures, time, solids. Nice and simple.

But, in 1789, someone with a telescope showed that Saturn represented only 'apparent' reality. In that year, Uranus was discovered, sending its shock waves throughout the astrological and astronomical world. Even more, this discovery was symbolic of the drastic changes going on in human consciousness itself. Reality itself could no longer be viewed as it had been.

Ever since then, definitions of reality were changed almost as often as someone with a coffee pot changes the coffee filter. Each new scientific discovery altered, sometimes even destroyed, whatever was the currently accepted view. The discovery of Neptune, and then of Pluto, only served to increase our awareness of how little we really did know of the true state of the universe.

And then came Chiron. With the coming into awareness of this little planet, an opportunity arrived to perceive what reality really is. As with any truths, what follows may be a bit controversial—especially if it shakes up your own personal concepts of reality. But then, wouldn't you rather be shaken up, than continue to believe in something that is in error in some, or many, respects?

Before I can show you how Chiron defines reality, I must first take you on a brief journey into the world of Quantum Physics. If you have studied this subject before, please bear with me.

From the beginning, the aim of physics was to produce a clear, detailed description of the universe and its laws. But as, step by step, smaller particles were discovered and examined, this aim became more difficult to obtain. After breaking down an atom into its components, such as electrons, protons, neutrons and the like, it was soon discovered that is IMPOSSIBLE to totally isolate such particles in both time and space. One can possibly measure the position of a particular particle with accuracy, OR measure the momentum of said particle—but one cannot do both. Measuring one automatically changes the other. [This is part of something termed THE HEISENBERG UNCERTAINTY PRINCIPLE, to the effect that to examine anything is to change its nature]. What it comes down to is that particles have only a 'probability' of being in a given place—we can never be certain. What is more, things such as protons and electrons are really impossible to isolate for study. There is no way to be certain whether an electron which we saw enter into an atom, is the same electron we watch leaving the atom. Imagine that—no way to be sure!

Now, electrons are termed 'probability fogs', and are studied by statistics. Keep this in mind for later.

There was a time that matter, and light [i.e., the electromagnetic spectrum] were seen as totally separate entities in the universe. But not anymore. A photon of light is seen as a little packet of energy—the foundation of all matter. It stores its energy through its angular momentum, and radiates light, not simply in a beam, but in whole units. These units can also be termed quantum of energy, so that by measuring light, we are also measuring stored energy. And, since it stores energy by the principle of angular momentum, the smaller it gets, the faster it spins, the more energy it can contain.

Now, light itself is special, for a number of reasons. When it moves from one point to another, it does not leave part of itself behind. What is more, photons always choose the path that gets them to their goal that takes the least amount of time. In fact, light is all over, and serves to connect everything to everything.

Lest you think I have forgotten about Chiron, it is time to bring the little planet back into the subject by bringing in the Chironic keywords QUALIFIER and WHOLENESS.

If you read the previous chapter, you will know that a Qualifier is THE whole that sets the limit to a category. For example, if the category is human being, we cannot take the iron out of a human, and call that iron the human. If the category is the element Gold, then we cannot take one of the electrons from an atom of Gold, and call the electron Gold.

Whenever there is an energy exchange at the atomic level, it is always in terms of whole quanta of light—or we can call them whole units of action. Thus, there is never a case that 1½, or 7¼ quanta of light are exchanged. Light—and action—comes in whole units. These units cannot be divided. THEY ARE THE SMALLEST WHOLES—THE PRIMARY QUALIFIERS OF THE UNIVERSE.

Have you ever heard of the term, 'First Cause'? Go to the Bible, and check out GENESIS 1:3: 'And God said, "Let there be light": and there was light.' Light is the first thing created—the oldest thing in the universe. From light, all things developed. Light is what ties all things together, making one whole.

Light is the qualifier of the basic building block of the universe.

Now we can, as I have said, equate a quantum of light with a unit of action. With this is mind, realize that, since action comes in measurable wholes, then wholeness must be the basic nature of each action. And if light is the primary force behind all creation, than wholeness is also the basic nature of all action with a purpose! The purpose of the action is the whole—it is not simply a sum of the parts.

Traditional science—shaped by Saturn—measures such things as mass, length, and of course, time. These are parts. Science can thus never really know the wholes that exist because of this type of measuring. The function of anything—be it a person, a car, or whatever—is only there in the whole. Take the whole apart, and the function is non-existent. Thus, the whole is actually greater than the sum of the parts.

CHIRON is the clue to this picture of reality, whereby the universe is a whole—all parts are interdependent—all parts composed of the exact same packets of light [action, decision]. To quote Teilhard De Chardin, 'The farther and more deeply we penetrate into matter, by means of increasingly powerful methods, the more we are confounded by the interdependence of its parts.' Chiron rules this whole concept of wholeness. It also rules the very idea of the qualifier, to distinguish the smallest article in a class. And Chiron rules the concept of this unit of light-unit of action.

Chiron rules the coming into awareness that a human body is composed of about 1,000,000,000,000,000,000,000,000,000 atoms—yet it is much more than simply a bunch of associated atoms. Chiron rules the concept stated by Alan Watts: 'Languages represent the world as if it were an assemblage of distinct bits and particles. The defect of such grids is such that they screen out or ignore (or repress) interrelations.'

Chiron also rules the concept that, the more complex something is, the more specialized something is, the less it can function if divided. Take for example, a plant. You may be able to grow a whole bunch of new plants by taking cuttings from a mother plant. Higher on the evolutionary scale, some animals can grow new tails if you cut them off, but they cannot grow many new animals from cuttings. Sitting higher up is the human species. While a person may be able to regenerate part of an organ, s/he not only can't (ordinarily) grow a whole new limb—but the ability to function under ordinary circumstances is lessened if a part is removed. Taking this one step further—the human species as a whole is greater than the sum of its parts—but functions that much more poorly, for each member who cuts himself or herself off from the rest, or for each member who is so damaged as to not be able to contribute to the whole.

Arthur M. Young has the concept that there are 7 stages in the universe—7 processes, seven steps, seven levels of freedom. The first stage—Light, spirit, and purpose, has the greatest potential freedom. This evolves into the second stage, of matter on the nuclear level. Here is the beginning of restraint, and the lessening of freedom. The next two stages—atoms, and then molecules, have progressively greater restraint, and lesser freedom. You can look at this process as the condensing of the energy of a photon into the mass of a particle, the joining of opposite charges to form an atom, and the linking of atoms to form a molecule. The remaining three stages show an increase in freedom, and a decrease in constraint. Stage five is the linking of molecules into the form of plants. Stage six is represented by animals, and the seventh stage is a class which includes humans—although Mr. Young says that we are not necessarily the only member of this class. The seventh stage has the greatest ACTUAL freedom, and once again is characterized by the word spirit.

Pervading each level of these seven is the over-riding sense of purpose— the universal energy that was put into motion when the creator said: 'Let there be light'.

But, while we are all linked together with the other six stages—only the seventh stage is capable of becoming conscious of this sense of purpose. Only the category that contains humans can make the conscious decision to take action to accomplish universal goals.

What sets the human species one step above the animals? Chiron. Chiron was not originally part of our solar system. One day, it entered our Sun's family, and will one day leave again. I propose the theory that it entered into its present orbit after animals were already roaming around the earth, but BEFORE the first human beings were born. Each type of plant, and animal, must have had a first specimen sometime. Thus, although we cannot trace them, each living creature has a horoscope for the birth of its species. Human beings, therefore, would be the only species to come into existence with Chiron in the species chart! Thus, what sets us apart is that, as a species, we were born with something extra.

CHIRON IS WHAT SEPARATES US FROM THE ANIMALS!

Think of the Chiron archetype—the centaur has the upper part of a human, and the lower part of a horse. He is an animal—yet one that has something extra—the potential to integrate his various animal traits and rise above them to the point of ruling them totally. Chiron was the example of what one can become.

And remember that most Centaurs were little more than animals. They were our other side—what to expect if we do not integrate Chiron into our being, but just respond to our ties to the lower levels in Mr. Young's steps.

The main key, to understand Chiron, and to perceive the true reality, has been given to you. The reality is that we are all one great whole. What you are looking at may or may not be a whole in itself, but you can be sure that, no matter what you are looking at, it is part of a larger whole. And how you perceive something simply depends upon your frame of mind at the time you look. As Alan Watts says, 'To the naked eye a distant galaxy looks like a solid star and a piece of steel like a continuous and impenetrable mass of matter. But when we change the level of magnification, the galaxy assumes the clear structure of a spiral nebula and the piece of steel turns out to be a system of electrical impulses whirling in relatively vast space.'

The coming of Chiron will open remarkable doors for those who want to grow. Chiron can enable you to change the magnification, both upwards and down—and not only in the way you perceive the world, but how you perceive yourself.

Chapter III: Chiros

Today's world is always caught up in TIME. Must not be late; set your watch; put this on your calendar. Time, like reality, has always been associated with Saturn. Or, when one talks about the time yet to come, one occasionally mentions Uranus as ruler of the future. In truth, both of these do represent aspects of time, and they are very valuable as the rulers of chronological time. Astrology itself would not be possible, if one did not take this element of time into consideration, nor would many other activities. The Bible, in Ecclesiastes 3, says, 'To every thing there is a season, and a time for every purpose under the heaven.'

Chiron, however, makes us aware of another kind of time—one that is outside of Saturn AND Uranus. We call this time Chiros.

Referring back briefly to Chapter II, we see that light is everywhere, and pervades everything that exists. Light has been existent from the instant the universe came into being. I put forth the proposition to you that light itself is outside of chronological time. Or, to put it another way, Time as we know it does not exist at the level of light photons.

This basic concept is not new. St. Basil is quoted as having said, 'Light is of a more general nature than time, for time is found only in the sensible world.' The key here is the word 'sensible', meaning perceptible to the senses, or to the reasoning powers. Time [that is, chronological time] ceases to exist, when one goes beyond just the ordinary five senses.

And it is more than just that. Our time sense varies by such diverse things as the state of our health, and even by the type of food we eat. For example, if our metabolism and temperature were higher than normal, two minutes of brain time might pass in only one minute of clock time—and we would think that time is dragging. This occurs, for example, often during a fever. Conversely, at night, when a person relaxes as s/he prepares for sleep, the body temperature declines, and time can travel faster and faster.

Furthermore, our time sense is less accurate when we are depressed, or mentally unstable. But when we are happy, we seem to be much more able to judge how long something takes to occur.

Another aspect of just how personal time really is stems from the part of the brain that records the sensory input. If we are conscious of a great deal of information coming in—if the input is complex, or in large amounts—intervals seem to be much longer than ordinarily. And this is how we remember them, too, when we look back upon them. The more the brain has to work, the longer an interval we believe we were exposed to the information. When we cannot remember much information, the time interval seems to have been much shorter.

Thus, the time measured by clocks—that we rely upon to conduct business in the material world—is the time ruled by Saturn. But Chiros represents the type of time that is beyond the chronometer. Chiron's time is not measurable by any clock—and may not be measurable at all.

When the planet Chiron passes over a natal position it brings the opportunity to enter into this Chiros state. A door opens, and time can seem suspended while one makes a major decision. At these crucial instants, one can truly be seen as having reached a turning point. What is decided during Chiros can change one's whole life.

The Chiron transit, however, is in itself neutral. The moment of Chiros is upon you. The decision is still your free will. You can choose to take a path which can lead you out of some Saturnian rut; you can choose one which enables you to correct an imbalance; you can even make the choice to stay on a path that will lead to the deterioration of your particular condition. But the choice is your own.

Chiron rules the concept of NOW. While the past [Saturn] exists, and we can learn from it—and while the future [Uranus] is definitely coming, and we can prepare for it—in truth, we only live in the present [Chiron]. As you are reading each of these words, it is the present. By the time the word has reached your brain, your eyes have already moved on to the next word—so the moment you read that word has already gone into the past.

Yet, how many people try to live in the past, or in the future—and thus miss the present that is around them? How many constantly replay the tapes in their memories, of things gone by, rather than smelling the flowers? Or, how many worry about the future, based upon past bad experiences, rather than paying attention to the present in order for the future to be more beautiful? This is one of Chiron's lessons to us—to live today, this minute, this second.

Look at Saturn and Uranus in the solar system. Both have been shown to have rings, and these rings can serve to become prisons if we let them.

But through Chiron, and the perception that we only live in the present, those rings can represent lenses, to magnify both the future and the past, magically—and to see them more clearly, when we need to.

Let us go back briefly into mythology. Chronus [Saturn] ruled the universe, until he was overthrown by his son Jupiter. Chiron was Jupiter's half-brother, but, even more, he taught one very important lesson: Honor Jupiter above all gods. Both of these aspects of the myths apply to our discussion of time. When Jupiter overthrew Saturn, it was a sign for wisdom, understanding, and personal growth to overcome the dictatorship of chronological time. And Chiron tells us to honor this view above all others—to become aware that growth will occur only when one can go beyond the limits imposed by the experiences of the senses, and when one can live in the now.

Further analogy comes from Chiron's astronomical position. Chiron in its orbit contacts the orbit of Uranus. Thus, Chiron contacts the future. And, Chiron actually crosses the orbit of Saturn, and moves closer to Jupiter than Saturn ever could. Thus, Chiron is not limited by Saturn, but can go both within and without its orbit—thus within and without chronological time. And when Chiron moves closer to Jupiter, it is the reminder of how important it is, to our very growth and evolution, that we are not ruled by Saturn.

As I mentioned, Chiron transits bring the opportunity to experience the moment of Chiros. Learning how to focus in upon one's natal Chiron can also bring about these moments of Chiros—and thus bring about the power inherent in these moments of Chiros when one chooses! One very good way to do this is to re-program your thinking to live in the present at all times. Other ways that have proven quite successful through time include deep meditation, and letting oneself become one with music.

While one's whole life contains opportunities for change and growth, one of the most important times occurs at the time of the Chiron return. This is discussed further in the next chapter.

But I think it important, before we end this chapter, to discuss the connection between the process of aging, and the concept of time.

Many scientists have concluded that the program for aging is encoded in one's hypothalamus-pituitary system. The evidence points to the control of hormonal release by the hypothalamus, and that as one gets older, this process gets more and more irregular. Even the body's immune cells are influenced by this, for they not only become less and less effective in fighting the body's enemies—but they may actually go haywire, and turn against the very cells they are supposed to protect. [We will discuss this at greater length when we look at Chiron and health].

But one of the primary results of this aging process is the decline in the rate of consumption of oxygen by the body—and thus a slowing down of metabolism. If you remember, a faster metabolism means that time moves slowly—and this is why time seems to take forever to a little child. But it is also why, when one gets older, time seems to move faster and faster.

The solution, or at least part of it, is taught by Chiron. Live in the now—the present. If you are not subject to the Saturnian consciousness, you will not have your time sense shaped by the state of your body and its metabolism. Do not become a Saturnian old man or old woman—become a Chironian being, living in the eternal now.

Chapter IV: The Chiron Return

Chiron has an unusual orbit, which is known to change throughout time. In the past, it has occasionally been as short as 46 years, or as long as 52 years. At the present time, the orbit is close to 51 years for one cycle. It averages out, over many centuries, to 49 years. I would like to discuss the Chiron return first from the standpoint of the 49 year average, second from its current cycles, and third as a return no matter how long the orbit is.

Anyone who has been involved with astrology even for a short while should know how important the number 7 is. At approximately age 7, a child experiences Saturn in square to natal Saturn, and then every 7 years thereafter Saturn again makes a hard aspect to its natal position. At age 28 [4 x 7], the Saturn return takes place for everyone, and this represents a major cycle for the archetypal human. [Of course, since the orbit varies slightly each cycle, and there are periods of retrograde apparent motion, Saturn does not return to its natal position in everyone's chart at exactly 28 years to the day, but varies with each cycle and with each individual].

And the orbit of Uranus is about 84 years, thus representing the symbolism inherent in the numbers 7 x 12. Again, it does not return at exactly 84 years to the day—but 84 does represent the archetype.

Chiron's orbit is represented archetypally by the numbers 7 x 7. This has many levels of symbolism, and basic numerology is outside the intent of this book. But a few points are worth mentioning.

First, with Saturn, it is a number 4 which is multiplied by the base 7 to get the orbit. With Uranus, it is a 3 x 4 which is multiplied by the same base. With Chiron, it is a 3 + 4 times base 7. With Chiron, the 3 and 4 are fused together to make a new number, unlike Uranus which has the 3 and 4 simply elevating each other to a new level via multiplication.

Not only that, but with Chiron, we have the unique situation of the number

51

seven being squared —thus elevating the whole number seven to a higher level. I will leave the further numerology of these numbers to those of you who are inclined in that direction.

I would like to make a comment, however, on humans in general at that age. Aristotle in his Rhetoric, said, 'The body is at its best between the ages of thirty and thirty-five; the mind is at its best about the age of forty-nine.' I agree with him, up to a point. In referring to the typical human being, his statement is very close to the truth. However, for those who truly comprehend the meanings of Chiron, the mind must continue to be 'at its best' for many, many years after age 49. More on this shortly.

The time around 50 or so is usually a time when old friendships are treated more warmly, and seem more worthwhile than ever before. The harsh relations with colleagues, caused by years of competition, usually begin to soften at this time. Even difficulties with relatives often begin to be less troublesome now. Physically, the average body begins to grow shorter. In the male, there is a marked decline in the level of testosterone, while in the female, more women begin menopause at age 51 than at any age between age 45 to age 55. Overall, there is a feeling at this time that one has completely formed one's personality. As George Orwell wrote, 'At fifty, everyone has the face he deserves'.

The Chiron return at the present time comes remarkably close to the time that the progressing Sun makes a Septile [1/7 of the zodiac, or about $51°25'43"$] from its natal position. Since I am a firm believer that all coincidences have some meaning to them, I feel that there must be a connection between the meaning of the Septile, and the discovery of Chiron while its orbit parallels this aspect. Let me elucidate on how I perceive the Septile:

A transit or progression of a planet making a Septile to anything in the native's chart brings out a sense of compulsion in regards to the natal body. There is a feeling of destiny—of some purely personal purpose that is larger than one's limited world. When it is a progression, the compulsion comes along with a need to link up the two planets, and bring about a change in the natal to make it more evolved, using the energies of the progressing body. When it is the Sun, progressing Septile to itself—there is the urge to bring about permanent change, or to remove any obstacle, in the person's sense of self, and in the life goals. It is like saying, 'O.K., I have had many different experiences. I know now pretty much who I am, and what I want for the rest of my life. Now I must make major decisions about changing anything I want to change—and pursuing the course I have in front of me for the rest of my life'.

There is much in the above paragraph which relates to the actual Chiron return. There IS a feeling of destiny and purpose for many at this time, and a time of major decisions. And what happens at the return DOES set the course for entire rest of life.

But in order to comprehend truly this time in one's life one must first go back and understand a little of Chiron's meaning at birth.

At birth, one's parents, and everyone else in the world, are worrying over some types of problems which relate directly to whatever sign Chiron transits. The obstacles they are trying to overcome are major issues, and pre-occupy much of the parents' minds. These obstacles can be things that have been let go for too long, and now MUST be taken care of—or they could be the result of changes in the world which cause restructuring, or redefining of issues and situations. But whatever the problems are, things must be dealt with.

Of course each family is different, so the individual problems a family faces will take on different aspects of Chiron's sign. For example, when the poor family was trying to stay alive during the Depression, Chiron in the sign Taurus brought out the Taurus survival instinct. But for a family that was wealthy at that time, entirely different Taurus issues had to be faced.

The common denominator of the Chiron sign, however, is the parents' pre-occupation. What happens is that the child's mind becomes imprinted with the importance of these particular problems. The child does not realize that s/he will have to face other problems later, which may be of equal or greater importance. Since More and Dad are so tense about what is going on at the time of the birth—the child becomes imprinted with the concept that solving these problems is 'priority one'.

The child learns that nothing must stand in the way of resolving any difficulties in these areas. This then becomes a deeply ingrained 'personal imperative' which stays with the child the whole life long.

As the child grows up, Chiron passes through each succeeding sign one by one, and thus eventually through every house of the chart. The child must deal with each type of new problem that develops, often coming from new or unexpected directions. Each new problem resolved gives the developing individual new experience, and serves to sharpen the problem-solving skills. Nevertheless, the individual still retains the basic personal imperative throughout each learning experience. When Chiron makes a hard aspect to its natal position, the individual learns that some other problems are also imperative. But never is the basic personal imperative altered—just sometimes adjusted or re-focused.

As the Chiron return approaches, the person has experienced every possible Chiron-to-Chiron aspect; passages of Chiron through every house, and through every sign. S/he has had to deal with it from every possible direction, and from all perspectives. Hopefully, the person has learned a great deal from all of these experiences in life. The past Chiron cycle has been a source of many, many lessons for the person.

When the Chiron return arrives, it can be an evolutionary leap. The person can now take off, and fulfill his or her purpose on earth. BUT, for many, it is too difficult. For many, the leap is not made.

Just as in the period around the child's birth, at the Chiron return, the world is contending with problems that relate to Chiron's current neighbors with anxieties in these areas; news reporters discussing related world issues; listen to co-workers discussing their difficulties in these areas. In other words, at the time of the Chiron return, the person is in effect coming home. What s/he has spent a lifetime dealing with, trying to resolve, trying to learn, is now plaguing everyone around the world. What will anybody do?

When Chiron makes ANY transit, the person can at least for a brief moment enter Chiros—the time outside of chronological time. At the Chiron return this no longer is an option—the person finds self forced into Chiros, maybe once, maybe several times. While these moments may be brief, they are now unavoidable.

The person looks around and sees others trying to overcome difficulties that s/he has spent a lifetime trying to deal with. People seem distraught, perplexed and confused. Yet, to the person having the Chiron return, many of the answers seem obvious—many of the problems easy to solve.

Now for Chiros. Major decision time. Should one help others with what one has learned? Should the Chiron-return individual become a guru, a teacher, or even become the mentor for a younger individual? Should the person begin to try to counsel others? OR, will the person attempt to make a profit from his or her knowledge and experience, becoming a creature of the material world, and selling the information? OR, will the person, perhaps, close up and withdraw, and not even try to help another?

No matter how one has lived up to this point, even if one has led a totally selfish or materialistic existence, one can now make that evolutionary leap. Note the word 'can', please. One has the greater free will under Chiros than under ordinary chronological time—but still one must make the choice.

For some people, the return is a very critical time in personal terms. They may develop a major illness, or a serious life-crisis. But even when the Chiron return comes on with such force, the purpose is the same. This crisis gives a major opportunity to make a major decision. Out of such crises comes great awareness, and the potential to become a truly gifted teacher, or even healer.

The story does not end here, of course. A few years later, and the person will experience his or her second Saturn return. What has occurred at the Chiron return will often set the course for what is to happen at the Saturn return.

To clarify this: if, at the Chiron return, one has made the leap to sharing the fruits of one's experience with those in need, then the Saturn return may be seen as the closing of one chapter in life, and the beginning of a new one. It will be seen as a stepping up, and life will be viewed as being truly grand.

But, if one did not step up at the Chiron return—if one chose a path of selfishness instead of a path of light—AND, one did not rectify this course during the years since the Chiron return—the Saturn return will generally be experienced as a great weight, and as the beginning of the downhill portion of one's life.

As I said at the end of the previous chapter—if you are not subject to the Saturnian consciousness, you will not have your time sense shaped by the state of your body and its metabolism. This should tell you that at the Chiron return one should work to develop an awareness of Chiros and learn to live in the 'Now', in order for the years after the Saturn return to be truly fulfilling and not years of deterioration.

At the Chiron return some people may feel rather superior to those around them, and quite self-justified. 'See, just as I have been saying all along', might be their attitude. Or they may feel that the 'know it all' in the areas of their natal Chiron sign. Such individuals can be heard saying, 'Now, you must do it this way.' Attitudes like this are not those that lead to taking the giant step upwards. They tend to irritate the very people whom the Chiron-return person is trying to help.

The most positive aspect of this time in life is achieved by linking the higher nature of the two signs which are frequently linked to Chiron: Libra [truly perceiving those you are helping as being your equals, not, inferiors, as well as looking at each teaching experience as your own learning experience, as well], and Sagittarius [sharing the knowledge and wisdom you have acquired, trying to share the true meaning of each experience, and wanting to understand what is going on in the minds of other people]. Perhaps we cannot say that Chiron has rulership over these, or any signs. But there is a definite affinity between Chiron and the signs Libra and Sagittarius.

The ancients had a definite awareness of the connection between liberation from Saturn—and the time around age fifty. In the Old Testament of the Bible, Leviticus 25:8-11, we find the following: 'And thou shalt number seven Sabbaths of years unto thee, seven times seven years; and the space of the seven Sabbaths of years shall be unto thee forty and nine years. Then thou shalt cause the trumpet of the jubilee to sound on the tenth day of the seventh month, in the day of atonement shall ye make the trumpet sound through all your land. And ye shall hallow the fiftieth year, and proclaim liberty throughout all the land unto all the inhabitants thereof; it shall be a jubilee unto you; and ye shall return every man unto his possession, and ye shall return every man unto his family. A jubilee shall that fiftieth year be unto you.....' [There is more, but this is the main part]. As you can see, every fifty years all slaves had to be freed, and liberty became the most important thing.

And in each person's life, the opportunity to achieve freedom from the Saturnian past, and freedom from anxiety about the Uranian future, comes around the fiftieth year—at the Chiron return. UNLESS, of course, one has opened up and truly embraced the principles of Chiron before the return arrives.

Wherever you have your natal Chiron, you tend to be most unaligned with any party or group—most on your own unique path. So you can see that, when Chiron returns, events and circumstances will focus attention on your particular path and stimulate your individualistic approach to the affairs of Chiron's natal house. Thus, Chiron as the door opener, opening up to your own special destiny. The Chiron return often brings about an awakening to your own singular purpose.

It can be a time of great power. You can overcome the most frustrating limitations now—the most mind-boggling obstacles. The house Chiron occupies indicates the area from whence the potential power can be drawn—and during the Chiron return you have the greatest potential to control and utilize this great power.

Chiron is often viewed as a way to TAP the power of this natal house, and at the return, the potential exists to turn the tap wide open. But consider carefully how you handle this-power. The best way, it seems, is:

1. Consider exactly in what ways you have let Saturn restrict you. How have you felt really secure behind some wall, so that you did not venture out into the world? Where have you ignored, or repressed, chances for growth?

2. Watch for ways to take true steps outside of your walls—they will be coming at the Chiron return.

3. Look for ways to be of real help to others, who can profit from your experience. But do it with light, not force and ego.

4. And, most important, learn to live in the NOW. If Chiron is tied into the universal light, and this light comes from the Creator of all things, then the light must exist in past, present and future. If you live for today, the other two will take care of themselves. Corinthians 2:17—'Where the Spirit of the Lord is, there is liberty'.

You might like to take example from a few people who made the giant step, accomplishing great things at or near their Chiron returns:

William Booth founded the Salvation Army.

Harold Carter opened the tomb of Tutankhamun, often considered the greatest find in archaeological history.

George Stephenson opened the first practical passenger railway in the world.

Charles Darwin published **The Origin of the Species**.

Henry Ford introduced the concept of the assembly line into his factory.

Henry Kissinger became Secretary of State and was awarded the Nobel Peace Prize.

Gerhard Schmatz became the oldest person to climb to the top of Mt. Everest.

Samuel Cunard established the first regular trans-Atlantic steamship service.

William Faulkner won the Nobel Prize for Literature.

Ernest Heinkel made the first successful flight by jet plane.

In closing this chapter, I must state that it is NOT over for those past their Chiron return who have not made that major jump. The lessons of Chiron can be learned at any age. The first step is to try to get into your own personal Chiron, and the next step is to try to learn the meaning of Chiros. If you learn to live in the present, age itself will cease to be a factor.

Chapter V: Myth

In ancient Greek and Roman myths, the various gods and goddesses can claim their ancestry to be the union of Uranus [the heavens] with Gaea [the earth]. Perhaps this represents creativity emerging from the grounding of the spiritual with the material ?

Anyway, Saturn was one of the children of the union. Through his match with Rhea, Jupiter, Neptune, Pluto, Ceres, Juno and Vesta were born. And, in what is typical of the gods, Saturn united with a nymph and produced Chiron. As you probably know, Jupiter overthrew Saturn, just as Saturn had over-thrown Uranus before him. Chiron never lost respect for his half-brother, so that when Jupiter took over as head of the gods, Chiron taught all of his pupils, 'Honor Jupiter above all others'. And, Jupiter had a great deal of respect for Chiron as well.

Another important aspect of the myth is the story of Prometheus. I am not going into detail about the crimes of Prometheus, since that does not directly relate to Chiron. But what does relate is his punishment.

Prometheus was chained to a rock, and each day a giant bird would come and rip out his liver. At night the liver would grow back. So he was in torture day after day. Chiron injured his foot, and was in constant pain. Both were immortal, so neither could end his suffering through death.

But Chiron appealed to Jupiter to spare Prometheus, and offered to die, that Prometheus might be freed. Jupiter saw to it that this was done, and also, to honor beloved Chiron, he placed the Centaur in the heavens as a constellation.

There is much to be gleaned from these myths, especially since they relate to Chiron's orbit in our solar system. Here follows some ideas that will give you food for thought.

One possible way to view the myths is to relate them to the archetypal human, from birth to adulthood. With this in mind, the union of Gaea and

Uranus would represent the union that led to the child's conception. It would refer to aspects of one's parents that the child might not see—aspects that the parents might have seen in each other, however—that nevertheless had an influence in shaping the child's makeup.

Uranus is overthrown, and Saturn becomes dominant. While the child is small, the planet Saturn is the main symbol of the male parent in most children's lives. The Moon represents the mother as the child perceives her—but not necessarily as the father perceives her. [For this, turn to the asteroid Rhea in the chart].

The child begins to grow up and think for him/herself—to question the parents, and form his or her own philosophy. This is the beginning of the rebellion symbolized in the myth as the war between Jupiter and Saturn. In this war, by the way, Prometheus sided with Jupiter, even though Prometheus was a Titan like Saturn, thus earning Jupiter's gratitude. This represents the beginning of a truly individual personality within the child.

After the war, Prometheus becomes chief advisor to Jupiter, which show the increasing importance of individuality in the growing youngster.

But the child grows more and more independent of the parents. While the child is slowly but surely learning to put Saturn in its place, the throne of Saturn still exists, only now it is occupied by Jupiter. The child no longer sees the parents as absolute gods—but still tries to hold onto the secure images s/he had of them, all the while still rebelling. This is represented by Jupiter getting angrier and angrier with Prometheus, as Prometheus teaches mankind one thing after another, making them less and less dependent on the gods. At this point, the youth has not fully developed a Jupiter of his or her own—but is still trying to put the parents on the central throne.

The major turning point in the child-parent relation ship begins now. In the myth Prometheus steals the cosmic fire from the gods, and gives it to mankind. This cosmic fire—the creative spark of the universe—means that mankind will no long be dependent on the gods. Relating this to the youngster—a time comes when s/he must act, totally alone, declaring personal independence.

Jupiter is outraged. The child's parents are furious—and the child finds it is getting close to impossible to keep the image of parents as the central rulers of life.

Jupiter chains Prometheus to the rock. Note the symbolism of the bird ripping out the liver— with the liver being ruled by the planet Jupiter. Jupiter showing his force—that he is still in control. Things are coming to a head with the parents.

Chiron frees Prometheus. This is the point where one comes of age. In some families, this can be a violent breakdown between child and parent, while in others, it can come as an agreement.

59

But now, the youngster is born anew—as an independent person.

Before Chiron gives his life, he teaches that Jupiter must be honored above all. Prometheus, once again free, again becomes a close ally of Jupiter. This is where the child has come to terms with his or her own Jupiter, has made it his or her own ruler, and no longer simply sees it as an extension of the parents. Hopefully, at this stage, the youngster makes peace with the parents, or at least with the images of the parents in his or her own head.

And of course, Chiron and Prometheus both had to suffer pain first—since true growth can only come out of pain and suffering.

The age when each step occurs varies from person to person. Some people never reach that final stage. Some never make peace with their parents, or do so only after the parents have died. And some get stuck in even earlier stages. As an astrologer, one's job would be to try to help each person move out of being stuck, and on towards the freeing of Prometheus.

Note, that when Chiron dies, he is placed with honor in the heavens, where he can always be seen—and where he can be sought for guidance. Long after one is freed [Prometheus unchained], one can always turn to Chiron for help and guidance.

Now let us take a look at Chiron's orbit, in relation to the myths. First, Chiron begins each cycle, when closest to the Sun, at perihelion. At this time it is closer to the orbit of Jupiter than Saturn can ever be. We can say that Chiron is conferring with Jupiter, and giving him the guidance he needs, as well as taking in whatever message Jupiter wants to give to the other gods.

Chiron crosses Saturn's orbit and moves outward. With Chiron's help, Jupiter becomes the dominant force in the solar system, as his message reaches out past Saturn, and is not stopped by Saturn's limits. This truly puts Saturn in his place.

Chiron then moves all the way to Uranus' orbit, and contacts said orbit. This, to me, represents the freeing of Prometheus. A number of authors have suggested that Uranus should have been called Prometheus, instead of Uranus. I submit to you that Uranus is its proper name, when referring to the child's past, where s/he came from, and why s/he was created—but Prometheus is the name of the planet once the child reaches adulthood.

After Chiron frees Prometheus he heads back toward Saturn. This is representative of his death, since Saturn was delegated to deep caves beneath the surface of the earth.

Finally Chiron reaches perihelion again—and Jupiter places him up among the stars.

In this last idea is the hint of the future for the planet Chiron. It will one day be forced to leave the solar system, and return to the stars from whence it came, when perturbations in its orbit throw it outward.

The orbit of Chiron is averaging at 49 years over its many cycles. As mentioned earlier, the Old Testament of the Bible perceives every 50th year to be the time to proclaim liberty throughout the land. This ties into the freeing of Prometheus once every Chiron cycle.

Some other aspects of Chiron's myths are equally important. He was the upper part of a man attached to the lower part of a horse—the man rising above, and controlling, his animal nature; and since the two were fused together, Chiron represented the fusion of both in a way that made the best use of both.

Chiron was a great teacher, teaching survival skills, as well as such things as healing, and music as a healing tool. Kenneth Negus says, 'One of Chiron's major roles was to teach the playing of the Kithara—a stringed instrument closely related to the lyre.' Chiron did not just teach music for the heck of it— he taught it so that his pupils could become more whole, and also so that they could heal others.

Chiron was also well known for his teachings of using herbs and other natural substances to bring about healing, and to help others become more at one with the universe. He even had his own flower which he used more often than any other herb—the Centaury. This flower comes in many varieties, such as the Blue Cornflower and the Giant Knapweed—used by herbalists to heal wounds.

Almost all the great heroes of myth were at one time or another trained by Chiron. He would withdraw with them to his cave, and the pupil would only come out when he was ready to face the world. Time, as we know it, would cease for those within the cave. Thus Chiron brings his pupils to an inner world, away from the world of everyday senses—and takes them where Chiros rules instead of chronological time.

In 1981, Richard Tarnas wrote an article for NCGR entitled Uranus and Prometheus. In this article, he mentions that the cosmic fire that Prometheus stole could be perceived as astrology itself, since 'the sustained study of astrology grants human consciousness the direct experience of clear, overwhelming indications of a divine intelligence of incomprehensible complexity and omnipotence.' Thus, by being taught astrology and science by Prometheus, mankind has the potential to become god-like.

Chiron was also known for the teaching of astrology to his pupils in the hopes of their becoming more at one with the universe. Chiron, the planet, is connected to the universal light which was born in the first instant of Creation. Could this universal light be one and the same as the cosmic fire? And, if so, can the freeing of Prometheus by Chiron represent the releasing of humanity's true destiny, after we perceive the true reality via Chiron, and thus perceive how we are all one? Astrology works because it represents the principle of 'As above, so below.' Is it this simple principle that will free us?

Chapter VI: Healing Heritage

Hippocrates was born around 460 B.C. Perhaps you are familiar with the abbreviated version of his Hippocratic Oath [adopted in 1948 by the General Assembly of the World Medical Association] which hangs in most doctors' offices. Anyway, Hippocrates is credited with separating the practice of medicine from religion and superstition, thus lifting it to a loftier plane. What many do not realize is that there are a number of translations of the Hippocratic Oath in existence, some of which advise the physician to consult the birth chart of the patient prior to making a diagnosis.

What is more, in the long versions—those closest to the original—there are such admonitions as: 'to reckon him who taught me this art equally dear to me as my parents; to share my substance with him and relieve his necessities if required; to regard his offspring as on the same footing as my own brothers, and to teach them this art if they shall wish to learn it, without fee or stipulation, and that by precept, oral teaching and every other mode of instruction, I will impart a knowledge of the art to my own sons and to those of my teachers, and to disciples bound by a stipulation and oath, according to the law of medicine, but to no others'.

Hippocrates recognized the importance of astrology to health. He also recognized the intimate connection between the teacher and his pupil, and the teacher and the healer. Perhaps Chiron [the planet] was unknown to astrologers in his day—but the inter-relation of its basic themes was very much on the mind of Hippocrates and those who followed him. There was a time when every doctor was also an astrologer. Many, in fact, would use the art of Horary Astrology in order to help their patients. While in today's world, we attribute medicine primarily to the sixth house and sixth sign—the ancient astro-physician would consider the actual physician at the seventh house.

There was a good reason to consider the physician as seventh house, rather than sixth. The doctor viewed his patient as an equal—a fellow human being—and not as the doctor's inferior. In fact, the doctor considered the work with the patient as a two-way street—by helping to restore the patient to good health, the doctor was in turn always learning, perfecting his art, and making himself more whole. What is more, the interaction was always two way—the patient never paid the doctor unless the patient got well.

Many people have suggested varying signs to be ruled by Chiron. It may be that Chiron does not 'rule' any one sign, but instead has an affinity with several. But if Chiron is to rule one specific sign, I vote for Libra, because of its connection to the seventh house, and Chiron's connection with the healer.

Place Libra on the cusp of the first house. Virgo on the twelfth thus represents the hidden assets and private resources that the doctor has to draw upon if necessary. Note, *if necessary*. The optimal role of the doctor has always been to teach people how to achieve and maintain balance in their lives. S/he resorts to tools to heal, if necessary, when a patient becomes ill. But s/he also is there to aid people to become whole. In fact, that is the doctor's primary function—and the healing of the ill is only a part of the larger picture. Thus, it is true that Virgo ties in to medicines, and healings. A doctor does use these, as necessary, to repair the damage done while a patient is out of balance. But once the patient is healed, then the doctor is bound to aid the patient to get onto the right track, toward balance and wholeness—this is the doctor's highest function. Thus, Libra as the physician.

To me, much of the confusion as to Chiron's' sign comes from disagreement over which sign(s) actually rule healing and medicines. I feel that Virgo does indeed rule the medicines a doctor uses to repair the damage to a system. But Libra represents the physician/teacher entity, and Chiron represents this side of Libra. When we begin to look at the function of a doctor, once again, as the one who enables us to balance our lives/ diet/fitness/health—instead of just the curing of ills, we will be able to see how Chiron ties in to Libra.

There is another rationale for tying Chiron to Libra, but I will get more into that later on.

Alan Watts has written a number of excellent things showing a correspondence between Western forms of psychotherapy and Eastern religions, with their emphasis on Liberation. He refers to the idea that they both are interested in 'bringing about changes of consciousness, changes in our ways of feeling about our own existence, and our relation to human society and the natural world.' Both are concerned with the transformation of consciousness—of releasing the individual from unconscious blocks, as well as from 'unexamined assumptions' and 'unrealized nonsense problems'.

Herein lies another key to understanding Chiron's nature. Watts points out that the underlying aim of Eastern cultures is this Liberation—and that such things as reincarnation, the occult powers promised, and other fancy things [while they may all be valid] can have the effect of acting to confuse the central issue. One can get lost in all the 'smoke screen', and miss the true purpose of the Eastern ways. And this true purpose is Liberation.

What is Liberation, really? As Watts says, 'Liberation does not involve the loss or destruction of ... the ego, it means seeing through them—in the same way that we can use the idea of the equator without confusing it with a physical mark upon the surface of the earth'.

Perhaps you have heard of one tool of this Liberation, the Koan. The Koan is a Chironic device—it is a tool from Zen Buddhism. The master would present his disciple with a problem to solve—a problem that could not be solved by the use of logic. The student would work hard at a solution to the Koan, struggling ever harder, getting more and more tangled up in his logic—until, hopefully, he would arrive at SATORI—a great insight from understanding the purpose of the whole lesson. But the insight did not come from understanding the specific Koan—the Koan was only a tool. Let us look at a bit of Buddhist philosophy.

All things, in this philosophy, are stated as falsely imagined, and having no reality of their own. Taken in the light of the connection with psychotherapy, we can view this as meaning that everything is relative—since nothing can be given any description, without relating it to something else, then nothing can be considered to have an independent existence. So this concept of 'nothing has a reality of its own' becomes perfectly valid in this context. This gives you a clue to the solution.

Another clue—some problems are really no problems—they actually have no solution. You can see this, over and over, when you are dealing with a neurotic person. Such a person keeps doing the same things, over and over, always without success—trying to solve such a false problem. S/he is trying to make sense out of something that cannot be resolved. For, you see, s/he does not see that this problem is nonsense—s/he sees it as important. [Sometimes, it goes to the extreme —s/he retreats from reality, into psychosis, unable to take any action whatever!]

This vicious circle is called Samsara. It is from this that Liberation releases us—upon Liberation we become aware that the problem we are trying to resolve is just plain meaningless. [Perhaps, in some cases, there may be a solution—but the basic problem is so absurd, when seen clearly, that such a solution is also nonsense.]

Back to the Koan. This was a tool, for getting the disciple to perceive his own vicious circle; to perceive that he was dwelling on nonsense problems—and to take the next step: to perceive that the whole problem of an existence independent from the world is one of the nonsense problems. This last thought returns us to Chiron, to the interconnection between all things, and to the ability to perceive that 'we are the world' [to borrow a line from a song].

Carl Gustav Jung said, '*We cannot change anything unless we accept it*'. This is also part of Chiron—it forces us to accept that something in us needs to change—then we can begin to perceive the direction we need to go to do so. Chiron has been equated with the concept of Guru. Some schools of philosophy insist that one can not reach liberation without a guru; some that some people need to do it totally alone; and some that a guru is not mandatory, but does make it easier. But in truth—there is always a guru. Oh, it may not be someone from India. It may not even be a living being. It may simply be a book. But somehow, some outside agency, some relationship, is necessary to put one onto the path.

Once on the path, however, one may never need the guru again. For example—let us say that a friend helps you to discover which train is the one going to a particular city. Once you have that information, you can get on the train yourself and ride all the way there without ever needing to refer to your friend again. And once you get to the city, you do not carry your train around with you—it got you there, but now, you no longer need it.

The ancients knew a great deal more than we give them credit for. Freud may have been a pioneer, but he was not going into uncharted waters.

With the Eastern ways to liberation, the maps were simply in a language Westerners could not understand. But even today, ways to Liberation, via psychotherapy, are often surrounded by smokescreens, albeit of a different kind—smokescreens of jargon, and technical language.

Go back into the past again, this time to Greece, and we perceive that the ancients knew about the mind-body link that we often forget. The very symbol of Chiron—the Centaur was a fusion of man [mind] and animal [body]. Tracing his ancestry far enough back, we hear universe was created out of chaos. This was not quite the word as we use it today, but rather the undifferentiated substance from which all things emerged. This could easily be seen as equating to pure light ['Let there be light'].

Chiron in mythology was a Maverick among the Centaurs. All of the other Centaurs were drinkers and carousers—Chiron rose above this. One way this can be interpreted is that we should all be this type of Maverick, rising above our animal natures, being different from the average human. But on another level, we can see Chiron as rising up above the social structure of the others. By doing this he was a Maverick in relation to society —but at the same time, wanting to be at one with a much larger structure—the universe itself. Thus Chiron was a symbol of one who has risen above the Samsara—one who has achieved the true Nirvana of seeing things exactly as they are, and how they interrelate.

Another perception of Chiron can be derived from the above, relating directly to physicians. View the general field of Medicine as the society of physicians. The Chironic factor—the Maverick among the 'healers'—is the one who truly places the welfare of the patient above the rules or 'accepted practices' of fellow doctors. Thus you can imagine the formally organized profession as being such a society—and those doctors who are willing to use unconventional therapies, as well as other healers who are not generally accepted amongst medical doctors, as being representative of Chironic healers. The individual —whoever s/he may be—spends life in a Quest for wholeness. For some this is totally unconscious, and for others it is a major conscious goal. But all of us search for this, one way or another. Chiron is the guiding force of the quest, leading one toward an understanding of one's destiny by showing how one truly fits in with the universe. The healer has the greatest potential for being the guide on this quest—once one has recognized the nature of the quest. But the healer must be guided truly by the Hippocratic doctrines—the whole ones, not the abbreviated versions. The quest leads to Self-transformation. This ultimate goal is what both laymen and physicians should strive to achieve. Many things can be truly used as tools in the quest. Chiron taught such things as music, diet, exercise, self-defense, and the use of herbs. [His own plant, the Centaury is used to treat wounds].

Since it is noted that you need not go to an actual guru to be set onto the path, you should realize that there are many things you can do all by yourself. Let us take a few examples:

MUSIC: Music can be used to put you into different moods, or help you out of moods. One of the most potent uses of music is to help you to enter into alternate realities by making meditation easier. With music, one can leave the realm of Saturnian time and enter Chiros, where major changes can be made and vision can be much, much clearer. The particular music depends on you, and your chart. One excellent method for selecting the music is to find a composer who has the Sun, Moon or a planet closely conjunct your natal Chiron—and, if possible the composer's natal Chiron on one of your personal planets, as well. Failing that, choose your music during a transit to your natal Chiron.

HERBS & DIET: If one is to be at harmony with the universe, one must be very selective about what one eats. Choose a time when your Chiron is being transited, or when you are receiving a Chiron transit, and revamp your whole diet.

To learn your real needs, try abstaining from some main item of food for a while, then notice very carefully your body's reaction when you resume eating it again. Keep on with this testing until you are sure of your body's responses to your diet. If a particular food really does not 'sit well' there is no great reason to keep on burdening your body with it. Try other things.

Not only should each meal be balanced, but all the meals in any one day must be in harmony. For some, eating six small meals a day is necessary to put the body in harmony. The body throws off what it does not use of some nutrients. For others, very specific requirements of food are the path. For myself, I have found that all red meats [beef, pork, lamb], all sugar, and caffeine must be totally avoided.

Keep in mind that the purpose of food is growth, when young, and fuel, when older. The purpose of Chironic diet is for the body to run in harmony with the universe. Go see a nutritionist or healer to prepare a diet that truly gives you what you need, if you are lacking the knowledge yourself. And one more thing—follow it, once you have found the path.

There are many things around you, which you may eat rarely, or not at all, but which should be integral parts of your diet—or which may be exactly what you need to balance out your system. Many people go to the doctor when they fail ill, and pay for expensive prescriptions full of strangely named chemicals. Yet in their own kitchens there are usually remedies for many, many ills.

Take for example raw onion. It contains phosphorus, calcium, magnesium, sulphur, sodium, potassium, and iron; starch, acetic and phosphoric acid; iodine, zinc and silicon; vitamins A, B, and C. What is more, it contains a plant hormone called Glueokinen, which resembles insulin in its ability to reduce the blood-sugar level; a substance which stimulates the digestive secretions of the pancreas; and, it emits [amazingly] Mitogenic Radiation—ultra-violet radiation which stimulates cell activity.

Being Chironic means opening your eyes to the world around you.

An excellent source of nutrients—and healing powers—is often overlooked, because it is seen as a weed: The lowly Dandelion! Did you know that only one ounce of this plant contains 7,000 units of Vitamin A? It also contains Vitamins B and C, calcium, potassium, choline, and two alkaloids which are very beneficial to the liver. Yet how many of you, by reason of social appearances, will not stoop to pulling up weeds for the purpose of eating them?

Chiron leads the individual towards becoming whole, but it also leads the medical field in general towards the same objective. Here are a few Chiron-related events, to show you what I mean:

Both Dr. Palmer, who discovered Chiropractic Medicine, and Roentgen, who discovered X-Rays, were born near the Chiron perihelion in the 1840's.

Fifty years later—1895—they made their discoveries, when Chiron was once again at perihelion. This perihelion is very important, for not only is Chiron closer to us than at any other time, but it is also within the orbit of Saturn.

Other things of interest in 1895: Dr. Freud began to publish his revolutionary theories on mental illness. The first Chiropody Law governing the study of Chiropody was enacted in New York. [This is the branch of medicine dealing with ailments of the feet—now called podiatry]. P. J. Roberts invented the first Medicine Bail. [Dr. Louis Pasteur died that year, although I am not sure how that relates, other than the fact that he made great contributions to medicine]. I could go on and on listing other events tied to Chiron perihelia, but I think you get the point.

As I mentioned earlier, I have other evidence of Chiron's relation to Libra. The ancient Greeks had another name for the sign Libra: Zugon, or 'yoke.' Zugon comes from the same root word as the biological term, zygote. This is defined as the stage in the development of an embryo where the sperm and egg cells [gametes] first unite, and true conception takes place.

Very early in the search for the meaning of Chiron a connection was discovered between Chiron and conception. A number of women with Chiron in their natal sixth house suffered miscarriages when transit Pluto made hard aspects to their natal Chirons. Time and time again, Chiron has proved prominent at conception, or other events related to the embryo and the pregnancy. The world's first 'test tube baby' was the result of fertilization of a human egg cell in a Petri dish at about the same time Chiron was discovered.

Now, this evidence does not, by any means, 'prove' that Chiron rules Libra. But it does point to a definite relationship between Chiron and the root word Zygos. And the Greeks did perceive Libra as being related to the same root word. Not proof—but definitely a worthwhile point of view to investigate further.

The word Yoke is a good place to close this chapter. Some of its meanings bear little relation to this topic, but some are very relevant. Yoke means to join, to tie, to link together. This is indeed an apt key for the union of sperm and egg. It is also very apt for the centaur himself—the fusion of Man and Animal. Just as the embryo is unique, and different from both sperm and egg—so is the centaur unique, different from Man or Animal.

Chapter VII: Healing the Wound:

Where Do We Go From Here ?

Medical pioneers have saved countless lives through the discoveries of wonder-drugs such as antibiotics. Each drug, in its turn, was a miracle cure, and came as a breakthrough. But time and time again, the medical profession did not heed the message of Chiron, to work toward the goal of bringing people toward wholeness. The Virgoan medicines—instead of being reserved as emergency healing tools, became freely [routinely] used on everybody.

With Chiron's entry into Gemini, the newspapers and magazines began to be filled with stories like this one: 'ANTIBIOTICS OVERUSED, DOCTOR SAYS: (Associated Press) The heavy use of antibiotics has produced bacteria resistant to control in infections such as gonorrhea, meningitis and blood poisoning .... Bacteria resistant to antibiotics thwart our present-day ability to treat even common diseases....The attitude that antibiotics cure everything pervades our culture. This mentality has to change....A report of one mother who gave antibiotics to a whole busload of children because one had a cold....Antibiotics alter the micro-environment to give advantage to resistant strains that can colonize those areas where competition from other strains has been eliminated by the antibiotics...'

Healing is a Chiron word. If antibiotics are being overused, and in inappropriate dosages, thus causing them to lose their effectiveness, some other source of healing must be in existence to be ruled by Chiron. The key lies within each individual, in something called the Immune System.

Perhaps you have heard of the case of Baby Fae, born in October, 1984. She was born with a defective heart. A drug called Cyclosporin-A was injected into her bloodstream. This drug so repressed her immune system that an operation was able to be done replacing her defective heart with the heart of a Baboon! Imagine—without the drug to suppress the immune system, the body would have automatically rejected that transplant from a different species. Chiron was prominent at this time.

The same month as the Baby Fae operation took place, another history-making operation occurred. A woman received a kidney from someone who had a different blood type. This had been thought to be impossible, as the immune system rejects any foreign object. The doctors used a new technique: they drew out components of the patient's immune system from her blood, thus avoiding this rejection. Chiron was prominent at this time too.

In fact, 1984 had a great deal of news about the immune system, from many different directions. For example, the findings about Acquired Immune Deficiency Syndrome [AIDS].

In 1984 Chiron made a station September 14, at 8°33' Gemini, activating the degree of a Solar Eclipse the previous May, and opposing the Uranus Station a few months later. [At the time of the above described operations, Chiron had returned to where it was at the time of the Uranus Station]

Anyway, now would be a good time to clarify just what the immune system really is. Protein molecules in the blood serum are the basis of the system. When some foreign body [termed antigen] is introduced into the system, the production of these protein molecules [antibodies] is stimulated. They work in several ways. They can work in conjunction with scavenger cells, to clean up the foreign element. They can puncture the wall of a bacterium, causing it to burst. They can cover up some structural component of a virus so that it cannot work, thus making it ineffective.

What is really remarkable about these antibodies is that they are very specific—when an antigen enters the system, the body produces a corresponding antibody that works only against that specific antigen, and no others. Just as with locks and keys—only the specific antibody fits with the specific antigen.

Immune cells are also involved in inflammation, as well as repair of body tissues.

Under ideal conditions the immune system works without problems. When the system is in balance it is enough to defend the body against any invader. The key here is that word, balance. Various things can occur to exhaust or suppress the immune system, or to impair its efficiency.

The immune system is powered by the general life force of the whole body. When the life-force is disturbed, the immune system is also disturbed. The main reason the life-force becomes imbalanced is a lack of harmony with the environment, and thus with the universe. The problem can arise from large amounts of toxins in the system from wrong diet, lack of exercise, and/or unfavorable climate [air pollution]. In youth, the body is able to cope, usually, with the poisons. Most toxins are absorbed from the system by the kidneys, liver and other organs of elimination. Eventually, the organs may become overloaded. At this point, other organs [not usually involved in this function] take over—the body becomes out of harmony with itself. Some parts of the body become less able to function. Of those that still can, some overwork, and some begin to work at 'wrong' tasks [malfunction] at the expense of their normal functions. Wastes then build up in the system, accumulating everywhere, so that eventually illness begins.

Other things beside toxins can disturb the immune system. Researchers at Ohio State University were studying the effect of diet on arteriosclerosis using rabbits for research. Several groups of these animals were put on an extremely high-fat diet, and each group was assigned to an individual student's care. One student really loved her charges—every day, she would drop in several times, hold and pet each rabbit. At the end of the experiment, a result came up that surprised all the researchers. The rabbits that had been picked up and petted had only half as much fat in their blood as all the other rabbits. Yet the petted rabbits had exactly the same diet! Just to make sure of the results, the experiment was repeated. The results were the same. It was repeated four more times, without any difference in the results. Thus it appears that tender loving care helps prevent arteriosclerosis.

In other researches in many other places, it has been shown that love, and being touched, actually give a boost to the immunity of the system. Dr. Harold Voth, of the Menninger Foundation, has said, 'It has been shown scientifically that people who are mentally run down and depressed are far more prone to sickness than those who are not. Hugging can lift depression, enabling the body's immune system to become tuned-up.' A neuro-psychologist, James W. Prescott, has said that studies have convinced him that 'the deprivation of body touch....is the cause of a number of emotional disturbances.' [And we know how interconnected the mind and body are]. In fact, hugging and touching can do more than just help balance the immune system—they can balance the over-all self-image, and thus the general state of the health. Pamela MCoy, P.N., has found that people who are often touched or hugged 'can often stop taking medication to get to sleep'.

Before you question the validity of these assertions think about this: The Hug Club [P.O. Box 453, Laguna Beach CA 92652] reports that a single section of skin, the size of a quarter, contains 50 nerve endings! Imagine how many nerves are activated when a person is being hugged—or hugging another!

Chiron functions to restore the balance in the system. A very simple statement, but the way it works can be extremely complex. I have seen Chiron act to bring another person into one's life when the imbalance is one that can be corrected by love and touch. This may explain the frequency of Chiron contacts when people meet future mates.

Under a major Chiron transit recently, Masayori Inouye, a biochemist at State University of New York, Stony Brook, was reported to be developing an artificial immune system. This is done by elongating partial viral RNA strands and inserting them into cells. When a virus invades the system, these cells bind to the invading viral RNA. This should not only stop the virus from reproducing, but this immunity should then be passed on to offspring! This procedure holds great potential for the future—but grave dangers, as well. For if the state of one's health truly depends on a wholistic attitude, this tampering with body cells could lead to far greater problems than the overuse of antibiotics. This can be a Chironic tool—but the danger lies in going too far with it.

Immunity also means freedom from illness. Chiron transits, more and more, are focusing on what we are doing to achieve this freedom, and how we are upsetting the balance through tampering with the system. For examples, the surgery cases described earlier in which the body's immune system was purposely repressed.

The cancer rate, world-wide, is alarming. Let us think a bit about cancer: The body attempts to defend itself against the spread of malignant cells— but something seems to go wrong with the immune system. Has it been repressed, thus allowing the cancer to start in the first place? Under a major Chiron transit, this news came out: Jorge Yunis, of the University of Minnesota, reported that he has been able to identify 51 fragile sites on human chromosomes that are liable to break. He believes that in a person who gets cancer, these sites are unusually weak. What is more, toxins, such as those in cigarette smoke, aggravate the weakness and make breakage more likely. When the chromosomes break cancer may result. The most important part of the news, however, is that it seems that certain elements in one's diet can strengthen the weak sites. For example, folic acid has been shown to do this when taken in foods [such as leafy vegetables and grains]. (Don't take a supplement without a doctor's advice, however—it can have side effects!)

Ever since the disease Acquired Immune Deficiency Syndrome [AIDS] was identified and reported, every breakthrough that has surfaced seems to occur under a major Chiron aspect. It is as though, now that Chiron has been discovered, we are being forced to focus our attention on exactly how the immune system works by confronting us with countless individuals in whom it has ceased to work. Chiron is thus teaching us about how the body must function as a whole by showing us what must occur when the body does it.

The AIDS experience will result in one very positive thing—we will learn a great deal from it about all humans, not just AIDS victims. Since AIDS is a disease in which a person's defenses just cease to work, we can see just how the immune system works by studying people in whom it no longer exists and comparing them to the rest of humanity.

[An interesting aside: Chiron has focused on the finding that hugging and contact tune up the immune system—yet the fear of contagion repels potential AIDS victims from this type of healing.]

72

CHIRON THE HEALER

David Carroll has written, 'The principal notion behind almost all forms of natural medicine is simply this: man's natural condition, his birthright, is a state of health; disease, despite its horrid prevalence across nations, is an aberration, an irregularity rather than a norm. This means that ill health 'is fundamentally a kind of imbalance, a disequilibrium, and that what a real medicine can do is set this balance right. Such is the basis of true healing.' David also says that because of this, 'medicine is only a catalyst, helping the body to help itself.' This is a point we must never forget.

Sleep itself is not ruled by Chiron. But, no matter what aspects of astrology you attribute to the rulership of sleep, Chiron does rule a very specific part of sleep—sleep as a healing tool.

Studies have shown that there are different stages in sleep and we all go through these several times per night. Two of these stages have a great deal to do with the body's ability to heal, and to stay healthy.

One such stage is termed REM sleep. This varies in length by how much went on during the day. You see, this stage is when you adapt to all that went on; your mind arranges your memories of the day, and the feelings that went with them, into places in your memory so that you can draw upon them in the future. Thus, the more that went on during the day, the longer your REM sleep. And REM sleep is the time when you have dreams.

You may not know all the physical changes that go on during this period. The brain temperature rises and the metabolism of oxygen is at its fastest. Time-sense is thus drawn out, and one can experience many minutes in only one of clock time. The cells in the hypothalamus are at their most active now and this means that these cells release a great quantity of the hormone CRF. This hormone commands the pituitary. The pituitary, in turn, sends out a hormone called ACTH which stimulates the adrenal glands. In response, the adrenal glands increase in sudden spurts their secretion of the steroids. [We thus awaken from sleep with the highest levels of adrenal hormones in our system. All day long, except under stress, these hormones decrease]. These hormones are essential for us to be at our peak fitness during the day, and necessary for us to be awake and energetic when morning comes.

So, in this stage of sleep, Chiron rules the changes that go on in our system to allow us to sort out the previous day by expanding our time sense, as well as the body's ability to judge just how much of the various hormones our body will need to face the new day. An ill-aspected Chiron could mean that one is not getting enough REM sleep to provide for the proper hormonal balance.

The other stage of sleep with which Chiron is connected is termed Stage

73

Four. A special hormone released at this time, HGH, regulates body growth, height and weight; it stimulates milk secretion in mothers; it stimulates the activity of the sex hormones; it lowers the blood cholesterol levels; it stimulates tissue growth by influencing the rate of protein synthesis. But the most significant aspect of this hormone is that it speeds healing. It even does this in bone fractures! [This hormone does get released at other times, but it reaches its peak in Stage Four sleep]. Thus, this stage of sleep is known as the body's time of repair and restoration. It is the deepest stage of sleep a person has.

Chiron rules the release of HGH by the pituitary gland, and thus the aspect of this sleep stage leading to normal repair and restoration.

Interestingly, larger quantities of HGH are released in children than in adults, because children need more for their actual growth processes. And, as can be expected, children have much longer periods of Stage Four sleep than do adults.

[An interesting aside—someone (not an astrologer) has likened Stage Four sleep to the time Chiron in myths took his pupils into his deep cave to prepare them for the world.]

To sum up: Chiron rules that aspect of sleep which leads to balancing the individual by sorting out the previous day's input; it rules the sleep that helps restore and repair the individual after the day's events; and it rules the hormonal release which enables the person to be at his or her best to face the coming day.

Since Chiron rules the balancing of the body to bring it into harmony with the universe—you can see how important the proper amount of sleep is. Any wholistic plan which leaves out getting enough sleep will not be truly wholistic, and thus not complete enough to be likely to do you any good.

In the previous discussion, I mentioned the hypothalamus. Chiron does not, most likely, rule this part of the body—but may have a lot to do with how it is triggered. Chiron probably does have some rulership over another part of the brain—the section that divides the right and left hemispheres and enables the two halves of the brain to communicate. As you probably know, the right half controls the left side of the body, and non-logical functions of thought. The left side controls the right side of the body, and the logical thought patterns. Chiron thus acts to intercede between them, to keep the mind and its functions balanced, so both can be used by the entity.

I mentioned food in the previous chapter. Some recent findings by Richard Wurtman of MIT will show you just how important balanced food intake is to healing.

Richard has shown that the proportion of carbohydrates in the diet indirectly determines how much of the chemical serotonin is present in the brain. Carbohydrates provide energy, but must first be broken down by the body into glucose. Insulin, released by the pancreas, controls the levels of blood glu-

74

cose. When you eat a lot of carbohydrates in a single meal, the pancreas must release more insulin to control and remove the excess glucose to maintain a proper balance. But insulin also affects the body's utilization of proteins. During digestion, proteins are broken down into amino acids which are recombined into new proteins suited to assimilation in the body. The amino acid Tryptophan has another purpose—it is also converted into serotonin inside of certain brain neurons. Serotonin is a chemical that triggers a response from other neurons, by the way. Anyhow, the specific brain neurons that produce this chemical are in the brain stem—and communicate with brain centers which control the onset of sleep, appetite and mood! [In other words, the release of serotonin will make a person feel sleepy, and less energetic].

Now, if you eat a diet rich in protein, the levels of both tryptophan and serotonin rise—but, believe it or not, the levels of these in the brain actually fall! But eat a diet rich in carbohydrates, and the brain levels of tryptophan and serotonin rise. Why does protein have this unexpected effect? Well, when you eat a high-protein meal, a number of other amino acids enter the brain, and somehow they keep most of the tryptophan and serotonin out. On the other hand, when you eat high carbohydrate diets, the pancreas produces more insulin, and insulin helps the tryptophan gain entrance to the brain!

Thus, it is important to be sure that your diet is higher in protein than in carbohydrates. Yet, you must be very careful here, for many high protein diets are also high in fats and cholesterol. An imbalance of this sort in the diet can produce an entirely different sort of imbalance in the health.

Any imbalance involving failure of the pancreas to produce enough insulin [diabetes may result] or over-production of insulin [tendency toward hypoglycemic reactions] is of great importance, deserving the most careful expert medical attention.

Another thing to note. Stress is a part of everyday life. It is even necessary. But the way we react to stress is controllable. If we let stress get to us, the impact actually impairs the ability of the body to utilize amino acids. This, too, will let more tryptophan into the brain, with the result of more sleepy, low-energy periods.

Conclusion? Imbalanced diet sets up conditions for a major Chironic turning point. Why not take initiative beforehand and control what you eat—so that Chiron transits bring about much more evolutionary turning points?

As mentioned before, there is a parallel between the purpose of Psychotherapy and the ancient Eastern ways to liberation. The essence of psychotherapy, no matter which school of thought, is still the liberation of the individual, so s/he can function as his or her true self. Yet, there are over 250 different kinds of psychotherapy. Can we truly accept that all are valid? or, that there is only one type that is the true way to liberation in the Western world?

Chiron is the answer to this quandary. Each person is unique. And each person has a unique Chiron, not just by sign and degree, but by house, aspects, retrograde or direct motion, midpoints, and even where it lies in relation to its perihelion or aphelion. [Just looking at sign and house position gives 12 x 12 = 144 different Chiron types!] Chiron, the healer, teaches us that each person's path is unique—the course one must follow to heal inner conflicts, and then go on to achieve wholeness, is different for each person. For one person, pure Freudian analysis may be the best course. For another, the archetypal approach of Jung might open the door. For still another, working with a Guru might be the most valid path.

Susan Gilbert has done studies to show that different kinds of therapy are effective for different people. For example, patients with a good education and a high level job respond more to group therapy, while those at the other end of the socioeconomic scale respond more to individual therapy. She has also shown that therapies which pose a lot of questions will be more beneficial to highly motivated people, while those who have low motivation respond better to a more sympathetic approach to healing.

Recent studies by a number of individuals have concluded that the position of Chiron in the chart of the healer is also important. It not only indicates the healer's preferred methods—but also those tools that the healer will find most successful in treating others. Frequently the therapist will have a blind spot here—since s/he has success with some particular method, s/he may perceive it as THE method which all therapists should follow. [Perhaps something similar exists in the charts of astrologers - Tropicalists vs. siderealists; Placidus vs. Koch?]

A case in point is Alma H. Bond, Ph.D., who is a Freudian psychoanalyst. Dr. Bond has, natally, Chiron conjunct Mars right on the cusp of the eighth house. In the Fall/Winter 1981 issue of Journal of Contemporary Psychotherapy, she published an article entitled, 'Counter transference as a Guideline in the Treatment of a Psychotic Patient'. The abstract of the article states: 'Presenting vignettes from a long analysis, the author describes many varieties of rage provoked in her (by the patient), and shows how the countertransference was the primary tool in helping to distinguish among the states, understand their origin, and work them through in the transference.' Dr. Bond describes countertransference as 'the total emotional reactions of the analyst to the patient in the treatment situation.' This includes 'the analyst's conscious as well as unconscious reactions to the patient, reactions to the patient's reality as well as his transference, and the analyst's reality needs as well as his neurotic ones. It implies that the emotional reactions of the analyst are intimately fused to those of the patient, and that while countertransference most certainly should be resolved, it is an extremely useful tool in gaining understanding of the patient.'

At a specific point in the analysis, Dr. Bond finds herself expressing her anger directly toward the patient. She had not done so up until this point, and of this she says, 'I think I knew intuitively that this was what (the patient) needed, and was now able to accept. Dealing with the rage of a psychotic parent is what made (the patient) ill, and she had to be able to withstand the full force of my rage before she could get well.' Here is a direct expression of the Doctor's Mars, being used as a tool for healing, as shown by the conjunction to Chiron.

What is also interesting is the great awareness Dr. Bond has of the whole Doctor/Patient process, and how it is truly a case of both being healed, not simply the doctor healing the patient. She says that the need for growth and development is strong in both the patient and the analyst. Also, 'When the analyst feels his emotional reactions are a strong therapeutic tool, he feels freer to face his own positive and negative emotions in the transference situation, has less need to block them, and can use them for therapeutic understanding.' [This view reflects perfectly Mars conjunct Chiron on the eighth cusp, naturally].

Dr. Steven Martin is a Jungian analyst who talks about the difference between anger and rage. Anger is a feeling, he says, but 'Rage is an emotion which rises in response to a threat'. Anger is something which is 'purposeful and works toward an end.' He perceives the necessity of transforming rage (whether open or repressed) into anger, where it can be dealt with constructively. 'I choose Hephaestus and Mars as two aspects of rage. Mars in his negative aspect moves outward, and seeks to avoid. In his positive aspect he is the god of fertility. Hephaestus is the depressive component of rage. In his negative aspect he rages and boils. His positive aspect is creativity. Both gods were born of Hera. They had no father; she created them in response to Zeus' birth of Athene'. They were born of her rage 'and of her incompleteness.'

Dr. Martin describes the second phase of rage as Aphrodite—married to Hephaestus, but a lover of Mars—and the third stage as Eros, 'the common child of Mars and Hephaestus. His paternity was never known.' It is interesting to contemplate all of this in regard to other parts of astrology—Hephaestus being the same as Vulcan [used by some astrologers], and Eros being an asteroid, also in use. But we are getting beyond the point.

The point is that Dr. Martin believes that the source of rage is the blocking of individuation which gives rise to feelings of indignation and revenge. This rage must be touched—dealt with—transformed into anger, before it can become constructive and healing-oriented. This rage can be Mars rage, in which you strike out, or Hephaestus rage, in which you feel imprisoned.

Chiron can be the tool to unblock the process—to transform the rage into a useful tool. In Dr. Bond's case it becomes a primary tool, due to the natal placement linking the two-body conjunction to the eighth house cusp. And, with other therapists, it can still be a major tool, although possibly not quite in the way nor to the extent that Dr. Bond utilizes it.

In some, rage/anger IS the block that keeps them from evolving. In others, it may be something else entirely. Once the individual has become aware of the block, it can then be a force for healing, instead of a negative energy. As Philip Sedgwick says, 'Chiron represents the one remaining thing that remains unresolved prior to the completion of a major transition. Once the conscious recognition of Chiron occurs, the dilemma flips and becomes a supportive aspect.' In the case of Dr. Bond and her patient, once Dr. Bond was able to express her own rage in the form of anger, she was free of a block that inhibited healing, and the patient was free to express her own inhibited rage.

This leads me to the idea of Chiron transits as TURNING POINTS. When Dr. Bond made the breakthrough in therapy, Chiron was significantly aspecting both her chart and the patient's chart. This is not unusual, but rather, it is a common occurrence: When someone in need of some type of healing, or some major step toward wholemaking reaches a turning point on the path to this goal, Chiron is almost always active in one of three ways—a transit of Chiron to something in the chart, a transit to the patient's natal Chiron, or a progression to the natal Chiron. Likewise, when a doctor or therapist makes a breakthrough with a client/patient, there is usually some Chiron aspect in the healer's chart—and frequently, to a part of the chart that is also in aspect to the client/patient's chart.

These turning points can be on many different levels. One may be the moment when the person actually realizes s/he has a problem that must be resolved. It can be at that moment when the person makes a conscious decision to work toward wholemaking. It may be when s/he makes the first contact with a doctor who will be THE person who helps. Or it can be the actual moment when the healing process begins. In many people, Chiron is active in more than one of these moments.

Chiron was discovered late in 1977, and since then there has been a great change in the consciousness of mankind about healing, and health in general. Many more opportunities are around for people to experience that first turning point to lead them toward becoming whole. For example, in 1977, the pharmaceutical manufacturing firm, Warner-Lambert, introduced the first home-pregnancy test, E.P.T. A woman can now find out much more quickly whether she is pregnant or not without depending on a doctor. This has the result, first of all, of putting more women more in touch with their own bodies, and more in control of them. But, even more significant—this was the start of a whole new wave of home tests! Kits for just about every type of health test are either now available, or will be soon. [Predictions are that, by 1988, the market for self-care kits will hit at least $1.8 billion!] Ingredient labels and health warnings are appearing on almost everything a person buys. [The Food, Drug & Cosmetic Act of 1938, as amended, continues to be enforced.] In every direction, the people are confronted with information that could lead to that first step, changing one's outlook, and moving toward a wholistic lifestyle.

Some correspondents have suggested that a very special method exists to deduce exactly what first step a person should take. Look at the sign and element of your natal Chiron—then, turn to the sign and element of transiting Chiron. Combine these, and look for something that fits the combination. For example, natal Chiron in Capricorn, transiting Chiron in Gemini—that is Earth and Air. Earth is very physical, material, while Air is mental, intellectual. Any therapy which emphasizes mind-over-matter would be favorable, as well as something that applies material things to influence the nervous system. [Possibly an example of this second approach might be magnet therapy].

A word of warning: Chiron is frequently found involved when actual problems develop, or health crises begin. In some cases, this seems to be because such a crisis is necessary, before the individual will take any action— s/he has been ignoring past Chironic openings. But in other cases Chiron is involved along with a number of negative aspects from what used to be called malefic planets. Chiron in such cases may be opening doors and removing obstacles. This serves to allow the hard aspects of Mars, or Saturn or another planet more opportunity to bring about trouble. Yet remember—Chiron is a healer. Even in such cases there is something you can do—represented by Chiron—to bring about a healing or more wholistic view, even if you cannot perceive it at the time. The hard aspects may be a convenient place to lay the blame, but FREE WILL is something we all have. Use it to tune in to Chiron.

Most of the readers of this book will be people living in countries where the standards of health care are modern, and fairly well up to date. But large areas of the world are still using medical practices we abandoned centuries ago, still suffering ills that have been eliminated in the more developed countries. Chiron nevertheless works in these areas, too. In places where the main healers are witch doctors, for example, Chiron can bring a turning point for the patient, using mind over matter, even though the methods are those we have given up as obsolete. What I am trying to say is this: utilizing Chiron's healing influence does not only mean using the most up-to-date scientific methods— rather, it means using any methods Chiron makes available to you. No matter what country you live in—no matter what lifestyle you live by—the key to Chiron is the realization that only by continually opening new doors will you grow toward wholeness. I like to quote a Dr. Sanford, who said, 'In all of us, the price of continued health is the continued development of consciousness.'

This process of 'continued development of consciousness' can be seen [slowly but surely] entering even the field of orthodox medicine. Many doctors have begun to take an interest in learning and playing music. They have begun to perceive that, as members of a very dehumanized profession [scientific medicine, with all its machines and meters], they need both the therapeutic and humanizing influence of music in their lives. Others are beginning to paint or create sculpture. These doctors perceive that it helps them to be more empathetic toward their patients because they can [with music or art] get more in touch with their own feelings, and thus understand more how their patients feel. [Statistic studies show this great need—a study sponsored by American Medical Association showed that a third of American physicians surveyed were "bitterly dissatisfied" with their work—and that the suicide rate for American doctors is well above the average suicide rate for Americans in general. Also, doctors have more drug and alcohol problems than the general population.]

So, the medical profession is moving to heal itself by simple humanizing approaches like these above. Colleges all over the country with medical schools have now, or are planning to add, courses in art, literature, ethics and other humanities. Another sign of this trend is the growing number of doctor/artist organizations that are springing up, and the shows and concerts given by doctors as musicians.

Astrologers, and many holistic healers have known for centuries about the importance of having the arts in one's daily living. Many modern astrologers, for example are also accomplished composers—the late Dane Rudhyar, for example. What is interesting is that the ancient Greeks knew this, and most likely they learned it from much older cultures.

And Chiron is the representative of this necessary union. In mythology, when Chiron taught his healing arts, he always included music as one of the most important. Kenneth Negus has pointed out that Chiron even had his own special stringed instrument, the Kithara, that he used all the time. Music [and art in general] is a major ingredient in the mixture necessary to align one's human and animal sides. 'Music hath charms to soothe the savage breast,' as Shakespeare said. Without art, for art's sake—healing cannot be complete. A sterile world is fine for keeping bacteria away—but not for the making of a whole human being.

Many astrologers are making progress in working with doctors of many specialties. [We could name names here, but shouldn't, for obvious reasons. There are many more than just the ones we have met.] There have been many successes in helping psychotherapists with their patients. Now the awareness of Chiron should increase the close ties between the healing arts and the 'music of the spheres'.

I opened this chapter by writing about how we have come to overuse antibiotics. I would like to close it with this information. In 1977, the year that Chiron was discovered, the Food & Drug Administration proposed the banning of penicillin and tetracycline in animal feed because it was believed that the practice could pose a serious health threat to humans. Congress, however, said not enough evidence existed to support this contention, and there was no ban enacted. Since then, facts and figures have been coming into print all the time—an avalanche of information since Chiron entered Gemini—such as the news that 25% of H. influenza bacteria are resistant to penicillin. The ban has once again been proposed and will be passed.

Section Two: The Application

♂ Chapter I: First Things First

The first thing to do, of course, is to locate your natal Chiron position. If you know how to use an ephemeris, the back of this volume has Chiron's position every ten days from 1900-2050.

If you do not know how to use an ephemeris, or if you would rather have someone else do the calculations for you, many computer services will now include Chiron in your chart if you ask them. Try Astro Communications Services Inc., ~~P.O. Box 34487, San Diego CA 92163-4487~~ U.S.A. They will draw your chart for you with their computer, and include all the symbols of the planets for you—including the symbol of Chiron if you ask.

If you have your own computer, and would like to get a program that calculates charts including Chiron, one place you can contact is Matrix Software, 315 Marion Avenue, .Big Rapids MI 49307 U.S.A. ~~Another excellent option is the CCRS program from Mark Pottenger, 838 5th Ave., Los Angles, CA 90005 U.S.A.~~

O.K., so now you have your chart with Chiron included. Where do you go from here? Well, you can start from any point you like, but I have found a particular procedure most beneficial in interpreting natal Chiron. Try it, and if you want to develop your own procedure after, go ahead. After all, Chiron is a Maverick, isn't it ?

Chapter II: Procedure

Set up your chart [or make a fresh copy], but leave out Chiron, Uranus, Neptune, Pluto and any asteroids. Now interpret it as completely as you can using only what is there. View this as your basic nature—your seed potential. Next put in Uranus, Neptune and Pluto. Continue the interpretation, expanding upon the seed, searching for ways to help it grow, and looking for how it fits into the universe.

Now include Chiron, and you are ready to begin its interpretation. Remember that Chiron is the bridge between Saturn and Uranus, and will help you to encourage the seed to grow, and flow with universal principles.

First, is Chiron direct or retrograde? If direct, Chiron is an accepted part of the personality since early childhood. The person views it as part of the self, whether s/he likes it or not. If retrograde, there probably was early resistance to Chiron in the person's life. In some area s/he was different, but did not want to be. What usually occurs is that, upon maturity, the person with retrograde Chiron not only accepts his or her Chiron, but is proud of being unique in some way. S/he may even go so far as to emphasize it in personality. This is especially true if it turns direct by progression.

Step Two. Where is Chiron in relation to perihelion and aphelion? Look for the place of your birthdate in this table.

Perihelion	Aphelion
March 16, 1895	June 2, 1920
August 29, 1945	December 7, 1970
February 14, 1996	

Chiron was moving from Aphelion to Perihelion from the mid-1860's until the first date on the table, if you were born back that far. Now that you have found which direction your Chiron was moving at your birth [perihelion to aphelion, or aphelion to perihelion], take note of another thing: Were you born within seven years before any of these dates? If so, make a note of that too. It will become important momentarily.

I. From Perihelion to Aphelion

If you were born during such a period, Chiron was moving away from Saturn and moving toward Uranus. The world was recovering from the effects of too much Saturn. Astrologically, when there is too much Saturn, it is necessary to increase Uranian vibrations to restore the balance to the world. The world in such periods moves toward the future, opening up, experimenting; an explosion of scientific advancement begins; public concern is for individual freedom, liberty and rights; the time is right to break with tradition. Born at such a time, your Chiron carries this orientation. The urge is to heal by going out beyond limits, expanding individual awareness, and helping others to get out of ruts. The need is to bring Uranus to Saturn—to help open the closed doors and revolutionize structures so they are more open and better suited to growth. You can look at the main thrust of your life as the desire to free Prometheus from his chains, and, by so doing, ending the pain or suffering of self and/or others.

I A. Born Within Seven Years Before Date of Aphelion

On the dates in the table, the direction of Chiron in relation to the Sun changed. [This is not the same as whether it appears direct or retrograde in apparent geocentric motion.]

We have found that if a person experiences such a change of direction of Chiron [toward or away from the Sun] prior to their first transit Saturn square natal Saturn around age seven, there is a terrific change in consciousness in the child. Initially, if you were growing up with Chiron moving from perihelion toward aphelion, an orientation toward Uranus—the shift in direction caused a corresponding shift in consciousness toward Saturn. World events around the time of aphelion show drastically the effects of too much Uranus in the world—no respect for values, nor laws, nor traditions; families without structure, society without cooperation. The aphelion comes with such intensity that it is indelibly etched into your psyche. The result: there are two conflicting orientations within you. Initially, the new one moving toward Saturn dominates your consciousness, with the old one relegated to the background. In fact, initially, it is stronger in you than in the people born during that direction. [More on this in Section II].

Eventually, a new awareness will dawn upon you—that too much of either Saturn or Uranus is an imbalance. By being born just before the change in direction, you have been gifted with the potential to develop a truly remarkable insight, and to pass this on to others—an insight as to how Saturn and Uranus can work in harmony. One better way to reach this true awareness is by

studying events in the world, and in your household, at the time of the aphelion. If you were only a few days old, it may not be possible to do so, unless
you can glean the information from older relatives. But if you can remember
events on your own concerning this time—your memories can greatly assist
you in coming to terms with the transition. You have seen Prometheus unchained, and now the major thrust of your life is responsibility to make the
most worthwhile use of this energy. It is very important that any sacrifices you
make be truly worthwhile and not a waste of energy. You have also seen,
symbolically, Chiron give up his life to free Prometheus. This vision tends to
develop in you a more sober, serious side than average, and a feeling of emptiness within you. There is the need to fill this emptiness.

II. From Aphelion to Perihelion

If you were born during such a period, Chiron was moving away from
Uranus, and moving toward Saturn. The world was recovering from the influence of too much Uranus. Astrologically, when there is too much Uranus, the
remedy is to increase the Saturnian vibrations in order to return the world to
balance. The world moves toward law and order, trying to find a structure to
build to put things back together. A cry goes out for a return to traditions;
conservative winds blow in society; public concern is for patriotism, concrete
values, curbing unrestricted behavior, protection for society rather than for the
individual. The time is right to bring back what was worthwhile from the past.
Born at this time, your Chiron gives you this orientation. The urge to heal by
teaching proper living is strong. Proper living includes such things as developing good habits and thoroughly knowing oneself and one's past. The urge
is to rid the world of its negative influences—to cleanse it of its problems. The
need is to bring Saturn to Uranus—to help channel individuality, and help the
person to use all talents to make a contribution to society.

You can look at the main thrust of your life as, first, the desire to achieve
perfection [since you are moving toward Saturn], and second, the desire to be
at one with the universe, as symbolized by Chiron being placed in the heavens.

II A. Born Within Seven Years Before Date of Perihelion

On the dates in the table, the direction of Chiron [in relation to the Sun]
changed. We have found that if a person experiences such a change of Chiron
direction prior to the first transit Saturn square natal Saturn around age seven,
there is a terrific change of consciousness in the child. While initially, you
were growing up with an orientation toward Saturn—the shift in direction
caused a corresponding shift of consciousness toward Uranus. World events
at the time of perihelion show drastically the effects of too much Saturn on the
world—dictatorships, slavery, restrictions, stagnation and over-regulation. The
perihelion comes with such intensity that it is indelibly etched into your psyche.

85

The result is that there are two conflicting orientations within you. Initially, the new one moving towards Uranus dominates your consciousness, with the old one relegated to the background. In fact, initially, it is stronger in you than it is in the people who are born during that direction of Chiron. [More about that in Section I.]

Eventually, a new awareness will dawn upon you—that too much of either Uranus or Saturn is an imbalance. By being born just before the change of direction, you have been gifted with the potential to develop a truly remarkable insight and to pass this on to others—an insight as to how Uranus and Saturn can work together. One better way to reach this true awareness is by studying events in the world, and in your household, at the time of the perihelion. If you were only a few days old it may not be possible to do this, unless you can glean the information from older relatives. If you can remember events on your own concerning this time—your memories can greatly assist you in coming to terms with the transition.

You have seen Chiron pass within the orbit of Saturn symbolizing his death and immortalization. And you have seen the cycle begin again, with Chiron once again becoming Jupiter's main advisor. The orientation for you is toward both endings and beginnings—achieving some great height, and moving on to some new quest. Never will you be satisfied with achievements. You will always have some new wall to scale, some new chain to break.

Step Three. Explore Chiron's position by sign. For this, you might like to read the appropriate section in my pamphlet, **Interpreting Chiron** (pgs. [37 - 40]). The sign position has a lot to do with the personal imperative you carry with you throughout your life. It ties into the problem that your parents [and the world around you] were concerned about at your birth. It might interest you to know that Chiron's eccentric orbit causes it to stay in some signs a great deal longer than in some other signs. It spends the least amount of time in Libra—less than 2 years. So, if you have Chiron in Libra, or in a sign near Libra, you are in a minority of the population. On the other hand, Chiron stays in Aries for over 8 years—so, if you were born with Chiron in Aries, or in a nearby sign, you have a lot of company.

Step Four. Study the particular degree that Chiron occupies. For this you will need a book that goes into the symbolization of each of the 360 degrees. There are several different books about degree symbols, but I am most comfortable with the Sabian Symbols as described in Dane Rudhyar's **The Astrology of Personality**. No matter which system you use to study the degree, you can glean remarkable insight from the images the degree symbol summons in your mind. Not only will the basic meaning of the symbol be important—but meditation upon it will help you make the best of it.

Step Five. Study the house position of your Chiron. Here again, you may wish to turn to the appropriate section in my pamphlet, **Interpreting Chiron**

(pgs. [21 - 30]), to better understand the house position. Keep in mind that whatever house your Chiron occupies will be an area where you have lessons to learn AFTER you have learned some Saturn lesson. There is often a feeling of immediacy in this house—of NOW. When problems arise here, nothing must stand in your way of resolving them immediately. Chiron can act to tune in to the basic energy inherent in the house and enable you to use it without limit. This can be good or bad. It can be energy you tap for healing—or energy you tap for negative purposes. The choice is yours—but remember Chiron's relation to Saturn and Uranus—the negative use of Chiron will eventually lead to disruption and breakdown, or restriction and punishment.

Step Six. Find the midpoint of Saturn and Uranus in your chart. No matter what house it falls in, and no matter if Chiron makes no aspect to the midpoint at all—the natal Chiron enables you to tap the energy flowing from the midpoint. Imagine the creative force that is released when the experiences of the past are united with the potentials of the future, and utilized right now, in the present? Well, by really getting to know your own Chiron, and developing it, you will begin to tap the energy of the Saturn-Uranus midpoint in whatever house it falls. You may also want to explore the degree symbol for this midpoint.

Step Seven. Now it is time to explore Chiron's aspects. The next chapter is devoted entirely to these angular relationships.

Chapter III: Aspects

In my pamphlet, *Interpreting Chiron*, I tried to give examples of how Chiron works natally in a number of aspects. Since that time, a great many people have written to request a more thorough coverage of the subject, and so, this chapter.

Chiron is a small body. True, it does seem to be as powerful as a major planet—but I have found that the orbs for Chiron aspects are a bit smaller than for regular-size bodies. A number of people have written to say they find my orbs too limited [and they may be correct], but I have not found any clear, distinct influences using greater orbs than shown in this table. However, if Chiron is part of an aspect picture, I do feel that you can extend Chiron's orbs beyond these.

ORBS FOR CHIRON'S ASPECTS

	Sun	Moon	ASC & MC	Planets & Lunar Nodes	Asteroids
Conjunction (0º)	5º	5º	5º	3º	1½º
Semisextile (30º)	2º	2º	2º	1º	0½º
One Eleventh (33º)	1º	1º	1º	0½º	0¼º
Semi-square (45º)	3º	3º	3º	1½º	0¾º
Septile (52º)	2º	2º	2º	1º	0½º
Sextile (60º)	3º	3º	3º	1½º	0¾º
Quintile (72º)	2º	2º	2º	1º	0½º
Square (90º)	5º	5º	5º	3º	1½º
Trine (120º)	5º	5º	5º	3º	1½º
Sesquiquadrate (135º)	3º	3º	3º	1½º	0¾º
Biquintile (144º)	2º	2º	2º	1º	0½º
Quincunx (150º)	2½º	2½º	2½º	1½º	0¾º
One Sixty-five (165º)	1º	1º	1º	0½º	0¼º
Opposition (180º)	5º	5º	5º	3º	1½º

Midpoints & Sensitive Points: For midpoints and sensitive points I use only conjunction, square and opposition, so cannot give orbs for other aspects to these points.

O.K., so now you have checked your chart out thoroughly, and you have found a few Chiron aspects that fit within these above orbs. How do you interpret them? Well, in the following pages I offer a few hints for Chiron in conjunction semisquare, sextile, square, trine, sesquiquadrate, quincunx and opposition to all the major planets, as well as conjunctions to both lunar nodes, and the four angular cusps. While I have observed Chiron active in other aspects, I have not yet made a thorough study of them. But here is a brief guide to the main Chiron aspects:

SEMI-SEXTILE (30°)

Don't overlook this little aspect. Chiron here gives a talent for maneuvering, over, under and around little obstacles, as well as a seeming sixth sense about where there are loopholes or chinks that one can go through. The planet that is being aspected is the tool that is used, or the part of the self doing the maneuvering. If Chiron is before the other planet, the maneuvering is usually subtle, often behind the scenes; others may never realize it is going on. If Chiron is after the other planet, the maneuvering is more open and matter of fact.

1/11 [UNDECIM]

This is my name for a little-used aspect that divides the circle by 11, and that is 32°43'38"+. This aspect and its multiples [2/11, 3/11 etc.] refer to the learning of, or becoming aware that one does not live in a vacuum—that there are times one must go outside of oneself to seek help, or to improve on something. I have found that the more Undecim multiples one has in a chart, the more social consciousness a person seems to have. Chiron in this respect seems to guide the person to seek outside help to heal or resolve problems related to the aspected planet. The Undecim [and its multiples] also seem to bring the aspected planet quite well into a group situation, to work with the group to help resolve difficulties.

SEPTILE (52°)

Chiron in such a person is often active even if it makes no other aspects anywhere in the chart. Whenever the individual has a reason to use the other planet in the aspect, Chiron acts automatically as well. The planet and Chiron may be concerned with entirely unrelated things at the time—or seemingly unrelated things. But the activation of one does not cause the other to activate—it just seems that one cannot become active without the other one also coming alive. In such people Chiron is so totally a part of their destiny that they must face it constantly and make it a part of their conscious world. Once they realize that Chiron cannot be avoided; once they consciously accept that Chiron must be a day-to-day influence, this person can become a great force for change in society and will perceive the Chiron septile as one of their greatest gifts. It enables the person to see beyond limitations, for example—when there is no awareness that limitations exist. It may cause a person to go off on a new path when there is no intention of so doing at first.

Don't forget the Bi-Septile (103°) and the Tri-Septile (155°), as well. The basic themes are the same, although in the Bi-Septile, the results of the aspect may be much more prominent and/or visible, while in the Tri-Septile, the results may express themselves in more subtle ways.

QUINTILE (72°)

The quintile, with any two planets, is an aspect of particular talent. With Chiron, the talent is that aspect of creativity whereby one goes out beyond the day-to-day world, beyond the limits of what one is working with, and finds alternative ways to do things, or finds other pieces to the puzzle that might otherwise be overlooked. This is an excellent aspect in the chart of any healer, as it gives the ability to come up with a therapy that works yet is totally different from what others would prescribe. What makes this aspect so positive is that once the person has found something beyond the present reality, they have knack for integrating it with what is already existent, as though it has always been a part of it.

The Bi-quintile (144°) works along these lines, too, except that there seems less awareness of this talent and more 'take it for granted' attitude about the results.

Still with me? Well, then I will go right to the interpretations.

The first thing to observe about Chiron in aspect [no matter which aspect] is that it seems to have a greater influence on the aspected planet than said planet does on Chiron. This MAY be due to the fact that Chiron is so recently a part of our consciousness that its effects are much more noticeable than those of traditional planets. Or, we may find that this will always hold true no matter how much we learn about the little body. But for the present, at least, Chiron is more of an influence than the object of influence.

The second thing to notice is that Chiron does not always react to an aspect in the same way as other planets do. Chiron, being the Maverick that it is, has the tendency to react in unique ways to each aspect. Thus, you cannot simply transfer the traditional meanings of the trine and sextile to Chiron, plug in Chiron keywords and leave it at that. You must, instead, look at each Chiron aspect as something special, different, and unique.

Let us begin the discussion with Chiron's aspects to the Sun, and then progress outwards from there.

The Sun is the source of life in the chart, and the basic, conscious self of the person. Any Chiron aspects to the Sun tend to set the person apart in the way they see themselves, and thus, in the sense of purpose s/he develops.

In the long run, this also makes the person stand out in the eyes of others, as someone following some special pathway s/he has marked out, rather than one society has marked for the individual. The hard aspects show this strongly, but even the 'minor' aspects produce somewhat the same effect. There is a tendency with Chiron/Sun aspects for the person to develop a 'superiority complex', although this need not occur [other factors in the chart may have much to do with this]. But even in those who do not see themselves above others, Chiron/Sun aspects produce a feeling of 'destiny' in some specific direction, or some intuition that they understand some specific vision, or some specific method of doing something, better than anyone else. Not that they are the best in their whole field [some feel that way], but that they are the only ones, or the best ones at understanding some specific aspect of their profession—or that they have a method that no one else can match. There is a very strong creative bent—these people have an originality that can make them famous. Usually there is some type of charisma, yet, at the same time, others tend to be wary of these people.

SUN CONJUNCT CHIRON

A very intense version of the traits described in the previous paragraph. These people are definitely originals, and frequently, originators. For the most part the are full of spirit and with a great wit; able to reach people on all levels as though they were equals. But there is, nevertheless, a kind of barrier around these people that few can pass through, close up. They may alienate many people, even groups of people, with the stands they take in life—but this is usually because those who feel alienated cannot see why the Chiron/Sun person does not buckle under, fit in, stick to the traditional rules. In truth, they DO disregard many rules, for themselves [although they usually won't begrudge you if you follow them]. They tend especially to ignore people who say, 'That can't be done' or 'You can't do it that way.' Not only that, but once they choose how they are going to express themselves, their goals, or their creative nature—they refuse to accept any obstacles in their way. This refusal to be stopped leads them into many new worlds—enabling them to bring together elements and ideas which others may never think of connecting. Most people with this aspect do have a great concern for people and people's problems—but frequently give the impression that they don't want to be bothered by the problems of an individual. [This may not be true at all—but it often appears that way]. To sum up, let us say that these people go through life forming two groups of people—those who like them, and those who don't. It is very, very difficult to be indifferent about this type of person.

EXAMPLES of people with Sun conjunct Chiron: Neil F. Michelsen, Jean Claude Killy, Huey P. Long, Vance Brand, Howard Cosell, Jean Cocteau, Jeff Bridges, Willie Mays, Mercedes McCambridge, Marlene Dietrich, Shirley Temple, Doris Day, Gale Storm, Kenneth Noland, Alene Duerk, Louis de Broglie, Rachmaninoff, Suzanne Sommers, Don McLean, Bernhard Goetz, Christopher

Atkins, Queen Elizabeth II, Minnie Riperton, Prince Charles, Prince Andrew, Barbara Streisand, Michele Cotta, Jerry Cantrell, Jon Bon Jovi, Mariah Carey, Michael Wilton, Pat Benatar, Sam Cooke, Teresa Brewer, Tom Hamilton, Tom Waits, Waylon Jennings, Harry James.

SUN SEMI-SQUARE CHIRON (45°)

With this aspect, there is something of a compulsion. Chiron seems to agitate the Sun, push it, stirring the person to take an active part in bringing about changes, opening doors, or rectifying imbalances. Such a person cannot rest—s/he must always be taking on some new challenge, some new obstacle. Deep within, it is almost as if s/he believe that obstacles can be overcome simply by force of will, or by a conscious belief that a way will be found to open doors. There is usually less of the self in this person than in people with Sun conjunct Chiron, because these people are so often preoccupied with their tasks that they don't even think about how unique they are, or who they are.

EXAMPLES of people with Sun semi-square Chiron: Francolse Gauquelin, Henry Kissinger, Zubin Mehta, Dennis Weaver, Rennie Davis, James Arness, William Blake, Giacomo Puccini, Bertrand Russell, John Anderson, Lloyd Bentsen, George Forman, Patricia Harris, Brian Wilson, Colonel Sanders, Phil Collins, Jean Houston, Harry Bellefonte, Van Cliburn, Keith Emerson, Paul McCartney, Dustin Hoffman, Andre Maurois, Amedo Modigliani, Billy Bragg, Bobby Brown, Buddy Guy, Charlie Watts, Danny Wood, Glenn Campbell, Jean Redpath, Jordan Knight, Lindsey Buckingham, Papa John Creach.

SUN SEXTILE CHIRON

These people use their distinctive characteristics as tools to help them get where they want to go. They go beyond walls, beyond limits, without very much difficulty, and seem to enjoy doing so. Perhaps because of this they seem to have an understanding—even an acceptance—of others who are different from the norm, and can work well with them if they choose to do so. Normally, a sextile implies that one can reap great benefits if one first puts forth the effort. This is true here, but with a twist: these people seem unable to avoid putting forth the effort. Chiron seems always to want them to do something else so they tend to get a lot done. They almost always have their followers—but tend also to have another group of people who do not care for them at all. The division is not as sharp as with the conjunction, but nevertheless exists.

EXAMPLES of people with Sun sextile Chiron: Dick Martin, Lawrence Welk, Edouard Lalo, Alfred de Musset, Gamal Abdul Nassar, Larry Csonka, Mike Schmidt, Kris Kristofferson, Robert Redford, Nathan Leopold, Paul Crafton, Aristide Briand, Merle Haggard, Norman Mailer, Sidney Poitier, Alan Watts, Jeck Lemmon, Jean Genet, Allen Ginsberg, Bobby Brown, Chubby Checker, Curtis Mayfield, Donny Osmond, Edgar Winter, Janet Jackson, Joni Mitchell, Kim Carnes, Mike Inez, Nancy Wilson (of Heart), Natalie Cole, Patti Smith, Quincy Jones, Rick Nelson.

SUN SQUARE CHIRON

This is a person who truly wants to change the world in some way, although s/he may or may not ever do anything about it. This urge stems from something very subjective—s/he has gone through at least one, but usually several major changes in the self-image and sense of purpose. Any Chiron square throws the other body off balance, and often, so that the person must make time to re-establish the balance. Once the Sun person has learned to leave a sense of 'ultimate purpose' open to change, and has learned that one's self-image must be allowed to adapt through new circumstances—s/he begins to thrill in self-discovery and in discovering more about the universe. At the same time this process goes on, s/he should begin to want to do something for the world in some way—correct an imbalance, open a door, teach, research. NOTE: Some people never do accept change—and are forced to cope with one disruption after another. If they continually fight the healing growth of Chiron, this aspect can become a symbol of feelings of persecution, as they nearly always see the disruptions as coming from external forces.

EXAMPLES of people with Sun square Chiron: Dr. Tom Dooley, Rudolph Nureyev, Art Garfunkel, J. Edgar Hoover, Albert Dyer, Charles Gounod, Louis Pasteur, Frank Sinatra, Susan Hayward, Henry [Scoop] Jackson, Ross McDonald, Gay Talese, Edith Custer, Sibelius, Robert Holbrook Smith, Nancy Reagan, Fernand Leger, Jack London, Alphonse Daudet, Richard Wagner, Leo Delibes, Vincent Van Gogh, William B. Yeats, Douglas MacArthur, Pierre Curie, James Joyce, J.R.R. Tolkien, Francois Coli, Charles Boyer, Andre Bergeron, Francois Truffault, Jean-Marc Reiser, Steve Allen, David Carradine, John Lennon, Dean Martin, Ryan O'Neal, Vincent Price, John Travolta, Al Green, Billy Squier, Bobby McFerrin, Bobby Vinton, Bryan Adams, Buck Owens, Dickey Betts, Eddie Cochran, Gladys Knight, Grover Washington Jr, Joe McIntyre, Joe Perry, Lyle Lovett, Mary Wells, Naomi Judd, Nina Carter, Vanessa Paradis, Warren Zevon.

SUN TRINE CHIRON

These people have a unique gift. Unless other features of the chart drastically outweigh this, they have a sense of wonder about life and a love of all the surprises life can bring. This wonder is contagious—they can bring it to other people just by being near them. There is also the ability in most of these people to portray this wonder creatively, through art or writing. This talent is not always tapped, however.

There is another side to this aspect. The Sun has a lot to do with self-image and sense of purpose, in addition to creative power. A Chiron trine is always opening up some new aspect of the person for them to develop, or some new world to be explored. In most people, this is seen as fantastic after a while. But for some time, there is an internal fight going on. At a young age they come to a firm conviction about who they are and what they are going to do. The Chiron trine brings these new aspects of the self from areas where the person was sure of having total self-knowledge. If such a person remains entrenched in a confirmed self-image, these new aspects tend either to become repressed [and then work on subconscious levels] or warped to fit in with the self-image that already exists. Once either of these things occurs, the process can snowball, as more insights are likewise repressed or warped. You can see the dangers of continuing this process for long. On the other hand, should a person refuse to explore new worlds that open, because s/he holds on tight to a very limited definition of purpose, the personal world will become less and less fulfilling, less and less realistic. Of course, if such a person can receive help anywhere along this process, the negative can be turned into a positive and bring a real enjoyment of life.

EXAMPLES of people with Sun trine Chiron: Luciano Pavarotti, David Cassidy, Errol Flynn, Anatole France, Andre Gide, Auguste Rodin, Judy Blume, Mike Love, Richard Speck, Chief Justice Earl Warren, Indira Gandhi, Bernard Baruch, Pete Townshend, Terry Gilliam, John Navin Jr., Paul Thayer, Goethe, Jean Anouilh, Josephine Baker, Gustave Dore, Erik Satie, Robert Schumann, Emile Coue, Alfred Dreyfus, Leon Daudet, Stalin, V.I. Molotov, Charles de Gaulle, Hirohito, Bruce Lee, Viven Leigh, Walter Slezak, Tom Smothers, Christine Ockrent, Bo Diddley, Bobby Fuller, Debbie Gibson, Donovan Leitch, Dr. John, Emmylou Harris, Ian Hunter, James Taylor, Jimmy Page, Marie Osmond, Tanya Tucker, Thomas Dolby, Wilson Pickett.

SUN SESQUIQUADRATE CHIRON (135º)

This is a lot like the semi-square. But there seems less of the compulsion, and more of a general restlessness to try new things, open new doors. One thing that does seem to come out of this is constant readjustments in life which slowly but surely help the person become a strong individual, full of courage and strength, spirited, with a good sense of humor. Such a person seems able to come back, time after time, stronger each time than before, no matter what frustrations have been encountered. Chiron here adds an always fresh approach to their manner which may make all the difference in success in the arts.

EXAMPLES of people with Sun sesquiquadrate Chiron: Giuseppe Verdi, Paul Verlaine, Bob Hope, Roddy McDowell, Robert Mitchum, Florence Chadwick, Charles Duncan, Billy Graham, Robert Six, Eric Idle, Peter Sellers, Guy Lombardo, Cher, Jonas Salk, Peter Lorre, Dostoievski, Fernandel, Peter Fonda, Henry Miller, Alexander Dumas, Auguste Lumiere, Paul Claudel, Charles Nungesser, Hermann Goering, Bob Marley, Bob Seeger, Cannoball Adderly, Charlie Daniels, Donnie Wahlberg, Elvis Presley, George Michael, George Strait, Gordon Lightfoot, Jerry Jeff Walker, Maurice White, Ray Charles, Robert Flack, Smokey Robinson, Tim Hardin.

SUN QUINCUNX CHIRON (150°)

These people get a real feel for the NOW—for what is needed at the present moment—in whatever field they enter. It is as if they can tune in to some subtle message that tells them, 'now is the time to do this particular thing'. However, with this aspect, there is a danger of getting stuck in that pattern—of staying with that vibration, even though it is time to move on to something else. These people have major lessons to learn about adaptation and versatility. Positively, if they can tune into the undercurrents, they can BECOME the vibrations—they can understand them so thoroughly that they identify with them, and other people will begin to identify them that way too. But they must learn to move on to another level, another role. Interestingly, while they are in tune with the vibrations, they can, if they so choose, use this attunement to direct, even control other people. If they learn to be adaptable, they are then capable of teaching others, and helping others to grow and adapt.

EXAMPLES of people with Sun quincunx Chiron: Leonard Bernstein, David St. Clair, Stanley Hiller, Representative Paul McCloskey, Bobby Short, George Peppard, Charles Bronson, Bela Lugosi, Candice Bergman, Bonnie Franklin, James Daly, Jack Valenti, Tom Bosley, Phil Ochs, Elie Wiesel, Ralph Waldo Emerson, Captain James Cook, Joan Jett, Dick Clark, Ellen Burstyn, Graham Nash, Jean-Francois Millet, Paul Cezanne, Rimski-Korsakov, Gaston Doumergue, Raimu, Maria Montessori, Andre Tardieu, Marcel Pagnol, Mohammed Reza Pahlavi, Alain Cuny, Al Hirt, Al Kooper, Big Bopper, Bonnie Tyler, Brian Jones, Dave Mason, Del Shannon, Elton John, Elvis Costello, Frank Zappa, Gene Pitney, Janis Joplin, John Lee Hooker, Layne Staley, Lita Ford, Liza Minelli, Lou Reed, Paul Revere (musician), Peter Gabriel, Phil Everly, Stevie Wonder, Tony Orlando, Whitney Houston.

SUN OPPOSITION CHIRON

Here is a fighter. The person perceives someone or something that needs change or beating, and will not stop until s/he has won. Of course, it may not be simply a physical fight—although this can be one expression. It seems s/he is always ready to take up some banner, fight for some cause. In the more evolved types, the causes are quite often the betterment of the human species: the enemy is disease, hunger, dictatorships or something along those lines. In any event, s/he is always competitive, and feels more alive when responding to a challenge or offering a challenge to someone else. As you might expect, people with this aspect make their share of enemies in life, yet most of their enemies grow to respect them. These are almost always people with strong principles, which they will not sacrifice simply to appease another. Other people are very important to those who have this aspect, usually, because aside from the need to compete or to fight, these people are also in constant need for more feedback—another viewpoint—another idea.

EXAMPLES of people with Sun opposition Chiron: Henry Cabot Lodge, John Voight, Rossano Brazzi, George Bernard Shaw, Alfred Lord Tennyson, Leon Spinks, Melina Mercouri, Leon Trotzky, Jane Fonda, Roger Daltry, John Koch, Andres Segovia, Terry Jones, Mark Twain, Dane Rudhyar, John Cage, Albert Camus, Johnny Carson, Mickey Rooney, George Sand, Raymond Poincare, Maurice Maeterlinck, Gilbert Becaud, Dag Hammarskjold, Bobby Goldsboro, Brian Eno, Clyde McPhatter, David Gilmour, Hank Williams Jr., Madonna, Petula Clark, Placido Domingo, Richie Havens, Ricky Scaggs, Stevie Winwood, Tommy James.

CHIRON IN ASPECTS WITH THE MOON

No matter what the aspect, these people simply do not feel comfortable doing things the normal, traditional way and do not appreciate being labeled as 'one of the crowd.' They cannot really relax, unless they are doing something a little different from what they did yesterday, and a little different from what others have done. Depending on which aspect it is, there may be only a mild anxiety, or a powerful need. Security is always tied in to a need for change, and a need to be different. In its most positive aspect, it shows in achieving security by helping others—improving their lives in some way. In its most negative, it can bring a powerful insecurity, unless the person can exert self and feel 'above' others as a way of being different. In many the Chironic need is not felt consciously here—but instead is an undercurrent in the day-to-day routines and habits. For such people, it is very important not to be too tied down to any one routine, with no alternative ways to do things differently if they so choose.

They have the ability to sense a particular mood, feeling, or emotion, tune in to it, understand it deeply, and make use of it. Depending on the evolution of the person, this can be a very positive force, or it can be a means of manipulating others. There is also the potential to sense vibrations on a much deeper level and work to understand these as well.

MOON CONJUNCT CHIRON

Vibrations of many types affect these people, so they must learn early in life some deep philosophy which takes into account unseen forces. This may be manifest in profound religion, but need not be. These people are also extremely susceptible to influence from their personal environment, and soon develop very unique criteria [tastes] about what it takes to make them comfortable. Many live in residences that are anything but normal; one may purposely seek out a place that is haunted; another may move into a house made entirely of rubber tires. Should they choose to, they can be great swayers of people's emotions because they can tune into some feeling common to everyone— some emotion everyone can identify themselves with.

It is often found that a person who has this natal aspect had a mother who was a pioneer in some way, or a researcher, or a specialized adventuress. It appears often that the mother has passed on to the child an abiding curiosity. It is also common that a person who has this aspect had a mother who was very much involved in health and healing, so that the child grew up with an instinctive understanding of how to help others. And, unless drastic indications in the chart point to the contrary, the Moon conjunct Chiron person usually feels very deeply the pains and sufferings of others.

EXAMPLES of people who have Moon conjunct Chiron: Jerry Lewis, Marjoe Gortner, Jules Lenier, Hans Holzer, Paul Verlaine, Robert Mitchum, Ross McDonald, Karl Malden, Patricia Neal, Sandy Duncan, Colonel Sanders, Terry Jones, John Denver, Carol Burnett, George Peppard, Barbara Streisand, Admiral Richard E. Byrd, Woodrow Wilson, Gaston Doumergue, Marie Curie, Francois Coli, Jean-Paul Sartre, Edmonde Charles-Roux, Farah Diba.

MOON SEMI-SQUARE CHIRON (45°)

These people are often very good people-movers. They often have the knack of stirring motivation in others, stimulating their feelings, arousing deeper emotions. They tend to enjoy trying to change the status quo, the arrangements people have let drift. It is very difficult for these people to keep still as they always feel that they must be doing something, either for themselves or for others. Many are 'do-it-yourselfers' because they don't want to sit still long enough to wait for someone else to do something.

EXAMPLES of people with Moon semi-square Chiron: Ray Davies, Kenneth Bergquist, Tom Aldredge, Dr. Martin Luther King Jr., Carl B. Stokes, Paul Joseph Goebbels, Eddie Albert, Jim Bailey, Karl Marx, Adelina Patti, Simone de Beauvoir, Andre Bergeron, Jacque Brel, Jean-Marc Reiser.

MOON SEXTILE CHIRON

These people have the knack and the understanding to represent the common human being, and thus can give others what they want. These people perceive others in a different light than most people do—more fine-tuned, more aware. They are usually perceptive of the ills and weaknesses of others; their strong points and talents; their needs and wants. Some may try to profit from this awareness, but the higher types truly want to help others. There is a hatred of unfairness both in their own lives and for others. If they perceive imbalance, it is second nature for them to fight to correct it, whatever the odds. They have a 'feel' or a 'flair' for giving things a personal quality. Whatever they create is one-of-a-kind.

EXAMPLES of people with Moon sextile Chiron: Mickey Rooney, Billy Rose, Arnold Schwarzenegger, Luciano Pavarotti, Malcolm Dean, Jean Anouilh, O. Henry, Bill Moyers, Edmund Rostand, Robert Goulet, Lula Alvarez, Betty Friedan, Mark Goodson, Mercedes McCambridge, Henry Perot, Nina Simone, Jane Fonda, Jacques Thibaud, Arthur Koestler, Elisabeth Kubler-Ross, Rex Harrison, Gregory Peck, Roy Rogers, Zubin Mehta, Pierre Loti, Enrico Caruso,

Igor Stravinski, Etienne Flandin, Krishnamurti, Salvador Dali, Indira Gandhi.

MOON SQUARE CHIRON

The relationship with the mother is usually quite unusual, either because the mother herself is 'different' in some way, or because of the circumstances in which the person is reared. This is more noticeable among women than among men. These people have a major lesson to learn about being adaptable—but until they do, it seems, time after time, that they stick to old habits until events seem to conspire to disrupt even the simplest routine. As a response, most develop either an abhorrence of any routine at all, or the ability to switch horses in midstream. This overcompensation may not develop for many years—the basic tendency is to stick to old habits even after they have outlived their usefulness. When such a person resists the change, s/he digs self deeper into habits and is less and less able to see that s/he is actually 'stuck' in the past. S/he can actually become totally dogmatic after awhile, refusing to see how stuck s/he is in old ways. Sooner or later one must pay the price for thus getting stuck, and it is usually painful when the moment of truth arrives. Some people with this natal aspect have a blind spot with simple everyday routine information, unable to see what is going on, thus often coming to wrong conclusions. For these people the lesson appears to be: Don't take your own perceptions as foolproof, and learn to be more observant.

EXAMPLES of people with Moon square Chiron: John Glenn, Mike Love, Tom McLaughlin, Brooke Shields, Herb Alpert, Wrong-Way Corrigan, Sandy Koufax, Liza Minelli, Billy Graham, John Dunlop, William Colby, Vance Brand, James Aking, Wendell Phillips, Modigliani, John Cleese, Prokofiev, Bobby Stone, Jon Voight, Cher, Prince Andrew, Derek Jacobi, Paul Lynde, Elvis Presley, Robert Redford, Nietzsche, Paul Choisnard, Gaston Bachelard, V.I. Molotov, Louis de Broglie, Walt Disney, Georges Brassens, Robert Badinter, Pierre Mauroy, Phillippe Bouvard.

MOON TRINE CHIRON

These people, through time, learn the lesson of not taking anything for granted—and they also learn that most other people do not learn this. It is because of this learning that these people make good teachers and problem-solvers. They can see that a problem may exist simply because things were taken for granted. They can help others to see this possibility. They develop the knack of simplifying complex situations, and for seeing things the way they really are. Most people with this aspect are not born with these skills. Rather, they are learned through many experiences in .their day-to-day lives. They learn that even in the most commonplace there may be things beyond their previous knowledge. They have the potential to develop the talent for coaxing people to see themselves as they really are, for good and for bad.

EXAMPLES of people with Moon trine Chiron: Fritz Perls, Donald Sutherland, Peter Ustinov, Willie Mays, George Moscone, Edmond Rostand,

Alfred Lord Tennyson, Tracy Austin, Alene Duerk, Denton Cooley, Robert Duvall, Redd Foxx, Charles Manson, Margaret Thatcher, Lawrence Welk, David Carradine, Sean Connery, Burt Reynolds, Oscar Levant, Zsa Zsa Gabor, Mick Jagger, Tom McLoughlin, Honore Daumier, Felix Faure, Sigmund Freud, Paul Doumer, Raymond Poincare, Arturo Toscanini, Lenin, Stalin, Charles Chaplin, Charles DeGaulle, Enrico Fermi, Marguerite Duras, Mohammed Reza Pahlavi, Serge Gainsbourg, Kareem Abdul Jappar, Louis de Funes.

MOON SESQUIQUADRATE CHIRON (135º)

These people may not necessarily be workaholics, but their restlessness is almost constant. If they are not involved in some project, they are not at all happy. Most of these people work better in fields where they have something to do with other people, in preference to working alone. An excellent sense of humor is usually noticeable—and even when it is not, these people usually enjoy a good joke and love to have fun. If they can combine a project with having fun, they are at their happiest. If not, it is still important that they keep active. 'Better to do something than nothing'.

One of the interesting side effects of this aspect is drastically different according to the sex of the person.

Throughout a woman's life, Chiron seems to teach an unending series of small lessons about her self, helping her to become well-rounded. After she reaches adulthood, she is often described as having 'class.'

In a man's chart, this aspect tends to bring out a sort of 'common man' side, for good or for bad. Whether or not the man becomes well-rounded and develops 'class' depends on how he deals with his Moon—how he deals with his anima. If he looks down on it, then the common-man side may simply develop as earthiness and uncouthness. On the other hand, if he comes to terms with his anima, he too will grow and develop sophistication. A woman, too, can be seen as this common type, but is less likely to be seen as un-couth—unless she totally identifies with her masculine nature and rebels against her feminine side.

EXAMPLES of people with Moon sesquiquadrate Chiron: John Travolta, Linda Blair, Billy Carter, Benjamin Disraeli, Marlene Dietrich, Ethel Merman, Rock Hudson, Elizabeth Montgomery, Alice Anne Bailey, Archie Griffin, James Counsilman, Robert Kastenmeier, John Scali, Debussy, Aristotle Onassis, Edna Ferber, Liberace, Montgomery Clift, Andre Malraux, Anatole France, Alexander Dumas, Octave Mirbeau, Edouard Lalo, Jean-Baptiste Corot, Matisse, Antoine de Saint-Exupery, Ernest Boulanger, Georges Clemenceau, Jacques Soustelle.

MOON QUINCUNX CHIRON (150º)

This aspect usually makes the native an instinctively keen judge of oth-ers. S/he can sense subtle moods, feelings and emotions as others experience them, that the average observer would miss. These people would usually expect nothing less from you than candor—they would rather have you say you dislike them than learn this from such cues as body-language, slips of the tongue, and the like. They usually also develop an instinctive sense of good timing, as if they almost sense all the currents going at any moment. They can draw others out, get them to say what is really on their mind. This can be a big asset in helping others. [It is hard to solve a problem if the person does not clearly explain what needs to be resolved.] It is not always easy to get close to people who have this aspect, however. Perhaps because they can see right through pretenses—they often insulate themselves from people after awhile, or at least become very selective about whom they deal with. The most negative expression of this aspect is a fearful view of the world in which everyone is seen as being deceptive. But, as with any Chiron aspect, this condition need not develop and can be changed when the person learns to distinguish between someone expressing different Levels of self [being inconsistent], as contrasted with someone being purposely deceptive.

EXAMPLES of people with Moon quincunx Chiron: Michel Gauquelin, J. Edgar Hoover, Katherine Hepburn, Sir Laurence Olivier, Walt Whitman, Oscar Wilde, Julie Andrews, Dave Brubeck, Phil Donahue, Peggy Fleming, Tom Bosley, Susan St. James, Edwin Lanehart, Sir Harry Lauder, Robert Bergland, Carmen Delavallade, Ralph Waldo Emerson, Arlo Guthrie, Jack Kerouac, Ryan O'Neal, Theodore Roosevelt, Harry Truman, Guy de Maupassant, Andre Tardieu, Simone Weil, Francois Mitterand

MOON OPPOSITION CHIRON

When this aspect expresses positively the people who have it are fighters for the people; but when negative they are fighters against the people, becoming quite defensive. The type of fighting they do depends on the sign and house positions, and, of course, the rest of the chart. In some there is a belief in non-violence, while in others, the opposite extreme prevails. In one way or another, this is the aspect of a real fighter's instinct. Many can penetrate problems quickly and go straight to the point. There is also a kind of charisma about these natives, and even their enemies can feel its influence. This aspect also seems to produce or bring out a multiplicity of feelings which may overwhelm an individual if s/he lets them. If this does occur the person may begin to dichotomize self, and project his or her own feelings onto others. Then the perception may develop that those 'others' are the enemy. Such a person must be guided to recognize the feelings s/he has, realize how many different levels of them s/he is experiencing, and how each emotional incident relates to the next one. For the people who do not let their feelings overwhelm them, this is an unbelievably creative aspect, leading them to experience a multitude of different feelings and moods which they readily integrate into their psyche. Perhaps it is this ability that makes them such capable fighters?

EXAMPLES of people with Moon opposition Chiron: Henry Cabot Lodge, Robert McNamara, James Dean, John Denver, Lord Alfred Douglas, Adolf

Hitler, Jean Didion, Shirley Hufstedler, Mayor Maynard Jackson, Jack Kemp, Stewart Mott, William Masters, Steve Allen, Elton John, Alan Watts, Fred Astaire, Prince Charles, Victor Hugo, Auguste Lumiere, Alma Cluck.

MERCURY

As you might expect, all Chiron/Mercury aspects have to do with a message the native must give, or an obstacle to communication s/he must overcome. Originality of thought and word is the key here, no matter which aspect between Chiron and Mercury is involved. It is not the originality of Uranus, which seeks to tear down the old, but the originality that simply seems to come from going off on a different path. There is an ability, with the turn of a phrase, or a few well chosen words, to open unexpected doors for other people. The mind is capable of reaching all diverse levels, which thus enables the native to communicate with people on all different levels. Whatever level s/he is talking on, s/he can make a listener feel that they are on equal terms. Usually there is a basic candor here, a tendency to say what is on their mind, without worrying about the effect this may have on others, OR, with the intent to open up others in spite of themselves. Along with this the person usually has the ability to know just what other people want to hear, and can use it if they choose—although it is extremely rare to find a person with any aspect between Mercury and Chiron who says things just to please others or butter them up.

MERCURY CONJUNCT CHIRON

While Mercury is usually looked at as being simply the logical mind, you will find that people with this conjunction have added concern for others into their thinking processes. It would take a drastically negative chart to really suppress this concern, although, in truth, other aspects can also serve to twist or pervert it into something else. These people usually comprehend how the average person thinks, and reach such people with their words and ideas. But, even more, they can think on many different levels, and thus reach many different sorts of people. They are not restricted to simple verbal communication or written words. Chiron takes Mercury out beyond its normal realm, enabling these natives to communicate on many non-verbal levels. Perhaps it is because their minds go places Mercury ordinarily doesn't go, but these people are truly original thinkers, coming up with ideas that seem farfetched, yet work wonderfully. They seldom overlook some piece of the puzzle because it is too small, or apparently insignificant. It is often such a piece that changes everything. Because their minds are not limited by convention, they can be quite controversial, but well worth attention. [In truth, it is difficult to ignore them, although you may not agree with them, or even like what they are saying]. These are the people to consult when you are blocked and need to find some way out—they can find the loophole, or think of a way to open the door for you.

EXAMPLES of people with Mercury conjunct Chiron: Troy Perry, Clive Sinclair, Ted Mack, B.J. Thomas, Edouard Daladier, Benjamin Disraeli, Yogi Berra, Governor Brendan Byrne, Nancy Dussault, Roman Gabriel, Dennis Hopper, Dwayne Hickman, Christopher Atkins, Nancy McKeon, Minnie Riperton, Sir Alec Guiness, Harry S. Truman, Chopin, Marie Montessori, Alma Gluck, Marguerite Duras, Amanda Lear, Billie Holiday, Bobby Darin, Don McLean, Doris Day, Herbie Mann, Jackie DeShannon, Mariah Carey, Muddy Waters, Neneh Cherry.

MERCURY SEMI-SQUARE CHIRON (45°)

Mercury wants to communicate, and with these people, incredibly so. These people leave marks on you—they reach you, often on many levels, and you do not remain quite unchanged. They all have unique individual styles, and their minds are NEVER idle. They must always be either thinking, talking, or taking something in, or be active in some other mode of communication. [The most drastic expression of this I have seen are those with Mercury in Gemini!] This aspect is a real asset if you are going into the field of music, for intense feelings can be communicated along with the lyrics, or through the music itself without words. The voices of these natives are truly special, individually distinct, but all expressing an urgency. Their tone almost always says, I have something you must hear. For those who are not in the communications field, nor involved in the arts, their minds must always be active, always seeking new fields, new ideas.

EXAMPLES of people with Mercury semi-square Chiron: Mario Lanza, Maurice Ravel, Carol Channing, Bruce Springsteen, Donald Kinman, Eddie Arcaro, Ernest Renan, Robert Holley, Rockwell Kent, Yehudi Menuhin, Grace Slick, Dal Lee, Rita Lavelle, Honore Daumier, Edgar Cayce, Pierre Mauroy, Curtis Mayfield, Donna Summer, Gary Puckett, Germaine Jackson, Grandmaster Flash, Helen Reddy, Janet Jackson, June Tabor, Mike Inez, Patti Smith, Quincy Jones, Roger McGuinn, Van Morrison, Willie Nelson, Wynonna Judd.

MERCURY SEXTILE CHIRON

One of the most positive aspects of this combination is the gift of being able to see the humor in almost any situation, and to be able to convey this vision to others. Here is another very active mind, although without quite the compulsion of the semi-square. The curiosity is very strong, and it is not limited to any particular subject—these people want to know about everything. Their minds are their greatest tool, and they must use them in every possible situation. And always, they want to go one extra step—whatever they discover, whatever conclusions are achieved, they want to go a step further, learn a little more. It is extremely rare to find anyone with this aspect who does not like to learn, and then it is usually because of conflicts in third house matters. This is an excellent aspect for a teacher, comedian, or orator, as well as for anyone involved in research. There is also inherent in this aspect a recognition of the potential inherent in all people, so that those who have Mercury sextile Chiron do not make distinctions between classes—they see the possibilities in everyone. It is for this reason, I think, that they appreciate others who are not considered 'normal', rather than discriminating against them.

EXAMPLES of people with Mercury sextile Chiron: Kirk Oates, Jack Paar, Alan Watts, Orson Welles, Orson Bean, Robert Bergland, Bob Gunton, Madeline Kahn, Paul Lynde, Katherine Graham, Eric Burden, Fats Domino, Leon Gambetta, Rabindranath Tagore, Erich Maria Remarque, Enrico Fermi, Richard Wagner, Dwight D. Eisenhower, Amy Grant, Buck Owens, Chaka Khan, David Bowie, Debbie Harry, Duane Eddy, Jesse Colin Young, Jilly Johnson, Joe Tex, Johnny Rivers, Joni Mitchell, Linda Ronstadt, Papa John Creach, Richie Valens, Tommy Roe.

MERCURY SQUARE CHIRON

These people exemplify the general description given in the Mercury/Chiron introduction section, but taken to extremes. Very original—true innovators. One-of-a-kind thinkers, and proud of it. [Very early in life they find out just how different their minds are from average, and it is rare to find one of these people unhappy over this discovery]. And they speak their minds! [Try to stop them!] Have you heard the song with the refrain, 'I did it my way'? That one is their theme-song. Some people love and admire them for their minds, and their words, but they have no trouble compiling lists of the enemies they have made among people who are too easily offended. There is even a tendency in these people to try doing particular things just to disprove some statement that these things are impossible, cannot be done. There is almost always a sharp wit; they can be biting if they choose. Rarely do you find anyone with this aspect who is not rather intelligent—Chiron seems to push Mercury to learn more, find out more, think more. Often, when these people were growing up, they had troubles sticking to certain lines of thinking, and discovering [sometimes traumatically] that they had to change their thinking. Once these people learn, through such forced changes, that their minds must adapt, be willing to try new ways of thinking, most of them relish trying new and experimental approaches.

EXAMPLES of people with Mercury square Chiron: Robert Stack, Michael Thomas, Paul Simon, Clarence Carvalho, Nancy Reagan, Geraldine Ferraro, Barbra Streisand, Ava Gardner, Hank Aaron, Kareem Abdul Jabbar, Amelia Earhart, Al H. Morrison, Toulouse Lautrec, Frank Sinatra, Zolar, Ezzard Charles, Howard DaSilva, Pauline Kael, Ross McDonald, James Taylor, Pablo Casals, Jimi Hendrix, John S. Pemberton, Dennis Wilson, Joe Louis, Stephen Foster, R.D. Laing, Edna Ferber, Arthur Rimbaud, Claude Debussy, Leo Delibes, Alexandre Scriabine, Etienne Flandin, Andre Bergeron, Barbara Streisand, Barry Manilow, Bill Haley, Chet Baker, Doc Severinsen, Gary Wright, George Michael, Howlin' Wolf, Jerry Lee Lewis, Jimmy Dean, Lyle Lovett, Paula Abdul, Percy Sledge, Randy Newman, Sting.

MERCURY TRINE CHIRON

One lesson these people usually learn, early in life, is that no one is perfect—that even our greatest heroes are human beings with faults. This aspect enables them to deal with people more as they really are, without any of the comparison of self to others that most people go through—neither worshipping another as being a god, nor looking down on another as being inferior. What is more, they are very good at making us see just how human we are as well. If need be, they can easily bring us down—and they are just as capable of showing us their own weaknesses if they feel that doing so will better enable us to relate to them. By recognizing their own humanity, and that of others, they are much better able to help people work toward becoming more whole. Of course, not everyone with this aspect becomes a healer. If the rest of the chart is full of problems, they might allow this ability to devolve into simply pointing out human weaknesses while doing little to help. But the ability is there, and can be tapped, with care. There are many avenues of positive expression for this aspect. Because the native sees no inferiors, they can work well with people who have emotional or mental problems, or other handicaps. In any communication-related field they can come across as a fellow human being, and thus reach others because they are easily accepted. In addition, this aspect does give originality to the thinking, and the realization that we should take no idea, no process for granted. It was probably someone with this aspect who came up with the saying, 'If you assume, you make an ass of U and Me.'

EXAMPLES of people with Mercury trine Chiron: Peter Sellers, Robert Culp, Phyllis Diller, Le Petomane, Yul Brynner, Florence Chadwick, A.J. Foyt, Peggy Fleming, Frank Gilford, Billy Graham, Claude Kirk, William Lipscomb, Karl Malden, Maria Callas, Isabel Hickey, Ursula LeGuin, James Beggs, Debbie Boone, James Caan, Sammy Davis Jr., Alan Alda, Walter Slezak, Emile Coue, Mauriac, Charles de Gaulle, Goering, Flaubert, Gauguin, Manet, Elton John, Arlo Guthrie, Peter Fonda, Ralph Bellamy, Roger Chapelain-Midy, Louis de Funes, Bob Marley, Chris Isaak, Dave Mason, Dionne Warwick, Donovan Leitch, Gladys Knight, Ian Hunter, Janis Ian, Jimmy Page, Joe Cocker, Keith Richards, Patti Labelle, Smokey Robinson, Steppenwolf, Tanya Tucker, Wynton Marsalis.

MERCURY SESQUIQUADRATE CHIRON (135°)

As in the semi-square, there is a restlessness of mind here, but usually without as much intensity. The need to keep mentally active, and to communicate, is very much present, but seems of a less imperative nature. The urgency of the semi-square is replaced here by a need to create, to tell a story, to put the pieces and bits together. [You can see the problem in case the Mercury is in, say, Virgo, where the tendency is to take things apart.] Negatively, this could express itself in telling lies, and possibly even believing them. Such a person needs a great deal of care, and help in finding outlets for creative impulses. With this aspect, a person is often confronted with some situation that is totally outside personal experience—and one in which current ways of thinking are inadequate. S/he must stop everything—seek help, or try an entirely new pathway—thinking must be re-aligned. Through time, and a number of such events, the person learns to approach each problem as something new. S/he learns to approach each problem without preconceived notions, and resolve it on the basis of new information inherent in the problem. S/he thus develops the ability to think while standing, innovate fluently, and be a real survivor. And, out of each such adaptation s/he goes through, the sense of humor grows and develops.

EXAMPLES of people with Mercury sesquiquadrate Chiron: Phoebe Snow, Dr. Louis Berman, Fernandel, David Brower, Giuseppe Verdi, Lee Evans, Jonathan Winters, Debra Winger, Raymond Donoran, Arthur Miller, Robert Schumann, Joachim von Ribbentrop, Fred Astaire, Alain Cuny, Bobby Fuller, Buffy Sainte-Marie, Dave Brubeck, Elvis Presley, Gene Pitney, Mary Black, Phil Ochs.

MERCURY QUINCUNX CHIRON (150°)

Here is promised minds that perceive many different levels going on in a situation at the same time. People who have this aspect perceive both the obvious and the more subtle processes as well. When solving problems their minds weave in and out among the different levels, discovering and connecting ideas and events that one-track thinkers never discover. The impact can be positive or negative. Positively, these people perceive multiple motives in others, and can help others to see themselves in better perspective. They see little bits others overlook, and add these extra data into their evaluations. Negatively, they can see too many levels, too many features, and sometimes so much that it cannot be sorted out. Too much information can be as bad as not enough. This aspect is very good to have if you are working to help others become more realistic, once its lessons have been learned. The search on many levels for information is natural, creative, BUT, one must learn to discriminate, sort out what one finds, and not just accept everything.

EXAMPLES of people with Mercury quincunx Chiron: William Saroyan, Arthur Janov, William Lamb, Roy Ash, Manuel DeFalla, Dane Rudhyar, Arthur Koestler, Mike Love, Dick Clark, Gustave Courbet, Camille Saint-Saens, Henri Michaux, Daniel Cohn-Bendit, Winston Churchill, Dag Hammarskjold, Cher, Aretha Franklin, Barbara Lewis, Big Bopper, David Mason, Del Shannon, Deniece Williams, Diana Ross, Eric Clapton, Fabian Forte, John Coltrane, Johnny Winter, Layne Staley, Mitch Ryder, Peter Frampton.

MERCURY OPPOSITION CHIRON

In some ways this one resembles the square. People who have this aspect have sharp minds and love to attack problems. In most, there is the love of a good argument or debate. They try not to let anything limit the range of their attention and often have very far-reaching ideas. This same stance works with people, too—they don't let others interfere with their explorations. No denial or refusal of information stops them. There is almost always an insatiable curiosity and a need to figure out both sides of any situation. [Give them a secret to uncover, and they are in heaven.] If you get into an argument with any of these people, do not expect to win easily. You can eventually convince such people only if you can make your side completely clear to them, and show them that you also understand their side. But they won't concede until they know you are really trying to see both sides [even when they know they are in the wrong.]

EXAMPLES of people with Mercury opposition Chiron: R.D. Laing, Jack Anderson, H.G. Wells, Stewart Mott, Margaret Thatcher, Jim Bailey, Lenny Bruce, Bobby Fischer, Gus Trikonis, Rimski-Korsakov, Andre Tardieu, Pablo Picasso, Henri Georges Clouzot, Billy Joel, Bobby Goldsboro, Branford Marsalis, Cyndi Lauper, John Lee Hooker, Lesley Gore, Stevie Nicks, Thelonious Monk.

VENUS

People with Venus and Chiron in aspect were put on earth to teach us a lot about ourselves and our value systems. In its most positive expression, these people can see clearly through false values, the conventions of society, and the role-playing people do. They develop the ability to see lasting values rather than those set up by particular cultures; to see inherent beauty, not simply beauty as defined by society; to see the value of people, not in arbitrary assigned roles based on class or gender. Yet, for the most part, they don't want to overthrow or disrupt society. Many just want to live life with real values. Still others simply want to pursue their own way [and, if you want to come along too, great].

A problem sometimes comes about with an individual who is uncomfortable with his or her own anima—the feminine principle. Especially if the native is male. Such a native externalizes the Chiron/Venus aspect, and sees it projected onto women. In the case of a male, there is frequently a powerful desire to assert masculinity, and a perception of women as threatening. In some cases, even a woman may follow this pattern. The thing to do is to help the person find a way to accept his or her own Venus—and the healing will follow.

VENUS CONJUNCT CHIRON

This aspect can express itself in a number of different ways. It gives, potentially, a great deal of love which comes spontaneously forth from the native as a real healing influence, giving most to those most in need. Here there can be a danger in that many people with this aspect are vulnerable to being easily hurt—their love is given without strings or expectations, without any defenses at all. It is, potentially, a very idealistic position. To quote from a popular song, 'The world was not made for one as beautiful as you.' If the aspect expresses itself this way, the native must be taught what the world is like, now, so s/he can deal with it realistically, and still give out love.

Another expression of Venus conjunct Chiron is a life quest for what is real, valuable, truly worthwhile in life—a quest for true beauty and value. This can lead the person to disregard society's values, or to try to select what is worthwhile out of all the fake values around. In this approach, s/he may acquire a set of personal values that does not quite fit with those of other people. Depending on the rest of the chart, s/he may keep this secret, or flaunt it. The special personal values are there, no matter whether hidden or displayed. Another expression of this aspect is a desire to understand what makes the real world tick—the laws governing material things. It is an excellent aspect for a scientist, for it seems that Venus is not passive when in this aspect—Chiron is trying to uncover as much about Venus as it can.

EXAMPLES of people with Venus conjunct Chiron: Francoise Gauquelin, Henry Winkler, Alan Ginsberg, Linda Blair, Hector Berlioz, A.E. Housman, Lloyd Bentsen, Bradford Dillman, Orville Freeman, John Sawhill, Raquel Welch, Bela Bartok, Al Jardine, Mama Cass Elliot, Teilhard de Chardin, Simone de Beauvoir, Edmonde Charles-Roux, Marilyn Monroe, Jacques Brel, Laurent Fabius, Morgana King, Barbara Mandrell, Bobby Brown, Dion DiMucci, Grandmaster Flash, Herbie Mann.

VENUS SEMI-SQUARE CHIRON (45°)

In its most positive expression, the person who has this aspect cannot rest while there is unhappiness around, or social conflict, or some imbalance. There is a desire to help the world, alleviate burdens, bring joy to others, which must be expressed. It may come out through some mode of social service, or through portraying the sufferings of others in the arts, or through active participation in political or social movements. No matter what level of evolution the person has reached, this aspect stirs the natal Venus and makes it very important in the life. When it is expressed negatively, the person begins to run away from Venus, or see Venus as threatening. There may still be the desire to bring joy to others, but it is twisted into a need to dominate or suppress his or her own Venus, and possibly anyone s/he may see as representing Venus in the world around the native. At its most negative, the native externalizes the Venus and focuses it onto some group or class or set of values, and decides the world would be a better place by the removal of this group/class/values. Such a person needs to be helped to get in touch with [accept] his or her own natal Venus to be healed.

EXAMPLES of people with Venus semi-square Chiron: Merle Haggard, Bob Dylan, Enrico Fermi, James Counsilman, Jeanne Crain, Dianne Feinstein, Eugene Fodor, Robert Hack, Franco Harris, Marlene Dietrich, Telly Savalas, Jean Cocteau, Bobby Riggs, George Lincoln Rockwell, Marc Edmund Jones, Nancy Reagan, Queen Elizabeth II, Zsa Zsa Gabor, John Lennon, Jack Paar, Edouard Daladier, Gaston Bachelard, Serge Gainsbourg, Jean-Marie Le Pen, Michele Cota, Bill Withers, Billy Squier, Bobby McFerrin, David Crosby, Edgar Winter, Gloria Gaynor, Harry James, Lyle Lovett, Nona Hendryx, Sam Cooke, Waylon Jennings, Woody Herman.

VENUS SEXTILE CHIRON

For some unknown reason, this aspect has been very under-represented in my study. Those people I have studied show a great deal of love for others, and caring—but it seems the Venus passivity is accented in this aspect. That is not to say that one cannot become successful with this aspect. But, unless other aspects point to the contrary, this sextile seems to express itself more quietly and subtly than most other Chiron aspects. These people tend to help others on a day-to-day basis, sometimes openly but seldom advertised. Chiron here does bring out the romantic side or the poetic nature of the person. There is a definite one-of-a-kind quality in any talent the individual has, and should other aspects propel the individual into the arts, the works will live long after the person passes on.

EXAMPLES of people with Venus sextile Chiron: Albert Dyer, Claude Kirk, Carl Sandberg, Michael Palin, Doris Chase Doane, James Beggs, Glenn Campbell, Walter Slezak, Igor Stravinski, Pierre Curie, Jacques Soustelle, Al Stewart, Billy Ocean, Bob Geldof, Bob Marley, Chet Baker, Frankie Valli, Helen Reddy, Jean Redpath, Linnea Quigley, Nina Carter, Richie Valens, Rick Springfield, Rickie Lee Jones, Roger McGuinn, Stevie Ray Vaughan, Teddy Pendergrass, Toni Tenille, Trini Lopez.

VENUS SQUARE CHIRON

When this aspect expresses negatively, it can be the most extreme case of being unable to deal with one's own anima. More than any other aspect of these two planets, the square will accentuate any imbalance the person has in sexual identity. In the male, it can bring extreme 'macho' behavior along with a lot of difficult relationships. Or, it could bring the other extreme, trying to resolve the square by total identification with the Venus, with the male becoming super-feminine—and still having trouble with relationships. As in other aspects between these two planets, the relief comes with getting the male to accept his anima, and giving him an outlet for it, as well as helping him put it into perspective with his animus.

It is extremely rare for this aspect to bring the same problem to a female. Rather, it tends to express itself as the female learning to deal with her own femininity, learning to put it into perspective, and rising above any social expectations or demands upon her because she is female.

No matter whether it is a man or a woman, the native has a completely unique taste in arts—such that it could lead them to create a whole new style or school of art [if promised by the rest of the chart.] The person finds beauty in objects others may overlook, look down on, or close their eyes to. When it comes to personal value systems, s/he is distinctly unique. Many people with this aspect follow their own path privately within society; others leave society altogether. For some there arises a personal imperative to show society where and how it is wrong—to teach others about false values versus true values.

EXAMPLES of people with Venus square Chiron: Peter Fonda, Marjoe Gartner, Bruce Lee, Liberace, Brooke Shields, Adlai Stevenson, Charles Addams, Vida Blue, Edgar Degas, Le Petomane, Louis Pasteur, Sophia Loren, Yvonne Burke, Judy Collins, Jimmy Ellis, Mark Goodson, Farley Granger, George Steinbrenner, Rimsky-Korsakov, Colonel Sanders, Fats Domino, Maxime Weygand, H.G. Glouzot, Ahmad Jamal, Bill Haley, Bobby Fuller, Bobby Vinton, Boz Scaggs, Chuck Mangione, George Michael, Jeff Beck, Johnnie Ray, Johnny Winter, Leonard Cohen, Lindsey Buckingham, Mary Black, Rick Derringer, Roseanne Cash.

VENUS TRINE CHIRON

This aspect can give that 'little something extra' that can make even a no-talent into a star, and someone with talent into a super-star. The individual has a self-invented style and no later imitator can do it justice. If people who have this aspect go into the arts, they often focus upon things people take for granted to get their messages across. Interestingly, when natives of this combination have major setbacks of any kind, they usually spring back, having learned a great deal, and are even stronger for it.

There seem to be two main types of people with this aspect.

Those with Venus 120° further along in the zodiac from Chiron tend to be either the artist, or one who is concerned with reaching and/or teaching children and protecting them, or one who has major lessons to learn about their own morals versus those of society.

Those with Venus approaching Chiron, with 120° yet to go before making conjunction, have more concern for ethics, esthetics and collective values of society, than for individuals.

EXAMPLES of people with Venus trine Chiron: Arlo Guthrie, Zubin Mehta, Ken Usten, Charles Bronson, Alice Cooper, Frank Zappa, Upton Sinclair, Truman Capote, Jimmy Carter, Don Ameche, Judy Blume, William Colby, Ronald Dellums, John Delorean, Justice William Rehnquist, O.J. Simpson, Phil Ochs, Mary Baker Eddy, Phil Collins, Balzac, Winston Churchill, Dwight D. Eisenhower, Alfred Dreyfus, Hirohito, Maurice Messegue, Jacques Mesrine, Fred Astaire, Josephine Baker, Helen Reddy, Jollivet-Castelot, Brenda Lee, Buster Poindexter, David Byrne, Donovan Leitch, Emmylou Harris, Grace Slick, Hugh Maskela,

Marvin Gaye, Paul Butterfield, Thelonious Monk.

VENUS SESQUIQUADRATE CHIRON (135°)

People who have this aspect have the ability to take the commonplace, everyday values and focus in on them—calling our attention to them, and also, to how far we have diverged from them or twisted them. These people can also bring us back to the simpler values—ideals that were important long before our present civilization—things we have forgotten. These people can help shape current values. There is, potentially, almost a genius capability for dealing with material things, such as the handling of money. [This would, of course, also depend on the rest of the chart—but the potential lies in this aspect.] There also seems to be a bit of theatrical talent for putting on whatever role is needed for a given situation, and then moving on to whatever other role the developing situation requires. The more elevated natives have a great deal of concern for others, and want to make sure that others can enjoy life. They will do whatever is feasible to bring happiness to all, and to help others overcome lacks and problems.

EXAMPLES of people with Venus sesquiquadrate Chiron: Art Garfunkel, Paul Williams, Errol Flynn, Rich Little, Rosano Brazzi, Elbert Hubbard, Montgomery Clift, Dorothy Hamill, Brian Mulroney, Mike Munkasey, Bernard Baruch, Arthur Miller, Mohandas Gandhi, Douglas MacArthur, Kareem Abdul Jabbar, Ralph Bellamy, James Dean, Gilbert Becaud, Brian Eno, Bryan Adams, Buddy Rich, Clyde McPhatter, Del Shannon, Eddie Cochran, K.D. Laing, Lesley Gore, Lionel Richie, Morrissey, Nick Drake, Petula Clark, Stevie Winwood, Tina Turner, Todd Rundgren, Woody Guthrie.

VENUS QUINCUNX CHIRON (150°)

People who have this aspect are very much aware of other people, and of all the different levels that exist in any relationship. Because of this perceptiveness, they have great potential to help others through problems in relationships by focusing on what approaches need change. They are very much aware of what people want—on many different levels—and usually know how to give it to them. They are capable of using this awareness to control, even re-shape other human beings. But they have many lessons to learn in relationships in which they themselves are involved. Their attitudes can run the gamut from general distrust of others, to looking down on others, to simply wanting to separate themselves altogether from society. On a more positive plane, they do develop some unique style in everything they do, working with reality in such a manner that it seems they become its master.

EXAMPLES of Venus quincunx Chiron: Paul Gauguin, Auguste Rodin, Malcolm Dean, Walter Mondale, Max Schmeling, Charlie Tuna, Mao Tse-tung, Robert Blake, Jim Bouton, Phil Donahue, John Dunlop, John Koch, Daniel Nathans, James Cagney, Saint-Exupery, Vittorio De Sica, Fernandel, Elvis Costello, Gene Clark, Jim Croce, John Fogerty, Lydia Lunch, Rod Stewart, Tommy

James, Wynton Marsalis.

VENUS OPPOSITION CHIRON

There appears to be two main types of individuals who have this aspect. One is the type that fights for rights and the values they cherish. This kind will be truly aghast at finding injustices, and will work to do something about them. The second kind seeks to change, control or even dominate whatever they associate with their own natal Venus. It may be simply trying to be in total control of their own feminine side, or it may be externalized as a feeling that they must control the women in their lives

If the person is of this last type, there seems to be a dominant Mars in the chart, and usually it is either afflicted, retrograde or in the 12th house.

In both these main types of individuals, the aesthetic sense is a bit unusual, and if they have artistic capabilities, they have no difficulty in developing a style that is uniquely their own. In relationships, both types have many lessons to learn, but the second type almost always has a great deal of difficulty in making relationships last. The potential here is for a very caring, giving person, once the individual has come to terms with his or her own natal Venus. Many people with this aspect are highly evolved and will go out of their way to see that others have any opportunities they need. They will give the proverbial 'shirt off their back', if they feel that it really will do some good.

EXAMPLES of people with Venus opposition Chiron: Michael Jackson, Diana Ross, Marty Balin, Paul Kantner, George W. Lippert, Aleister Crowley, Roger Staubach, Kevin Rowland, George Bernard Shaw, Greta Garbo, Francois Mitterand, Louis de Funes, B.B. King, Carole King, John Lee Hooker, Lou Reed, Mark Lindsey, Mel Torme, Ray Charles, Roberta Flack, Tim Hardin.

MARS

Those who have an aspect between Chiron and Mars have a great potential for overcoming immense obstacles. What is interesting is that this seems to be true for all, no matter what the aspect is, even if it is one of the so-called 'minor aspects.' The trait is stronger in those with the major aspects uniting Mars and Chiron. These two bodies have a special relationship to each other that is not often discussed in literature on Chiron.

This relationship stems from the chart for the moment of Chiron's discovery in which Mars and Chiron are closely linked by a square aspect (*see pg.* [44]).

Seen in this light, any aspect between Mars and Chiron echoes the discovery chart, and this is an extremely important part of the natal chart. Each person with one of these aspects, whether it is 90°, or some other arc, is having to deal with problems and situations that are not only basic to the meaning of Chiron itself, but even more, directly related to major problems in the collective conscious/unconscious of mankind today.

Tradition has it that when a planet is discovered its meaning ties in closely to major events at that time. So this is true, of course, with Chiron's basic nature. Even more explicitly, the Chiron/Mars aspect represents very specific problems mankind must face, now.

The late Marc Edmund Jones often said that when a new planet is discovered, there is required a rise in cosmic consciousness. [Involving all of the human species.]

Chiron, among other things, denotes trying to rectify imbalances, and trying to heal illnesses. Applying this to Mars, there are many areas that come to mind. I will take just a few, but you can apply this principle to every other Mars concept that comes to your mind.

The world is having to deal, more and more, with sexual stereotypes. It is no coincidence that the first-ever convention of the National Organization of Women (NOW) took place around the time of Chiron's discovery. So, one major problem Chiron/Mars people have to deal with is the whole concept of sex roles, and of imbalances in equality based on these roles.

Taking it one step further, one must realize that every woman has a Mars in her chart, and every man a Venus. Chiron is focusing on the need for people to come to terms with their 'opposite sex' planet—for a man to recognize the positive nature of his own Venus, and for a woman to become aware of the positive qualities in her own Mars. So, these are major issues for people with aspects between Mars and Chiron.

There is a great deal of violence in the world today, from petty squabbles to actual wars. Richard Nolle has pointed out that there is a definite connection between Mars square Chiron and terroristic incidents. Mankind itself seems to be heading for major war that could end all life on this planet. As we move closer and closer to such a horrible possibility, we must face a very real issue—find a way to resolve our martial conflicts peacefully, or face annihilation. On a personal level, individuals with Mars and Chiron in mutual aspect must deal with similar lessons—to find a way to resolve conflicts without resorting to violence [either physical or verbal.] They have major lessons to learn about temper, and about resolving issues in general.

The last area I want to mention here is that of one's modus operandi—the method of procedure an individual takes to attack a problem, or resolve a difficulty. In society as a whole, standard procedures are being questioned, one by one, in all areas of life. Every method that has been relied upon for years seems now to be no longer taken for granted. The whole fabric of society is changing as people are questioning the reasons for various procedures [customs], and finding holes in the logic of others. On the individual level, people with Mars/Chiron aspects have major lessons to learn about relying upon traditional methods, and usually develop unique, often innovative ways to attack problems. But many must first learn to see when it is all right to use traditional methods. There is a tendency to pursue a different approach without even giving the traditional way a second glance.

MARS CONJUNCT CHIRON

There is an incredibly strong tendency in the people who have this aspect to do things their own way. If your child has such an aspect, you probably are in the habit of saying, 'All right, do it your way. Don't listen to me.' And yet, this very same child WILL accept advice from some person s/he sees as a mentor—if s/he can find such a mentor. So this child must be very careful as to whom s/he turns to for advice. In the adult, there is still the same need to follow one's own path to resolve problems, although s/he will be more likely to listen to your advice—if you can show that the advice comes backed by some authority noted for special or unique insight, rather than just from your own opinion or some arbitrary authority. Once these people tap into it, they seem to have a remarkable ability to find the key to overcome other people's problems—and they usually are very concerned with doing that. In their own lives, it is usually different. They tend to have continual or recurrent problems with Martian things, over and over, until they learn some major lessons. After that, they can not only work to attack their own problems in unique ways—but they also develop a remarkable insight into what makes other people tick.

There is almost always a unique view of sex, and of sexual roles, that is totally of their own. This is not to say that it is abnormal or unnatural—but merely that it seems to be one they have found for themselves, often a bit beyond socially accepted traditions. It is very unusual for such a person to go through life without making some enemies, or at least alienating some people. This is never done intentionally— but rather, it happens incidental to their tendency to pursue their own ways.

EXAMPLES of Mars conjunct Chiron people: Henry Perot, Zsa Zsa Gabor, Huey P. Long, Benny Hill, Bob Crane, Paul Newman, Joseph Goebbels, Walt Disney, F.A. Bartholdi, Marc Chagall, Pierre Mauroy, Billie Holiday, Billy Preston, Daryl Hall, Jackie Wilson, Jackson Browne, Johnny Paycheck, Muddy Waters, Nat King Cole, Ninah Cherry, Roger McGuin, Tony Bennett.

MARS SEMI-SQUARE CHIRON (45°)

Never say, 'you can't' to people with this aspect, because it is usually enough to provoke them to prove you wrong. Of course, it may be the best way to get them to do something—good psychology—but only if you can actually make them to believe you really think they can't. Mere words are not enough—they can usually see through that. More than this, they cannot tolerate the thought that anything may stand in their way when they are trying to complete some personal task, solve some problem, or uncover some information. Chiron is always stirring up Mars here, pushing it to do more, accomplish more, release more energy. Mars does not seem to be able to refuse. Instead, these people seem to be constantly active, constantly busy. Their need not to be stopped pushes them to keep trying new methods, new slants, new angles, going around, or even ignoring obstacles. They usually have a major lesson to learn about their temper, since Mars is so active in their lives.

It seems there are two distinct types of people with this aspect—those who are just plain aggressive or assertive, and those who have channeled the energy into fighting for some-cause. Of course it is possible to be both—but quite often, the latter type has found a way to tone down their assertiveness until they are actively involved in their cause. One thing that seems to occur with all natives of this aspect is very definite tastes—either they really like something, or they don't like it at all. They usually have no hesitation in telling you how they feel. This aspect seems also to add to sex appeal—perhaps because the Mars is so active. In its most negative expression, some lower sides of Mars, such as sadistic tendencies, may show. In some women it may lead to over-expression of masculine traits. But when the lower side is expressed, it is usually due to an imbalance of the male and female qualities of the person, and can be brought into balance, with help.

EXAMPLES of people with Mars semi-square Chiron: Omar Sharif, Keith Emerson, Dr. Martin Luther King Jr., Wilt Chamberlain, O. Henry, Bertrand Russell, Greta Garbo, Bishop James Pike, Miles Davis, Redd Foxx, Joel Grey, Madeline Kahn, John Knowles, George Lucas, Bette Midler, Claude Debussy, Raymond Donovan, Robert Redford, Cat Stevens, Joe Chambers, Frederic Chopin, Alphonse Daudet, Jules Massenet, Maurice Maeterlinck, Marconi, Charles Lindbergh, Barbara Mandrell, Cannonball Adderly, Eddie Jackson, Herbie Mann, James Brown, Michael Bolton, Sinead O'Connor.

MARS SEXTILE CHIRON

People who have this aspect have little doubt in their minds that they can do anything they set their minds to do. While they are not usually the type to do things merely to prove someone wrong [as in the semi-square], the thought rarely enters their heads that any given project might be too difficult. Likewise, they take it for granted that anything they choose to do they will be allowed to do. It is not that they are, by nature, lawbreakers—unless other aspects in the chart point to that. Rather, when they choose to do something, it just seems natural to them that they be allowed to do it. If you have a child with this aspect, you can see how imperative it is that the child grows up with a good sense of values in hopes that the child will choose not to pursue antisocial activities. These people have a great deal of talent in controlling and using Martian energy, no matter what field they enter. And they usually have a great deal of energy, often seemingly coming from nowhere. They have a remarkable ability to manifest Mars as a tool, whether they are skilled with scalpels or carving knives, one-of-a-kind athletes or hard hitting politicians. Whatever they do, their methods carry with them their own personal brand—their own unique patterns.

EXAMPLES of people with Mars sextile Chiron: Tom McLoughlin, Larry

Csonka, Auguste Rodin, James Blish, Dave Brubeck, Eleanor Carter, George Foreman, Elizabeth Koontz, Kate Millet, Cindy Williams, Carl Wilson, Katherine Graham, Leopold Stokowski, Daniel Berrigan, Percival Lowell, Aretha Franklin, Ben E King, Brad Whitford, Cher, Dave Brubeck, Edgar Winter, Felix Cavaliere, Jimmy Buffet, John Lennon, Kim Carnes, Patti Smith, Phoebe Snow, Ray Charles, Steppenwolf.

MARS SQUARE CHIRON

One of the major lesson that this person must learn is to be adaptable—to try new methods when they come along—to experiment. Some learn it early in life while others apparently never learn it. But, until they learn, the following sequence of experience usually comes: The person finds some method that works—some plan of action. S/he uses it continually, getting into a rut [habit]. After this goes on for awhile, Chiron comes along and throws a wrench into the process—the success formula doesn't work any more, or it produces negative results. When this occurs, the person may fall down, and fall hard! Even when s/he doesn't actually fall, s/he is definitely thrown off-balance, and must re-orient self. At this point in time, the person usually chooses one of three alternatives.

1. Make an adjustment, and then go back to some routine method of doing things. If this approach is chosen the person will once again have to go through the same process in the future, and again each time s/he refuses to learn. Eventually, this repeated stress can have an influence on the health, producing stress-related ills.

2. Learn part of the lesson. If this is the case, the native learns the virtues of trying new methods, new ways of doing things, but not the 'why' of the lesson. S/he begins to revel in each new method. S/he may seek out and try to experience every new act that can be found, every new experience and sensation that exists. S/he is even capable of inventing brand new ones. If the person continues along this course s/he will still be confronted with Chiron throwing a wrench into the act—but the native will see it as just one more new experience, or as a temporary setback. Continued long enough, this person may go to excess with destructive results.

3. The person learns to be adaptable. S/he learns to try new things, and learns to discriminate, so that s/he also knows when the old methods are still valid. S/he uses new ways of doing things when the time is right. S/he thus builds up a broad repertoire of methods and experiences we draw upon, and is seen by others as extremely resourceful and multi-talented. Should s/he turn great personal energy toward helping others, s/he finds a knack for coming up with the right solution for each individual's problems, and often uncanny insights into what makes people tick. S/he welcomes each new experience, but sees it as a means, not an end.

EXAMPLES of people with Mars square Chiron: J.R.R. Tolkien, Linda

Blair, Spiro Agnew, Alan Alda, Jerry Lewis, Malcolm Dean, Rockwell Kent, Sir Harry Lauder, Percy B. Shelley, Rod Stewart, Jim Morrison, Tom Aldredge, Florence Chadwick, Ezzard Charles, Nanette Fabray, Billy Graham, Valerie Perrine, Roger Staubach, Gay Talese, Peter Graves, Michael Jackson, Glen Scarpelli, Nancy Reagan, Terry Gilliam, Terry Jones, Marlon Brando, Jack Lemmon, Rex Harrison, David Cassidy, Cezanne, Stravinski, Balzac, Jean Genet, Jean-Claude Killy, Aleister Crowley, Billy Idol, Bonnie Raitt, Bryan Ferry, Charlie Daniels, Chet Baker, David Bromberg, Dollie Parton, Donna Fargo, Doris Day, Dr. John, Geoff Tate, Johnny Winter, Meatloaf, Odetta, Paul Butterfield, Peter Frampton, Peter Gabriel, Phil Everly, Randy Newman, Rod Stewart, Sade, Stevie Nicks, Stevie Wonder.

MARS TRINE CHIRON

People who have this aspect seem always to be seeing glimpses of innovations they can make, improvements they can add, even when they are not looking for them. It is almost as though there is some sentinel in their unconscious always on the lookout for new breakthrough opportunities even while their conscious minds are content with working with what they have at hand. On a positive level, therefore, these people are fluent innovators, seemingly able to open new doors with little effort. When they make a deliberate effort to research problems, they seem to be able to make obstacles almost melt away. When hard work is required, they are usually willing to devote much energy to the tasks at hand—unless other aspects point to the contrary.

There is another side to this aspect. As natives are growing up, the unexpected seems to happen to them in areas of life that they thought they knew—that they had taken for granted. These unexpected events test their Mars. There may be tests of their masculinity, or tests of their stamina, or tests of their ability to attack a problem, tests of their ability to assert themselves or even tests of their ability to take the first step in some new situation. With Chiron in trine to anything, unexpected lessons come because we usually feel comfortable with areas 120° away from a planet—we feel we can express ourselves freely there, and that we can take the area for granted—that it is never going to pose a challenge. But Chiron reacts differently here than any other type of trine. Doors open up in areas in which we had no idea there were any doors. Since Chiron in trine teaches one not to take anything for granted, many people learn this lesson quickly and profit by gaining the ability to look into places others ignore—to try methods others would not expect to be valid [too commonplace, or too ordinary, or simply not 'worthy' of consideration]. (When someone with this aspect comes up with a new procedure, you might find yourself saying, 'Now why didn't I think of it—it was right in front of me all the time?')

There can be a hazard in this aspect. Some people are insecure, and when these unexpected doors open to them, they become scared, defensive. They tend to try to erect walls—barriers—in the areas influenced by Chiron—to try to shield Mars from the unexpected. This has the following result: Mars, which needs these lessons to evolve, begins to deteriorate. Possibly, it even may become distorted. In such an event, the person may express Mars in strange, sometimes anti-social ways. The unexpected events none-the-less occur [in a context made less favorable by the person's defensive reactions], but the person misinterprets them in relation to the walls s/he has built up. This vicious circle will continue until the person sees that s/he must tear the walls down. This happen with the help of someone in the role of guru or healer, or it may happen [spontaneously] when Chiron makes a hard aspect by transit to its natal position.

KEEP IN MIND that this is only one of many expressions of Chiron, and much less common than the more positive expressions of this trine.

EXAMPLES of people with Mars trine Chiron: Helen Reddy, Karl Ernst Krafft, Richard Speck, Wendell Wilkie, Richard Daley, George W. Lippert, Conrad Moricand, Alfred DeMusset, Henri P. Petain, Jacqueline Onassis, Phil Donahue, Robert Gilruth, Glen Tetley, Anne Tyler, Shelly Winters, Beau Bridges, Sharon Tate, Natassja Kinski, Christopher Atkins, Mike Munkasey, Michael Erlewine, Admiral Robert E. Peary, Marie Osmond, Keith Moon, Sir Alec Guiness, Jonas Salk, Jack Kerouac, Paul Simon, Ferand Leger, Marguerite Duras, Robert Schumann, Sigmund Freud, Fred Astaire, Mistinguett, Jean-Paul Sartre, Valery Giscard d'Estaing, Bernard Pivot, Jane Fonda, Becky LeBeau, Debbie Gibson, Del Shannon, Eddie Rabbit, Emmylou Harris, Joan Baez, Peabo Bryson, Percy Sledge, Sting, Gene Clark.

MARS SESQUIQUADRATE CHIRON (135°)

This aspect seems to be almost identical with the semi-square of these two planets. So, for the most part, refer to that description [page 120]. However, it seems to be a bit less compulsive and takes on a more personal level than that aspect. The need to be constantly active is there, but the native seems to make a more personal, deeper commitment to whatever cause is involved. People with this aspect may not come on so aggressively, but they do attack problems more thoroughly and put more of themselves into it. They have much spirit and can seemingly survive just about anything that happens to them. They often develop a sense of humor that can be biting or sarcastic—or at least direct to the point, in the way that a scalpel in the hands of a skilled surgeon gets right to the spot. Many of these people develop keen insights into human nature. These sometimes serve as verbal scalpels.

EXAMPLES of people with Mars sesquiquadrate Chiron: Ray Stevens, Neil Diamond, Harold Robbins, William Casper, Kathryn Grayson, Eartha Kitt, Telly Savalas, Flip Wilson, Debra Winger, Vincent Van Gogh, Vaslav Nijinski, Humphrey Bogart, Ryan O'Neal, George Gershwin, Amy Grant, Buddy Rich, Carly Simon, Chick Corea, Debbie Harry, Don Henley, Harry James, Joe Tex,

Randy Travis, Rick Springfield, Roy Harper, Robin Trower, Sonny Bono.

MARS QUINCUNX CHIRON (150°)

These are the people who go off the beaten path to do their search. They look into things that are not ordinarily the province of their professions, yet are not completely alien. They may end up going to extremes because there is a tendency to continue further and further down the path, diverging farther and farther away from standard acceptable practices. Thus, one of the lessons of this aspect is to know how far to go; to know when it is profitable to go off on a sideline, and when to stop. The danger here is that these people can get trapped in their tangent, and not only be unable to return—but not see any necessity for returning. Those who are late sorting this situation out do come back to reality with skills at helping others turn around. Most of these people somehow manage NOT to go to extremes, although the thrust of this aspect is almost certain to push them into being pioneers of one sort or another.

EXAMPLES of people with Mars quincunx Chiron: Eleanor Bach, Brian G. Marsden, Sally Kellerman, Dr. Sam Sheppard, Jean Anouilh, James Hilton, Lana Turner, Joseph Alioto, Alene Duerk, Daniel James, Sammy Lee, Eric Burden, Geraldine Ferraro, John Stamos, Paramahansa Yogananda, Rachmaninoff, Shostakovitch, Dick Clark, Kevin Rowland, Ritchie Valens, Anne Bancroft, Camille Saint-Saens, Georges Clemenceau, Foch, Alfred Dreyfus, Enrico Caruso, T.S. Eliot, Gustave Dore, Billy Joel, Dan Fogelberg, Gene Pitney, Grace Slick, Morrissey, Roberta Flack.

MARS OPPOSITION CHIRON

This aspect produces real fighters, and what they fight for depends on the sign and house of these two planets. The more elevated types can go all out in the fight for those less fortunate, or for those oppressed. In the lower types, the fighter instinct is developed into a strong feeling that they can improve their stations in life by a fight. There are major lessons to be learned here about one's own masculinity, which hopefully, they have learned very early. If not, there may develop an overpowering need to assert the self, to the point that the overcompensation distorts the lifestyle. On the positive side, these people enjoy finding special ways of doing things, and a clear feeling of being different from ordinary people.

EXAMPLES of people with Mars opposition Chiron: Luciano Pavarotti, Manuel DeFalla, Marcel Proust, Pearl S. Buck, Leon Spinks, John V. Lindsay, Thomas Bradley, Maria Callas, Ursula LeGuin, Winston Churchill, Dustin Hoffman, Louis de Funes, Hugh Maskela, Marvin Gaye.

JUPITER

The aspects between Chiron and Jupiter have a very big influence on how well a person learns, and how well s/he passes on wisdom to other people. No matter what the aspect, s/he learns best in loose situations, without any formal structure. The more rigid the rules, the more difficult it is for such people—especially if the aspects between Jupiter and Chiron are hard aspects. These people always seem to have original ideas—and unusual ways of teaching them to others. They are capable, if they choose, of making major impacts on the belief systems of others. They have a unique slant on life, and a truly individual way to interpret the world around them, that sets them apart from other people. In maturity, these people develop great self-assurance and strong convictions. This aspect is rarely seen in 'wishy-washy' people, unless it is overwhelmed by contrary indications. People with this combination can go to the other extreme in their over-compensations, and become too sure of the correctness of their beliefs—too sure of the rightness of the stands they take.

JUPITER CONJUNCT CHIRON

There are problems in teaching those who have this aspect. It is not that they do not want to learn—in fact, they want to learn, more intensely, and a broader range of lessons, than the average. The problem is with structure. Getting them to a particular place, and at a particular time, is often very difficult—especially if they must do so on any regular schedule. Unless other things point to the contrary, these people are at their best when they can teach themselves—or at least pick the subjects, and the times and places to study them. These people profit greatly from individual tutors more than from regular schooling. Another expression of this aspect is the tendency of these people to be certain in their beliefs —they have little or no doubt at all that their convictions are correct. This tendency can be directed positively, or negatively, depending on what their convictions are. This leads to another point: these are people who find meaning in events—in life—that is not quite the same as what others perceive.

They often can perceive significance in things that others overlook, or in ideas others find trivial. Thus they have the potential of reaching others, to help others find meaning in their own lives. This special vantage point can also come out negatively—they may notice great significance in many unpleasant or negative events, and weave a philosophy built upon despair or sadness. Or they could see the meaning of the negative, and develop a philosophy of change—of the sort needed to alter negative conditions. One lesson many who have this aspect must learn is to see the bright side in situations, and to see the good side in people.

EXAMPLES of people with Jupiter conjunct Chiron: Jules Lenier, George Peppard, Henry Winkler, Roddy McDowell, Edmond Rostand, Frank Sinatra, Orson Welles, Moishe Dayan, Tracey Austin, Robert Bergland, Bob Gunton, James Hodgson, Don McLean, Jascha Heifetz, Elie Wiesel, Arthur Rimbaud, Bob Crane, Kareem Abdul Jabbar, Clark Gable, James Joyce, Arthur Miller, F.D. Roosevelt, Picasso, Pierre Mauroy, Bernard Blier, Anne Murray, Barry Manilow, Bette Midler, Bryan Ferry, Cannonball Adderly, Cher, David Bromberg, Ian

Hunter, Jimmy Dean, Linda Ronstadt, Neil Young, Paula Abdul.

JUPITER SEMI-SQUARE CHIRON (45°)

A person who has this aspect seems to be compelled to learn, compelled to try to understand life, everything around him. S/he is never content to rest, never comes to the impression s/he knows everything. Instead s/he wants to understand more, always growing, always expanding. In its most negative expression, this can be a simple urge to expand the self and its world at the expense of others. In such a case the person can grow distant from others—cut off from reality—seeing only the self. Such a person can be helped by stirring interest in sharing wisdom with others. This usually makes the person aware of worlds other than his or her own. Positively, such a person can be a major influence on the beliefs of others, and on the self-esteem of fellow human beings. S/he must be careful, as well, as there is always the urge to push one's own philosophy, or one's views, onto others as a way of helping them grow. This can be irritating to others.

EXAMPLES of people with Jupiter semi-square Chiron: Joan Crawford, Scott Baio, Joseph Goebbels, Rex Harrison, Ahmad Jamal, Amy Grant, Bonnie Raitt, Bruce Springsteen, Curtis Mayfield, Donna Fargo, Eddie Money, Nick Lowe, Tammy Wynette, Tommy Roe, Wynonna Judd.

JUPITER SEXTILE CHIRON

People who have this aspect really make you stop and think. They are capable of coming up with insights about you, about humanity, or about life in general, that are remarkable for clarity and accuracy. They have the ability to tune in to the 'flavor' and interests of a particular time and interpret them as a part of a larger picture. Depending on the level of evolution of the individual—and also depending upon the culture they are living in, they can interpret the positive, uplifting aspects, or the negative, depressing aspects. By being able to perceive the basic character of the culture, for the particular time, a person with this aspect is capable of using personal knowledge to manipulate, even control others, if the rest of the chart is bent in that direction. No matter what the rest of the chart is like, there is a tendency to get caught up in philosophical ideas and not realize they are too abstract to really use well in the real world. This may take the form of trying to create a world that fits their abstract concepts and not realizing just how far from reality they are straying. Should they be able to realize and avoid such hazards, this is an excellent aspect for any sort of teaching or enterprise in which one's personal interpretations are essential.

EXAMPLES of people with Jupiter sextile Chiron: F. Scott Fitzgerald, James Hoffa, Richie Valens, Richard Nolle, Edouard Daladier, Auguste Piccard, Ottorino Resphighi, Ted Mack, Josef Stalin, Vance Brand, Steve Cauthen, Eleanor Clark, Eugene Fodor, Franco Harris, Roger Staubach, Beau Bridges, Eric Burden, Paul Kantner, Katharine Graham, Joan Jett, Johnnie Ray, T.S. Elliot, Balzac, Oscar Wilde, Woodrow Wilson, Gaston Bachelard, Prince Andrew, Jack

Paar, Billy Squier, Bob Dylan, Bobby McFerrin, Bono, Brian Jones, Carole King, Eddie Jackson, Eddie Rabbit, Edwin Starr, Lena Horne, Lionel Richie, Lou Reed, Maurice White, Odetta, Paul Revere (musician), Ray Charles, Richie Valens, Teresa Brewer, Woody Herman, Tim Hardin.

JUPITER SQUARE CHIRON

Early in life there is a basic tendency to become too relaxed and comfortable about what to believe—and how to interpret nearby events. The universe—it seems—abhors any resistance to change, so the person with this aspect goes through periods of upheaval, as traumatic events come to challenge the validity of the personal belief system. And the results usually go one of two ways: a tendency to make some adaptation, but basically to keep the same beliefs, OR a realization that to grow, one must be open to new ideas, new concepts. If the first pattern is followed, there will be many more such challenges, until the person learns to adopt the second pattern. Sometimes a person will build up a shell to shield self from these new challenges—but such shells are almost always shattered by the next challenge. On the other hand, if the person can grow to accept the idea of growth and acceptance of new ways, s/he can often perceive hidden meanings that others never dream about. Compared to the average person, the Jupiter square Chiron individual [even the negative side] has a unique way of interpreting things. The developed type is good at any area in which it is important to convey a slant that differs from the ordinary. Such a person can be an ideal teacher, able to get the meaning across in complex subjects. In public service the native of this aspect will go beyond the system to enable the truth to emerge.

EXAMPLES of people with Jupiter square Chiron: Albert Dyer, Rosalind Russell, Marcel Proust, Percy B. Shelley, Rudolph Valentino, John Cage, Henry [Scoop] Jackson, Dan Rather, Gay Talese, Nancy McKeon, Carlos Castenada, Sheena Easton, Camille Claudel, Francois Truffault, Hubert Reeves, Anne Bancroft, James Caan, Sammy Davis Jr., Jack Sheldon, Donald Sutherland, Jane Fonda, Jerry Cantrell, Johnny Cash, Lydia Lunch, Morrissey, Nat King Cole, Randy Travis, Tom Hamilton.

JUPITER TRINE CHIRON

There is a lot in common between this aspect and the sextile between these two planets. With the trine, it seems initially that it is easier to fall into the negative tendencies, especially the tendency to control or manipulate others. Of course, this is not necessary—and many individuals rise above this trait. But it is a hazard here. Part of the problem lies in the early years of life. The person has experiences—both good and bad—that force revision of the belief system. The experiences come from the most unexpected directions—from areas where s/he assumed s/he knew pretty much all there was to know. These experiences made the person learn much, quickly, about other people, and what makes them tick—and what others believe. S/he frequently gets remarkable insights, too often taking them for granted after a while. In this there is a hazard—by taking insights for granted, s/he tends to feel free to use these insights any way s/he wants. Such a person needs a lot of guidance, at least initially, in using insights to help others. On a more positive note, s/he is able to catch even the smallest nuance of any situation, or of a person's behavior, and make good use of what is perceived. In the arts, or communication, s/he can use this ability to make others see themselves or some very specific aspect of themselves.

EXAMPLES of people with Jupiter trine Chiron: Henry Mancini, Vincent Price, Peter Hurkos, Marion Brando, Leo Guild, Giacomo Puccini, Lucille Ball, Mao Tse-tung, Governor Brendan Byrne, Alene Duerk, Stanley Miller, Jack Kemp, Kenneth Noland, Cathy Rigby, Ron Ely, Prince, Arthur Koestler, Dag Hammarskjold, Arthur Conan Doyle, Louis de Broglie, Edmonde Charles-Roux, Jean-Paul Sartre, Marc Chagall, Octave Mirbeau, Bill Withers, Chaka Khan, Charlie Parker, Doris Day, Duane Eddy, Linnea Quigley, Sarah Vaughan, Theodore Bikel.

JUPITER SESQUIQUADRATE CHIRON (135°)

One of the most positive influences this aspect gives is a feeling that nothing is impossible—a basic philosophy that those who have it can do just about anything they set their minds to do. On a positive note, this aspect does seem to give its natives a little something extra—they can often do what others think impossible. But, with this aspect, it is very easy to overdo, to the point of recklessness. These people do have major lessons to learn about accepting advice from others, and about the fact that they are yet human, despite a seeming 'guardian angel' which appears to protect many of them even from their own follies. On a spiritual level, they are not afraid to go off exploring new worlds—in fact, their curiosity is amplified by this aspect. The less evolved also have this compelling thirst for knowledge, but may seek it vicariously, in the affairs and lives of others, or in purely mundane areas.

EXAMPLES of people with Jupiter sesquiquadrate Chiron: Robert Horton, Christopher Reeves, Shirley MacLaine, Rich Little, Conrad Moricand, Sophia Loren, Maria Callas, Robert Goulet, Benjamin F. Bailer, William Colby, Sammy Lee, William Lipscomb, Kate Miller, Ted Turner, Paramahansa Yogananda, Evel Knievel, Buddy Holly, Paul Thayer, Ian Fleming, Mohammed Reza Pahlavi, Zola, Clemenceau, Goering, Manuel de Falla, Stephen Foster, Ben E. King, Bonnie Tyler, Eddie Cochran, Gordon Lightfoot, Leonard Cohen, Nina Carter, Tina Turner.

JUPITER QUINCUNX CHIRON (150°)

Those who have this aspect, through time, grow to have a deep understanding of the many levels of other people's thinking. They learn how others have many aspects in their thinking, some extremely subtle. And they learn to tune in to the belief systems of others and work with them, even if the native is of an entirely different mind. Expressed in a negative fashion, this aspect leads its natives to use their own beliefs to manipulate others and shape the ideals of others. This aspect is excellent for teachers, as it gives the ability to project understanding and comfort. There is also promised the ability to transform the ideas of others into much more positive expressions. [Evangelical editing.] People with this aspect often feel that they are beyond traditional rules and traditions in matters of growth and expansion. If the chart is basically well-balanced, this aspect allows an individual to grow without inhibitions and achieve truly great heights. In the more negative expression, the individual can go to extremes in disregard for structures, to the point of being considered totally unscrupulous by others. This aspect can enable the person to develop great resources—even in the material realm—but s/he must be wary of the temptations inherent in going beyond the rules.

EXAMPLES of people with Jupiter quincunx Chiron: Nelson Rockefeller, Aristotle Onassis, Donald Sutherland, Philip Berrigan, Ava Gardner, O. Henry, Ezzard Charles, Robert Six, Arthur Taylor, Edith Custer, Geraldine Ferraro, Eddie Murphy, Charles Manson, Shostakovitch, Alan Freed, Bill Cosby, Mickey Rooney, Peter Ustinov, Jean Anouilh, Admiral Richard E. Byrd, Richard Wagner, Felix Faure, Andre Tardieu, Stalin, Henri Georges Clouzot, Pierre Curie, Jacqueline Nourrit, Michele Cotta, Billy Idol, Celine Dion, Gene Chandler, Harry Connick Jr, Howlin' Wolf, Mariah Carey, Steve Lawrence.

JUPITER OPPOSITION CHIRON

On the one hand, this aspect gives its natives the ability to see many, many opportunities that are missed by most people. They often perceive so many that it is difficult for them to decide which to pursue. In its more negative expression, its natives are tempted onto new pathways simply because they are new or different, without regard to where they may lead. In extreme cases, the natives get carried away by their initial successes, and lose touch with their surrounding reality. Then Chiron brings circumstances which force them to alter their whole belief-systems, drastically. On a positive level, these people usually have a great deal of spirit and a love of life. This is often contagious so they bring up the moods of other people. One very intriguing gift of this aspect is that its natives can usually develop an incredibly complete insight into the nature and doings of some particular type of person, or the workings of a particular philosophy. You can see how this profound understanding could be an asset to a teacher in specialized areas, or to an actor portraying very specific characters.

EXAMPLES of people with Jupiter opposition Chiron: Zubin Mehta, Dr. F. Regarde, Giuseppe Verdi, Doris Day, Nancy Dussault, Darlene Hand, Kris Kristofferson, Burgess Meredith, Shelley Winters, Brian Keith, Gale Storm, Adam Ant, Rimsky-Korsakoff, Colonel Sanders, Jean-Baptiste Corot, Balzac, Adelini Patti, C.G. Jung, Etienne Flandin, Charles Chaplin, Adolf Hitler, Charles de Gaulle, Dwight D. Eisenhower, Bill Wyman, Charlie Daniels, Donnie Wahlberg, Stevie Ray Vaughan, Germaine Jackson.

SATURN

As you might expect, any aspect between Saturn and Chiron is immensely important. As Chiron represents the going beyond Saturn, any connection these planets have will have a major impact in shaping the individual's whole concept of reality itself. People who have aspects between Saturn and Chiron all have lessons to learn about self-limitations—there is an initial tendency to set too many limits on the self, but then Chiron comes along and teaches them how to go beyond limits. With some, the lessons are learned early in life, and with others, not until adulthood, but the lessons must be learned, nevertheless. Once past this stage, these people usually grow to accept a basic attitude that anything that must be accomplished can be done—that nothing important is impossible. In most cases—especially with the hard aspects—there is definite conflict with authority in childhood, and often one or both parents are extremely difficult to deal with. Such a child usually learns quite early that parents are not gods. Many times there is a great deal of resentment toward one or both parents. In some cases, however, the child develops a severe double-standard—s/he knows that the parent is imperfect, yet the parent, in action, still is perceived as though s/he were 'pure' or without flaw. Thus, a lesson that must be learned is about one's own judgement—many do not trust their own ability to judge people, situations, or themselves, because of this 'double-vision' arising from the parental conflict. On a positive note, once the native comes to terms with this, and has learned to cope with it, s/he is capable of going beyond the ordinary ways of doing things, at will. S/he can work with any structure and transform it by showing how it must be changed. S/he recognizes that reality is only apparent—and changes with new information.

SATURN CONJUNCT CHIRON

This aspect is a rare one. It has occurred exact only once this century [1966], and so has not produced a great many cases to study. In a recent survey of individuals born during this conjunction, the following information was found:

All seemed to have an extremely low opinion of their fathers, and this included those who lived with stepfathers and adopted fathers. On the other hand, there was a common feeling of warmth toward their mothers. Many of the individuals had parents who were extremely unusual, both in their general attitudes toward parenting, and often in the differences between marriage partners, [such as drastic differences in age.] This unusualness was apparent to others, not just to the child. The number of fathers who abused their children seemed to be higher than average expectancy. But not every case included abuse. Once the native has come to terms with this conjunction, it promises a remarkable ability to delve into the most hidden aspects of life's most basic forms, or society's most deeply ingrained institutions, or the structures that permeate all levels of a culture. It denotes an individual who learns to make his own reality, if need be. And it indicates one who never lets self be a prisoner to any structure, nor a prisoner of the past.

EXAMPLES of people with Saturn conjunct Chiron: Gustave Courbet, Walt Whitman, Glen Scarpelli, Nancy McKeon, John Keynes, Jean-Paul Sartre, Bela Lugosi, Tom McLoughlin, Bobby Fuller, Janet Jackson, Jerry Cantrell, Mike Inez, Sean Kinney, Edie Brickell Simon.

SATURN SEMI-SQUARE CHIRON (45°)

With this aspect, we have a person who is never content with the way things are, but who always wants to be accepted. There is frequently a dislike of any authority whatever, although it may not reach the point of hostility. When the person overcomes his irritation with those in charge, s/he can quickly rise to authority. The hazard here is in a tendency to become too authoritarian—overcompensating—and alienating people. When this occurs, there will usually be a series of frequent Chironian events which ought to bring the person back toward a more even-handed approach. But it will be the person's own choice whether s/he learns from these events or not. For those who do not gain positions of authority, or do not allow themselves to go overboard, a big plus here is an ability to see humor in almost any situation, and to be able to step out of an oppressive situation, to get their heads together, and to see it more clearly.

EXAMPLES of people with Saturn semi-square Chiron: Chief Justice Earl Warren, Wendell Willkie, Max Baer Sr., Steve Cauthen, Richard Wagner, Charles Nungesser, Claude Levi-Strauss, James Caan, Henry Miller, Bono, Branford Marsalis, Eddie Jackson, Joan Jett.

SATURN SEXTILE CHIRON

In most individuals, it appears that Saturn dominates Chiron in this aspect. Instead of the person using a planet as a tool to bring about Chironian objectives of balance, healing, and the like, as in other Chiron sextiles, with Saturn, there is a tendency to use Chiron as a tool to bring about Saturnian objectives. Note that I said 'tendency'—many people rise above this and allow Chiron to shape their Saturn. But this tends to give two basic types of individuals.

The Saturn-type wants to bring about changes in structures, or society, that help rid them of faults [as they see them], in order to make them more truly Saturnian. They tend to see Saturn as the most important part of day-to-day existence, while they see Chiron as a tool to be used to benefit Saturn. This type of person truly appreciates the virtues of the individual, but only as s/he can be utilized to improve life in some way without altering the basic scheme of things. The Chiron-type wants to Chiron-ize Saturn—to bring about changes

125

in the basic structures of things and society to bring about fairness, rectify imbalances, and open opportunities. This type will use any conventional methods that seem necessary for their goals but will not restrict themselves to them. They see Saturn as something that must be changed—must be improved—and will not fit in with any group or society that is unwilling to make needed changes. They will, however, fit in when they see doing so as necessary—but only as far as it is necessary. Both types relish experimentation.

EXAMPLES of people with Saturn sextile Chiron: Jacques Cousteau, Robert Cummings, Jean Anouilh, Alfred DeMusset, Maurice Ravel, Ronald Reagan, Jean Harlow, Nancy Lopez, Frederick Seitz, Capt. James Cook, Michael Jackson, Bernard Baruch, Thomas Mann, Jean Genet, Howlin' Wolf, Kate Bush, Linnea Quigley, Lita Ford, Madonna, Prince, Richie Valens, Tanya Tucker.

SATURN SQUARE CHIRON

It is a rare person with this aspect who did not as a child have a great deal of difficulty with parents. Since this aspect seems to stay within orb for many years, it seems to represent more people, whole generations, rather than single individuals. Thus, a great many people came from homes where there was difficulty dealing with authority. Between 1935 and 1952, Chiron and Saturn were exactly square each other 21 times, and in orb most of the rest of the time. A great many people were born in those seventeen years. This aspect is the most significant of any Chiron square, except possibly the square from Mars. First, it expresses itself as a tendency to get set into some routine, or some effort to build a structure that is impervious to change. The person has a clear-cut idea of reality, and while s/he might not like it, it is secure. Even in the severest cases, where the parental symbol was an extreme tyrant or dictator, the child feels, 'This is the reality.' But Chiron comes along and throws the person totally off his/her feet. S/he may easily feel that s/he has been zapped! The world picture is suddenly different from what s/he had thought it was, and reality must be drastically redefined. At this point, the person usually goes one of two ways. 1. Fear becomes dominant. S/he withdraws, doesn't know whom or what to trust. Feelings of persecution may arise. S/he knows that what s/he had counted on no longer works, but s/he is too afraid to look for something that will work. S/he may seek guidance—the best thing s/he could do—but frequently s/he allows self to be almost crushed before seeking help. 2. This is the more positive expression. The person recognizes that it is up to self to put the pieces together to form a more coherent personal definition of reality. S/he pulls self together—sometimes seeking assistance from a counselor, psychologist or guru—and attempts to construct a more workable life system with a structure that will withstand whatever comes. At this point crucial decisions are made. Some go so far as to establish a new, tight, secure foundation for themselves, and then hide behind it. If this path is chosen, the individual must eventually go through the catastrophe all over again as s/he discovers that the new reality is faulty, too. Some go to the extreme of disregarding conventions, structures, and any definition of reality altogether. They may become totally anti-authority. These people, too, will one day reach a critical point where everything collapses around them—only for them, it may eventually be the coming of a very heavy Saturn event [imprisonment, poverty, ostracism] causing a great loss of personal freedom. If they do not learn from such experience, the cycle can repeat. The most positive path, however, is the acceptance of any definition of reality as temporary, and any structure as useful, but only as a means to an end. By learning to accept change, accept authority as necessary to a particular situation [but not as all-powerful], accept that those in power are also human, the person reaches a great equilibrium. S/he can use Saturn when needed, and go beyond it when necessary. In fact, s/he can create his/her own structures to fit the occasion, and discard them when they're no longer needed. One of the people with this aspect, Robin Williams, said it best as the title of his album, REALITY IS A CRUTCH.

EXAMPLES of people with Saturn square Chiron: Tom McLoughlin, Jay North, Vance Packard, Robert Redford, Lance Reventlow, Burt Reynolds, Phoebe Snow, Noel Jan Tyl, Herb Alpert, David Bowie, Joe Louis, Hector Berlioz, Edwin Lanehart, Robin Williams, Andy Kaufman, Eleanor Clark, Larry Csonka, Leonard Dawson, Tom Dempsey, Don Drysdale, Mia Farrow, William Lamb, Liza Minelli, Stewart Mott, Jane Fonda, Carl Wilson, Arlo Guthrie, Phil Collins, Anatole France, Jim Bailey, Jose Feliciano, Uri Geller, Diane Keaton, Tome Smothers, Suzanne Sommers, Gus Trikonis, Sir Alec Guiness, Juliette Drouet, Jacques Mesrine, Gerard Depardieu, Barbara Mandrell, Billy Ocean, Bob Marley, Bonnie Tyler, Buddy Guy, Buddy Holly, Carl Perkins, Connie Francis, Cyndi Lauper, Dan Fogelberg, David Mason, Dollie Parton, Don Everly, Donna Summer, Donovan Leitch, Edgar Winter, Gordon Lightfoot, Huey Lewis, Jimmy Buffet, Joel Grey, June Tabor, Kenny Loggins, Lesley Gore, Lionel Richie, Liza Minelli, Meatloaf, Melissa Manchester, Mitch Ryder, Naomi Judd, Natalie Cole, Nick Drake, Patti Smith, Peter Wolf, Robin Trower, Rod Stewart, Ron Wood, Sonny Bono, Stephen Stills, Tina Turner, Todd Rundgren, Tom Petty, Warren Zevon.

SATURN TRINE CHIRON

This aspect can make a difficult childhood because one of the parents continually surprised the child. Just when the child thought s/he knew what was expected of him/her, the authority symbol would pull a rabbit out of a hat, and the child would have to change his/her mental picture. This also meant that the child had to change his/her own self-image, and his/her concepts of his/her own limits. The surprises could be good or bad—but were surprises because they came in some area that the child had felt secure in taking for granted. This experience can bring about a number of possible results. For some, there seems to be a very shaky self-image because s/he looks for a parent s/he can rely upon as stable. In this case the person grows up with basic

127

insecurity, and may feel that other people have 'the answers' but that s/he may never find them. For others, there will come a powerful desire to seek a totally unchanging parent figure, such as a guru, or religious leader, or even a strict God-figure, to model themselves after—so that they can once again relax, and take for granted what 'should be.' And for still others, the choice is to integrate the concept of change into the self-image, and even enjoy it. For these, the world opens up as a place to explore and self-discovery becomes a great pleasure. This path also usually leads to the ability to get along with those in power because of an inner understanding and sympathy with them.

EXAMPLES of people with Saturn trine Chiron: Dean Martin, Jack Sheldon, Steve McQueen, Anthony Armstrong-Jones, David St. Clair, Arturo Toscanini, Ingrid Bergman, Paul Anderson, Richard Boone, Gwendolyn Brooks, Yvonne Burke, William Casper, Lawton Chiles, John Connally, Bradford Dillman, Robert Haack, Cardinal John Krol, Carol Lawrence, Katherine Graham, Gustave Dore, Edouard Manet, Ernest Boulanger, Pierre Loti, Maxime Weygand, Paul Claudel, Marie Curie, C.G. Jung, Paul Choisnard, Morganna King, Arthur Miller, Octave Mirbeau, Chet Baker, Clyde McPhatter, Donny Osmond, Herbie Mann, Lena Horne, Lyle Lovett, Odetta, Petula Clark, Richard Harris.

SATURN SESQUIQUADRATE CHIRON (135°)

I call the people who have this aspect 'The Testers' because they will always be testing their limits, testing the rules, testing traditions. It is not that they are out-and-out rebels—in fact, they may be model citizens. But they don't believe in sacred cows—if something is in need of change, they feel it should be changed. On the other hand, if something passes their test, they are usually very happy to accept it and go on to something else. If they see some rule or regulation that is not valid in a particular situation, they usually see no reason to be bound by it. But they will work with rules that make sense to them. You can see how they may have trouble with authority, however, unless authority gives them a great deal of freedom. These people always feel the urge to push limits back further, further, further. And they don't believe in the phrase 'I can't.'

EXAMPLES of people who have Saturn sesquiquadrate Chiron: Francoise Gauquelin, James Earl Ray, Toulouse-Lautrec, Princess Grace of Monaco, Frank Borman, James Lovell, Fats Domino, Ursula LeGuin, Raymond Donovan, Sean Connery, Gore Vidal, Yehudi Menuhin, George du Maurier, Maupassant, Ferdinand Foch, Sigmund Freud, Robert Badinter, Serge Gainsbourg, Jean-Marie Le Pen, Big Bopper, Bo Diddley, Buck Owens, Pete Seeger, Ray Charles.

SATURN QUINCUNX CHIRON (150°)

For these people, the search is on for some version of true reality — something beyond what the world around them perceives as the way things are. They do not accept the idea 'this is the way things must be', unless it comes from what they conceive as an indisputable source. And, very rarely can they find any such source. This aspect seems to work as almost a compulsion to seek truth, to seek the answers to whatever questions or problems they are concerned with. As a result, they can become extremely knowledgeable on a great many subjects .... but most especially, on the one particular topic that is their quest. On a negative level, they can become the very thing they cannot easily accept in others—they can come to consider themselves as indisputable sources. Even if they don't actually perceive themselves this way, they can appear to other people as though they think that way. On a more positive level these people almost always become figures of respect in their fields—even if you do not care for their attitude.

EXAMPLES of people with Saturn quincunx Chiron: R.D. Laing, Earle Besserer, Jerry Lewis, Oscar Wilde, Art Arfons, Howard Cosell, Billy Graham, Claude Kirk, Sammy Lee, Patricia Neal, Peter Graves, Carlos Castaneda, Paul Lynde, Robert Stack, John D. Rockefeller, Arthur Conan Doyle, Alexander Solzheneitsyn, Emile Coue, Valery Giscard d'Estaing, Gilbert Becaud, Charlie Parker.

SATURN OPPOSITION CHIRON

On a positive level, these individuals seem to triumph against impossible odds. They are definitely fighters, and usually have very strong principles for which they fight. No one, nor anything, is going to stand in their way when they are striving for some goal. They often perceive life, or at least part of it, as a war between what is, and what should be, and they are convinced that what should be is the winning side. Negatively, they can be quite ruthless in their methods, if necessary. They tend to follow the philosophy, 'The end justifies the means.' If other aspects also point in this direction, they can become truly dangerous foes, and potentially dangerous to society as a whole. There is a tendency with those who have this aspect to become totally convinced of being right on some issue, and then become closed off from any information that points to the contrary. But, as in all Chiron aspects, when such a person goes too far along this line, drastic events will come along to shake his/her closed world. The normal reaction is one of two things: Either to pull the walls more tightly around self, and thus begin to see others as enemies—or to recognize that no human being can ever know all the facts on any subject. If the latter path is chosen, the person has the chance to develop a keen eye to search for new information, new facts, new data where others do not go.

EXAMPLES of people with Saturn opposition Chiron: Robert Horton, Jack Anderson, Dr. Christiaan Barnard, Eva Marie Saint, George Bush Sr., Maria Callas, Steve Allen, Philip Berrigan, Dick Martin, Goethe, Theodore Roosevelt, Rabindranath Tagore, Kurt Vonnegut, Auguste Lumiere, Maurice Messegue, Andre Bergeron, Al Hirt.

URANUS

Chiron's relationship with Uranus is the most unusual of any planet-to-planet relationship. For one thing Chiron has been pretty much in orb of opposition to Uranus since 1952, and will be until 1989. [Chiron makes 41 exact oppositions to Uranus during this time period.] So we have for study countless examples of people with this opposition.

But as for the conjunction—there is no conjunction of Chiron with Uranus in this whole century. We cannot study vast numbers of individuals who have Chiron conjunct Uranus, as there are none so born in the 20th Century. Another consideration: Chiron's orbit brings it all the way out to nearly touch Uranus' orbit. So some Chiron-Uranus aspects are much stronger than others, depending on how far from aphelion Chiron is at the time of the aspect. The Chiron-Uranus oppositions in 1952 were much less powerful, distance-wise, than those of 1970 [the year of Chiron's aphelion].

The actual influence of Chiron-Uranus aspects appears to be an amplification of the basic Uranian traits in the person. It is extremely important for these people to be distinct individuals; to feel truly that they exist as separate entities, unique, one-of-a-kind. When any Chiron-Uranus aspect is natally prominent, they tend to be true anomalies, with usually many eccentricities as well. Those who have prominent Chiron-Uranus aspects seem to have something extra—some talent or traits that are extra special and make them stand out. Even if the aspects are not prominent there appears to be something about these people that makes them difficult to categorize—you are not quite sure how to label them. There is almost always a hatred for hypocrisy. They would rather be hated than two-faced. There is also a tendency to believe that nothing is sacred—that anything can be changed, no matter what it is.

Since Uranus is so unconventional in the first place, I thought I would break with the pattern of the rest of the chapter and go through the aspects in reverse order, beginning with the opposition and ending with the conjunction.

CHIRON OPPOSITION URANUS

As I have written elsewhere, this opposition seems to tie into the ever-quickening pace of scientific breakthroughs that began in the early 1950's. Actually, one of the problems is that science is making discoveries faster than they can be integrated into society—even faster than proper safeguards can be devised for our protection from side-effects and from the discoveries themselves. This same 'vibration' seems to be part of the nature of individuals who have this aspect. There is a thirst for the new, for discovery, for experiences, that often outweighs the taking of any precautions. This is especially true when the opposition is prominent in the chart. You dare not try to curtail the freedom of such an individual—the consequences are not pleasant. The urge for independence in such a native is so strong—especially if the aspect is prominent—that s/he frequently has trouble in relationships. S/he needs a relationship with someone who will give him/her 'their own space.' It is difficult to find someone sufficiently secure to give a partner that much freedom. It seems that these people are always so full of life, and spirit—they may be down, but never for long.

EXAMPLES of people with Chiron opposite Uranus: Leon Spinks, Tracey Austin, Mark Fidrych, Archie Griffin, Tatum O'Neal, Michael Jackson, Adam Ant, Debbie Boone, Amy Grant, Billy Idol, Bobby Brown, Brad Whitford, Bruce Hornsby, Bryan Adams, Celine Dion, David Byrne, David Lee Roth, Donny Osmond, Elvis Costello, Germaine Jackson, Harry Connick Jr, Janis Ian, Joe Jackson, K.D. Laing, Layne Staley, Lyle Lovett, Mariah Carey, Marie Osmond, Pat Benatar, Peabo Bryson, Rickie Lee Jones, Ricky Scaggs, Tanya Tucker, Thomas Dolby, Cyndi Lauper, George Strait.

CHIRON QUINCUNX URANUS (150°)

If anything, these people are more one-of-a-kind than the other Chiron-Uranus aspect natives. They do not seem to be able to do things any other way than 'their way', whether this turns out good or bad. They are not types you would ever forget once you have met them. They usually burn an indelible image upon your mind. They truly want to find some niche—some career— some path, that is so totally theirs that they never need search again. They feel a very powerful need to search for what specifically embodies themselves and no one else—no matter what it takes. And they never seem to stick by convention—much to the chagrin of their associates.

EXAMPLES of people with Chiron quincunx Uranus: Alice Cooper, Malcolm Dean, Vida Blue, George W. Lippert, Mike Schmidt, Bruce Springsteen, Auguste Rodin, Prince Charles, Brian Eno, Glenn Frey, Gloria Gaynor, James Taylor, Kenny Loggins, Lionel Richie, Rick Springfield, Steven Tyler, Stevie Nicks, Stevie Winwood.

CHIRON SESQUIQUADRATE URANUS (135°)

RESTLESS! Always looking for something new to try, preferably something that others say they can't do, or shouldn't do. Such a native will never be content, no matter what s/he has, or what s/he discovers—s/he will always have to go on and try to do something else. And it seems that, for these people, life is full of unexpected events. They tend to get used to this after awhile. Once convinced that the unpredictable is a way of life, they can accomplish the unimaginable. This aspect also gives the natives the ability to deal with problems quite well because nothing seems impossible and nothing catches them totally unawares.

EXAMPLES of people with Chiron sesquiquadrate Uranus: Uri Geller, Larry Csonka, Carl Wilson, Emile Zola, Pierre Loti, Ferdinand Foch, Raymond Poincare, Marconi, Jose Feliciano, Jollivet-Castelot, David Bowie, David Mason, Edgar Winter, Jimmy Buffet, Marc Bolan, Patti Smith, Ron Wood, Tommy James.

CHIRON TRINE URANUS

Those who have this aspect seem able to fit square pegs into round holes, and vice versa. They are often attracted to careers that seem totally out of character for them—and yet they do quite well in these seemingly inappropriate fields. It is rare to find an individual with this aspect who has not made major career changes. One reason often given for such a change is that the initial vocation put their basic integrity in jeopardy—that it was not honorable, or not completely honest—and that they would have to sacrifice what they viewed as themselves in order to stay. On the other hand, they see nothing wrong with going into some field that is not totally open and above-board—as long as they feel that they can remain themselves while they are there. Their motto could be, 'Be true to thyself. On a negative level these people may find it very difficult to admit being wrong about something. They often have large lessons to learn in that area.

EXAMPLES of people with Chiron trine Uranus: Troy Perry, Fernand Leger, Carl Sandburg, Oscar Wilde, Josef Stalin, Goldie Hawn, Candice Bergen, Joe Greene, Bob Gunton, Pablo Casals, Anatole France, Arthur Rimbaud, Winston Churchill, Manuel de Falla, Cher, Lawrence Welk, Jack London, James Joyce, Felix Faure, Jules Massenet, Trotsky, Douglas MacArthur, Francois Coli, F.D. Roosevelt, Raimu, Laurent Fabius, Al Green, Barry Manilow, Bette Midler, Billy Preston, Dave Mason, Ian Hunter, Lesley Gore, Neil Young.

CHIRON SQUARE URANUS

There can be a great deal of conflict in the life of anyone who has this aspect. For one thing, s/he is always his/her own person—never submitting to the dictates of others. This is another of the truly 'one-of-a-kind' individuals, especially if this aspect is prominent. On a positive level this is the individual who will try something new even if they have full knowledge that others will offer ridicule. Of course s/he would prefer acceptance—but s/he would much rather achieve success, or discover the truth, than worry about the opinions of others. On a negative level s/he can attach him/herself to any guru or teacher who promises real fulfillment of his/her true purpose in life. Then s/he can be just as uncaring of the ridicule of others as s/he follows the teacher. One thing that seems extremely important to everyone with this aspect is that s/he discovers the truth—both about self, and about life—and then, once s/he has found it, to reveal it to others if possible. The methods chosen to do this will, of course, relate to the signs and houses of Chiron and Uranus.

EXAMPLES of people with Chiron square Uranus: Hans Christian Andersen, Baudelaire, Sir William Crookes, Honore Daumier, Gustave Flaubert, Thomas Huxley, Alfred DeMusset, John Ruskin, Ray Davies, Prokofiev, John S. Pernberton, Mama Cass Elliot, Jim Croce, Dostoyevski, Gustave Dore, Edouard Manet, Balzac, Pasteur, Abraham Lincoln, George de Maurier, Leo

Delibes, Josephine Baker, Stephen Foster, Michael Nesmith, Boz Scaggs, Gladys Knight, Janis Joplin, Joe Cocker, Marilyn McCoo, Mike Bloomfield, Patti Labelle, Paul Butterfield, Steppenwolf, Steve Miller.

CHIRON SEXTILE URANUS

Those who have this aspect seem to put themselves into any message they try to get across to others. There is usually a very strong need to improve the world or at least the part of it that they live in—because they can perceive some very real ways that the world can be changed for the better. Negatively they can easily get so caught up in their individual perceptions that they do not realize that there may be other valid views. Even when they go this route, they usually give 'lip service' to the right of the individual to take his/her own stand. It is rare to meet an individual with this aspect whom you later forget— something of the person always stays with you. It may be a mannerism, or some nuance in their philosophy, or even a look in their eyes—but you do not forget them.

EXAMPLES of people with Chiron sextile Uranus: Ritchie Valens, Wolfgang Amadeus Mozart, August Picard, Lee Trevino, Roman Gabriel, Martin Sheen, Raquel Welch, Mike Love, Eric Burden, Bob Dylan, Bobby Vinton, Charlie Watts, Chick Corea, Ginger Baker, Grace Slick, Harry Nilsson, Leon Russell, Ringo Starr, Roy Harper, Wilson Pickett.

CHIRON SEMI-SQUARE URANUS (45°)

Both Chiron and Uranus are here amplified to the point where the person who has this aspect is in a class of just the one. S/he is usually able to make inroads into a field that others of similar background have failed to enter, and s/he also seems to have some type of charisma for which people find no full explanation. S/he really 'follows a different drummer', and may be lucky enough to interest others in the same tune as s/he hears. Whether s/he goes it alone, or leads the way for others, s/he will be no one's puppet. It is easy to see how, in some areas of life, this trait could quickly irritate others who want obedience in their associates. This person works best in a field where s/he is rewarded most for experimenting and trying new things, and where s/he works in some capacity to make life better or more pleasant for other human beings.

EXAMPLES of people with Chiron semi-square Uranus: Dustin Hoffman, Rudolph Nureyev, Brian G. Marsden, Rudolph Valentino, Bobby Seale, Judy Blume, Maynard Jackson, Ron Ely, Brian Mulroney, Gary Hart, Jeddu Krishnamurti, Zubin Mehta, Bill Cosby, David Carradine, Bill Withers, Bill Wyman, Buddy Holly, Charlie Daniels, Don Everly, Duane Eddy, Gene Chandler, Jerry Lee Lewis, Phil Everly, Waylon Jennings.

CHIRON CONJUNCT URANUS

If you know someone with this aspect, s/he probably has a great deal to tell you, for s/he has lived a long, full life. S/he has experienced both the Chiron return, and the Uranus return, and life has been full of remarkable events. That seems to be one of the hallmarks of this aspect—a very eventful life. If you can imagine Chiron as a lens that focuses the planet at high intensity you can get a good idea of the effect of this conjunction on its native. There is an unbelievable thirst to 'live'—to experience life to its fullest. There is also a powerful need to make a mark; to do something which will be remembered long after the native has died. But it is not out of vanity—rather, from an overwhelming need to have one's life mean something in the grand scheme of things. If you ever meet a person with this aspect who never amounted to anything—you will find a person full of stories of major failures that will amaze you. A conjunction is the beginning of a cycle, and the Chiron-Uranus cycle is quite a long one. Such a person has often been at the forefront of revolutions, or events which changed the world into what it is to this day. If you talk of someone who believes in overcoming insurmountable odds—this is the person. It can be felt in the personality—an underlying belief that good, or right, will prevail in the end. Unless there are serious aspects to the contrary, the individual is/was very concerned with the quality of life and the problems of humanity.

EXAMPLES of people with Chiron conjunct Uranus: Chou En-Lai, Golda Meir, Liu Shao-Ch'i, Norman Vincent Peale, Leo Szilard, Ariel Durant, Emmet Kelly, Paul Robeson, Bertold Brecht, Erich Remarque, Ben Shahn, George Gershwin, E.Y. Hatburg, Fred Astaire, Bessie Love, Eugene Ormandy, Molly Picon, Lily Pons, Gracie Fields, Dorothy Gish, Oscar Homolka, George Jessel, Zasu Pitts, Cyril Ritchard, William Boyd, Sidney Blackmer, Ernest Hemingway, Charles Boyer, Humphrey Bogart, James Cagney.

NEPTUNE

Those with Chiron in aspect to Neptune are truly tuned in to the problems of others. This can be on a small level or a larger one. Other natal aspects can encourage action, or repress the urge to help—but this concern is always there. On a negative level it is often the case that the person can get carried away by the concern and get wrapped up in some quite illogical scheme to help others, perhaps doing more harm than good. The initial intention is the solution of the problem. If the Chiron-Neptune aspect is strong, there is something 'otherworldly' about the individual—and yet the native projects the feeling that makes others 'want to go to this 'other world.'

Chiron tends to enhance the imagination here as well as the sensitivity to suffering. Because of this the native often takes the road of building blocks and walls to shield self, lest s/he become overwhelmed by the pain and anguish s/he is capable of feeling. Once s/he learns to deal with it without hiding behind a wall, Chiron-Neptune aspects enable one to experience true empathy and be a real spiritual teacher, healer, or guide. Even if the aspect is not prominent natally, there is an element of the dreamer in every one who has a Chiron-Neptune aspect.

CHIRON CONJUNCT NEPTUNE

If this aspect is prominent the individual who has it has the ability to influence large masses of people. Depending on spiritual development, s/he can do so on an emotional, or a spiritual level. Negatively the healing and wholemaking qualities of Chiron can be distorted by Neptune, making the individual see his/her role as that of a changer or influencer of people, yet not realize that the power s/he is tapping is not his/her own but universal forces. This can be dangerous to the native and to others. Positively there is a keen sensitivity to the needs of others and a basic understanding of how to give them what is needed. It is a powerful position for any teacher for it gives the ability to convey much more than just words, and much more than the pupils may realize they are learning. There is a super-sensitivity in every one born with this aspect, but if the environment s/be grows up in does not allow him/her to admit to having feelings, this aspect can be repressed, much to both personal and society's loss.

EXAMPLES of people with Chiron conjunct Neptune: Jose Feliciano, Fernand Leger, Ottorino Respighi, Upton Sinclair, Josef Stalin, Leon Trotsky, Dennis Wilson, Don McLean, Bela Bartok, Robert Holbrook Smith, Sandy Koufax, Albert Einstein, Douglas MacArthur, Francois Coli, Herman Hesse, Al Stewart, Bob Marley, Bryan Ferry, David Bromberg, Rod Stewart, Stephen Stills, Van Morrison.

CHIRON SEMI-SQUARE NEPTUNE (45º)

Chiron gives these individuals the feeling that, in order to become truly whole—to be truly balanced, the answers lie in the unknown, in the mysterious, in the mystical. This fascination for the hidden side of things makes them excellent explorers, assuming other aspects enable them to keep a clear head. When they do not go in for exploration, they do seem to enjoy stirring up murky waters in the hopes that the good stuff will become more visible, as well as the bad. The hazard with this aspect is that it is easy for those who have it to become swept up by their fascination with unknown worlds and lose touch with the real world.

EXAMPLES of people with Chiron semi-square Neptune: Admiral Robert E. Peary, Sigmund Freud, Elbert Hubbard, Richard Speck, Benjamin Disraeli, Ann Tyler, Brian Wilson, Otis Redding, George Sand, Philippe Petain, Woodrow Wilson, Vaslav Nijinski, V. M. Molotv, Bob Dylan, Helen Reddy, Chubby Checker, Curtis Mayfield, Eddie Rabbit, Edwin Starr, Gene Clark, Glenn Frey, Maurice White, Paul McCartney, Paul Revere (musician), Percy Sledge, Roger McGuinn, Steven Tyler, Tim Hardin, Tommy Roe.

CHIRON SEXTILE NEPTUNE

This aspect creates a real longing in the individuals for whatever 'utopia' is described by the sign and house of natal Neptune. This dream, or fantasy or ideal is seen as the cure to most [if not all] of their problems. If they project this perception, it is also seen as the cure-all for the problems of others as well. Positively they can do a great deal for others because of their idealism and imagination. There is a great deal of 'soul' in these people, and they really can see a world that 'could be.' Negatively, if Neptune is too strong, they can lose themselves in the search for the ideal and even come to believe they are living in such a world now—living in a world that others perceive simply as fantasy. There is a great potential for healing here, as well as for psychic perceptions.

EXAMPLES of people with Chiron sextile Neptune: Mike Love, Ryan O'Neal, Ritchie Valens, Arthur Bremer, Gene Pitney, Ray Stevens, Neil Diamond, Michael Moriarty, Martin Sheen, Phil Ochs, Richard Wagner, Van Gogh, Charles de Gaulle, Jean-Marc Reiser, Ringo Starr, Aaron Neville, Billy Ocean, Bob Dylan, Bobby Goldsboro, Bobby Vinton, Buffy Sainte-Marie, Buster Poindexter, Ginger Baker, Graham Parker, Huey Lewis, Joan Baez, Joe Perry, Joey Kramer, Leon Russell, Natalie Cole, Ninah Cherry, Placido Domingo, Richie Havens, Wilson Pickett.

CHIRON SQUARE NEPTUNE

This aspect seems easier to deal with than the soft Chiron-Neptune aspects. Perhaps because it was within orb for many years, it is something that we have grown to accept as part of everyday life. The most common expression of it is the tendency to have some dream that is totally you—some image of the ideal self that is the way you want to be—and then to believe totally that you can be this. The magic of believing in yourself. This aspect does not denote success or failure at achieving this dream—only the very strong belief that this is what you could be—even should be. There is also, if the aspect is strongly emphasized, a desire to overcome any obstacle that interferes with your understanding of life or of the universe. For some, however, Neptune is too hard to deal with—perhaps because of the environment in which they grow up. For these people the tendency is to go overboard into the real world—to submerge themselves into material things—in order not to have to deal with the unknown [which they truly fear.] Yet such people can open up, with guidance, to their real dreams, but only if they are helped to overcome their fear of the unknown.

EXAMPLES of people with Chiron square Neptune: Jerry Reed, Adlai Stevenson, Donald Sutherland, John Travolta, Noel Jan Tyl, Luciano Pavarotti, Glen Campbell, David Carradine, Tom Snyder, Baudelaire, Gustave Flaubert, Charles Gounod, Louis Pasteur, Walt Whitman, Julie Andrews, Craig Breedlove, Wayne Embry, Mark Fidrych, Archie Griffin, Ken Kesey, Dennis Hopper, Geraldine Ferraro, Gary Hart, Adam Ant, Jimi Hendryx, John Paul Getty, Karl Marx, Guy de Maupassant, Auguste Bartholdi, Fiodor Dostoyevski, Zubin Mehta, Warren Beatty, Billy Carter, Van Cliburn, Merle Haggard, Jack Nicholson, Tom Smothers, Bob Geldof, Bobby Darin, Bonnie Tyler, Bruce Hornsby, Chaka

Khan, Cyndi Lauper, Don Everly, Frankie Vallie, Germaine Jackson, Jackie Wilson, Jean Redpath, Jerry Lee Lewis, Leonard Cohen, Lou Rawls, Michael Bolton, Nancy Wilson (of Heart), Phil Everly, Reba McEntire, Rickie Lee Jones, Ricky Scaggs, Sam Cooke, Steve Lawrence, Stevie Ray Vaughan, Trini Lopez.

CHIRON TRINE NEPTUNE

This is another aspect in effect for many, many people. It is a little like the sextile. But, unlike that aspect, the trine gives the individual a tendency to take for granted that the dreams s/he dreams are ideals that will lead to a whole life, and may not be consciously aware of how important these dreams are. If the individual in childhood is allowed to dream and express the dreams, as an adult s/he will feel very comfortable exploring matters of alternate realities and ideals which could slowly change the world. On the other hand, if the person was told in childhood to stick to the real world, the dreams they take for granted will be just the dreams instilled in them by others. Check up on sign and house placements and you can see what sort of dreams the person feels will guide them truly to a whole, balanced life. Check other aspects—especially from Saturn, and you can often see if s/he is following his/her own dreams or those learned from others.

EXAMPLES of people with Chiron trine Neptune: Hal Holbrook, Liberace, Robin Moore, Sam Peckinpah, Troy Perry, Ira Progolf, Peter Ustinov, Jonathan Winters, Carlos Castaneda, Dr. Tom Dooley, Philip Berrigan, William F. Buckley, John Michael Addey, Pope John Paul II, Edgar Degas, Walter Schirra, Yul Brynner, Melina Mercouri, Margaret Thatcher, Jimmy Carter, Howard Baker, James Blish, Doris Day, Alene Duerk, Stanley Hiller, Pauline Kael, Elizabeth Koontz, Sammy Lee, Patricia Neal, Shelly Winters, Gale Storm, John Stamos, Nancy McKeon, Benny Hill, James Beggs, Truman Capote, Sammy Davis Jr., Jack Lemmon, Gore Vidal, Daniel Berrigan, Marlon Brando, Lenny Bruce, Johnny Carson, Mick Jagger, Jack Kerouac, Paul Newman, Sidney Poitier, Bobby Stone, Leo Delibes, Jean-Paul Sartre, Simone de Beauvoir, H.G. Clouzot, Claude Levi-Strauss, Edmonde Charles-Roux, Valery Giscard d'Estaing, Maurice Bejart, B.B. King, Bobby Brown, Celine Dion, Charlie Parker, Chris DeGarmon, Doris Day, George Michael, Harry Belafonte, Jerry Cantrell, Joe McIntyre, Johnnie Ray, Jonathan Knight, Mel Torme, Paula Abdul, Sarah Vaughan, Scott Rockinfield, Sinead O'Connor, Stan Getz, Theodore Bikel, Vanessa Paradis, Whitney Houston, Wynonna Judd.

CHIRON SESQUIQUADRATE NEPTUNE (135°)

This aspect gives a person who feels compelled to make his/her dream a reality, and will never rest until s/he does so. The hazard here, of course, is in the nature of the dream. The aspect in itself does not denote good or bad ideals, only the compulsion to act on them to bring them into manifestation. Yet, frequently along the way, events will come along to throw a wrench into the works—to put a block in front of the goal. Here the person goes through a crisis which usually results in a major change in what s/he wants to make happen—a change in his/her ideals. Quite often it is a major disillusionment that causes the shift. But whatever it is, s/he seems to be even more compelled, after such a crisis, to bring the new dream into reality.

EXAMPLES of people with Chiron sesquiquadrate Neptune: Leo Guild, Jacques Cousteau, Robert Cummings, Jean Anouilh, John Mitchell, Bishop James Pike, Jackie Coogan, Frederic Keitz, James Hoffa, Thor Heyerdhal, Dylan Thomas, John Cage, Dean Martin, Alan Watts, Howlin' Wolf, Woody Guthrie.

CHIRON QUINCUNX NEPTUNE (150°)

A person who has this aspect tends to allow self to commit his/her whole life to the pursuit of some dream, especially if the aspect is prominent. And the more s/he goes into the dream, the more s/he changes to fit it. It is very difficult to persuade such a person that s/he is on a wrong track, unless you can reach the person when s/he first begins to fail under the spell of the dream. There is a great deal of charisma that seems to come from this aspect—perhaps the spell is contagious. If the native is not spiritually elevated, s/he may be tempted to use this charisma to control others—and usually succeed in doing so.

EXAMPLES of people with Chiron quincunx Neptune: Don Loper, Clifford Oders, Amelia Earhart, Aristotle Onassis, Ian Fleming, Erich Maria Remarque, Ralph Bellamy, Oscar Levant, Auguste Renoir.

CHIRON OPPOSITION NEPTUNE

People who have this aspect seem to be convinced that the reality they were brought up to believe in is not quite right—that the ideals they were taught to strive for are not those that really will make them happy. Or, that the general image of the universe taught them is not correct—that it has holes or inaccuracies in it. As a result, they have an inner discontent which leads them to search for a clearer picture of the universe, or for something to believe that will truly bring them inner peace. There is a great potential for helping others here, but frequently the individual must overcome inner confusion before s/he can open up to consider other problems

EXAMPLES of people with Chiron opposition Neptune: Karl Ernst Krafft, Andre Malroux, Vittoria DeSica, Charles Richter, Marie Osmond, Paul Verlaine, Enrico Fermi, Anatole France.

PLUTO

When Chiron unites in aspect with Pluto, it gives the individual an awareness of untapped potential in a situation and how much power would be available if the potential were brought out. In itself, of course, the aspect is completely neutral. Where the person perceives this potential, and how s/he makes use of it when s/he finds it, would be learned from viewing the whole chart. The person also gains insight into how to turn entire situations around to make better use of what is available. In the evolved type the awareness is directed toward finding the way to transform a situation, to bring about healing, and to make the most out of the least. In the unevolved type the awareness is used to discover how to gain the most control over the situation, to reap the greatest personal benefits. In either case the potential is here to bring about a healing of critical situation-problems by taking them through a catharsis, cleaning out dead wood, and going off in some new direction to breathe new life into them. At the best, aspects from Chiron to Pluto enable the individual to use Pluto's transformative powers in some new way to bring about true wholemaking. At the worst, Chiron aspects to Pluto reinforce the obstinacy of Pluto by giving the person the feeling that s/he is on the correct path, merely because the path s/he follows is not accepted by most people.

CHIRON CONJUNCT PLUTO

Pluto's urge to bring about total transformation is focused through Chiron, giving the individual a highly specific area in which s/he feels transformation must occur. The sign is of importance here, but, even more, the natal house—it is here that the person will concentrate a powerful urge for transmutation. It is important for the individual to be highly evolved with this aspect. If s/he is not, the result could be the equivalent of turning someone loose with a death ray. If s/he is of a more evolved type Chiron has the focus of a sophisticated symbolic laser, enabling the person to cut away that which has lost its value; then taking what is left, rearranging it and making it work in a brand-new way, unlike anything that has gone before. This aspect also enables the person to tune in and focus on hidden or obscure data and bring them to the surface. Pluto always intensifies and in this case, it intensifies the person's need to follow his/her own path, and the need to seek out what needs to be changed in the pursuit of wholeness. Such an individual seems to be very much aware of the general pains afflicting humanity, as well as the deep need of mankind to find solutions to our basic problems, to find release from the pains some way.

EXAMPLES of people with Chiron conjunct Pluto: Karl Marx, Benito Mussolini, Gustave Courbet, Auguste Piccard, Walt Whitman, Michael Moriarity, Michael Erlewine, John Keynes, Terry Gilliam, Charles Gounod, Pierre Laval, Edouard Daladier, Harry S. Truman, Raimu, Alma Gluck, Bela Lugosi, Billy Joe Thomas, Coco Chanel, Bruce Lee, Vikki Carr, Chuck Mangione, Cliff Richard, David Crosby, Dionne Warwick, Dr. John, Frank Zappa, John Lennon, Martha Reeves, Phil Ochs.

CHIRON SEMI-SQUARE PLUTO (45°)

The person who has this aspect seems compelled to change things, or people, or else to seek total power. If s/he is of the elevated type the power s/he seeks will simply be control of his/her own life. Such a person has a great deal to give, both by example, and by teaching others how to master their own lives as well. If s/he is not the higher type, however, Pluto tends to dominate Chiron so that the individual gets carried away with a desire to seek power and control. The end result is like opening a door to Pluto and putting no restrictions upon where it goes.

EXAMPLES of people with Chiron semi-square Pluto: Lance Reventlow, Burt Reynolds, Darlene Hard, Kate Millet, Charles Manson, Allen Ginsberg, Alan Alda, Henri Matisse, Alfred Adler, Barry White, Bobby Darin, Carly Simon, Glenn Campbell, John Fogerty, Lou Rawls, Nona Hendryx, Steve Lawrence.

CHIRON SEXTILE PLUTO

This aspect usually makes the individuals strive for a high order of efficiency and professionalism in their lives. It is not, as a rule, out of ego or desire for self-aggrandizement that they act this way—rather, it is deeply ingrained in them that if something is done right the first time, it won't have to be redone later. Also, they know that some things can only be done once. This is another excellent aspect for the researcher since it endows its native with an insatiable curiosity; a love of finding out what makes things tick. It also seems to strengthen the individual's confidence in his/her own abilities. This usually brings admiration from associates. On the negative side [or maybe it is not so negative] this aspect gives a tendency to be brutally frank. If ever you ask for an honest opinion, you will get it from one who has Chiron sextile Pluto.

EXAMPLES of people with Chiron sextile Pluto: Neil F. Michelsen, Willie Mays, Neil Armstrong, William Ball, Alan Bean, Vance Brand, Henry Perot, Dan Rather, George Steinbrenner, Raymond Donoran, Camille Claudel, Gabriele d'Annunzio, Anne Bancroft, Bill Cosby, Sean Connery, Omar Shariff, Jack Sheldon, Henry Winkler.

CHIRON SQUARE PLUTO

This aspect has a number of different expressions, and can be quite difficult to deal with. For one thing, there is a very strong need to be the master of one's fate—the captain of one's own ship. There is almost the feeling that 'it can not be any other way.' On a positive level the person develops a great deal of self-control and a thirst for new and better ways to improve the self. In the negative expression of this aspect the person is extremely sensitive to the environment and to anything s/he feels is intruding upon his/her 'space.' Others could be seen as trying to take power out of his/her hands, and thus, as the enemy.

Another expression of this square is the need for continual self-discovery, and, if the person is evolved, a great deal of curiosity to delve into the unknown. The negative expression is an anxious concern that others are delving too deeply into personal affairs, interfering, invading privacy. Still another manifestation of this aspect is the desire for a world in which every person should have the right to manage his/her own life, as the native does. Positively the person will go out of his/her own way to help others do this, striving to secure for each individual the same chances. In the negative expression the person who has this aspect divides people in to 'us and them', and tries to give opportunities at the expense of 'them.'

EXAMPLES of people with Chiron square Pluto: Mario Lanza, Liberace, Mickey Rooney, George Wallace, Charles Bronson, E.W. Demara, Hugh Downs, Steve Allen, Carol Channing, Eleanor Bach, Sigmund Freud, Elbert Hubbard, Auguste Rodin, John V. Lindsay, Huey P. Long, Ray Bradbury, Howard Cosell, Nanette Fabray, George Forman, Betty Friedan, Pauline Kael, Elizabeth Koontz, Edith Custer, Admiral Robert E. Peary, John Paul Getty, Bernard Goetz, Lloyd Bentsen, James Counsilman, Minnie Riperton, Paul Thayer, Alan Freed, Felix Faure, George Bernard Shaw, Francisco Franco, Edmonde Charles-Roux, Georges Brassens, Maurice Messegue, Andre Bergeron, Yves Montand, Kurt Vonnegut, Montgomery Clift, William Holden, Dick Martin, Al Hirt, Charlie Parker, Dave Brubeck, Nat King Cole, Pearl Bailey, Pete Seeger.

CHIRON TRINE PLUTO

Davy Crockett used to say, 'Be sure you're right, then go ahead.' That could be the by-word for all those who have this aspect. They are not quick to form an opinion, usually [there are exceptions, of course, as indicated by other natal aspects], but once they have chosen what they feel is the right approach it is nearly impossible to make them change their minds. As you can imagine, this trait can be both positive and negative, depending on their opinions and the situation. One of the most positive expressions of this aspect is that over a period of time, those who have it impress people with their personal convictions and their ability to remain true to themselves. There is usually a definite awareness of subtle intricacies in situations—details the average person misses.

EXAMPLES of people with Chiron trine Pluto: Dr. Walter Koch, Tom McLoughlin, Phoebe Snow, Ian Fleming, Eddie Albert, Bette Davis, Max Baer Sr., Joseph Joffre, James Stewart, Orville Freeman, Cardinal John Krol, Marc Edmund Jones, Sir Laurence Olivier, Herbert Von Karajan, Balzac, Jules Massenet, Jean Genet, Alain Cuny, Anatole France, Andre Cayatte, Simone Weil, Bernard Hinault, Rex Harrison, Burl Ives, Billy Ocean, Buster Poindexter, Deniece Williams, Graham Parker, Huey Lewis, Joe Perry, Joey Kramer, Natalie Cole.

CHIRON SESQUIQUADRATE PLUTO (135°)

One common denominator here—it seems that every native with this aspect has been deeply hurt at least once. The place of the hurt can be found from the signs and houses of Chiron and Pluto. This pain serves to give the person a burning desire to make things right again, and with maturity, it usually develops into a desire to make the world right again. If the pain is too deep, however, or if the person is unable to find a way out of the pain by perceiving some positive features in the world, it is possible that the native will withdraw within self, running from the pain that is too hard to face.

EXAMPLES of people with Chiron sesquiquadrate Pluto: F. Scott Fitzgerald, Christopher Reeves, Jean P. Sartre, Lotte Strahl, Janis Ian, Mark

Goodson, Aristotle Onassis, Clark Gable, Ralph Bellamy, Alan Watts, Melissa Manchester, Nina Carter, Phoebe Snow, Russell Thompkins Jr, Tom Hamilton.

CHIRON QUINCUNX PLUTO (150°)

It appears that this aspect denotes an individual who does not begin to discover a sense of purpose in life, until there is some major traumatic event—often the death of someone close—and learns to integrate the experience into his/her life to make it acceptable. Prior to the trauma the individual is often light, even child-like, and may even be irresponsible. The traumatic event starts the process of change. The person may go through years of 'hell' trying to deal with it, unless s/he can find someone who will open up and encourage expression of the pain, rather than trying to repress it. This must be someone with whom the native feels very secure. Once the person has been able to deal fully with the hurt, needing no further work on it, there comes a compelling sense of destiny which stays with the native for the rest of the life.

EXAMPLES of Chiron quincunx Pluto: Kirk Oates, Mark Fidrych, Archie Griffin, John Travolta, George Sand, Tom McLoughlin, Adam Ant, Bob Geldof, Bonnie Tyler, Bruce Hornsby, Chaka Khan, Germaine Jackson, Michael Bolton, Rickie Lee Jones, Ricky Scaggs, Sam Cooke, Stevie Ray Vaughan.

CHIRON OPPOSITION PLUTO

This aspect seems to express itself in one of two ways. In some natives it shows up as a great need to overcome some powerful inner hostility stemming from early childhood. This hostility may come from being constantly thwarted by parents, or from being a recipient of hostility from others in the environment. Whatever the cause, there are major lessons to learn about opening up, getting in touch with the inner rage, and then cleansing it once and for all from the system. In other persons, rather than anger, the expression is a need to win—to overcome obstacles and to beat any opponent. In some cases it seems that actual people must be beaten; in other cases an abstract opponent will do.

EXAMPLES of people with Chiron opposite Pluto: William Cullen Bryant, Steve Cauthen, Vanessa Williams, John Stamos, Matt Dillon, Eddie Murphy, Fred Astaire, Annabella Lwin, Bono, Joe McIntyre, Jon Bon Jovi, Michael Wilton, Ninah Cherry, Paula Abdul, Sinead O'Connor, Taylor Dayne, Terence Trent D'Arby, Vanessa Paradis.

LUNAR NODES
CHIRON CONJUNCT NORTH NODE

Like Donna Van Toen, I feel that the North Node is a point of growth, a point of untapped potential . . . To get at this potential you have to work darned hard. With Chiron here . . . the individual must work even harder, initially. [I'll explain, later.] At the South Node, on the other hand, are those talents and abilities that are so much a part of you, that you do not need to develop them further. If you use them for yourself, you get into a rut, and end up feeling that you are going nowhere. If you use them for other people, it is like taking money from an unlimited trust fund—you always have enough more to give.

Now any person has the tendency to rely upon the South Node, rather than to strive in the direction of the North. But the person with Chiron on the North Node has a double difficulty: not only the normal human nature to follow the South—but also, it takes a conscious effort to search for the pathway represented by Chiron—to seek the teacher, the guru, the light. The average person born with Chiron conjunct North Node tends to talk a lot about how s/he wants to achieve the great things represented by the natal house occupied by Chiron—but constantly returns to doing things as s/he has always done them at the South Node. S/he may often seem to be on the verge of taking the big step forward, only to revert to the prior line of least resistance. However, should that person actually take that Step—and many do—there develops a particular talent bordering on genius. S/he becomes very conscious of the needs of others and can become a great teacher in his/her own right. And s/he follows a truly unique path.

EXAMPLES of people with Chiron conjunct North Node: Bobby Fischer, Dick Clark, Jimi Hendrix, John Travolta, George Moscone, Herb Dennenberg, Robert Duvall, Thomas Eagleton, Jean Cocteau, Harry Chapin, Johnny Rivers, Michael Nesmith, Marty Balin, Gary Hart, Eddie Murphy, Paramahansa Yogananda, Maurice Ravel, Dmitri Shostakovitch, Eric Idle, Jim Croce, Dick Clark, Edwin Aldrin, Warren Beatty, Pierre Curie, Sessue Hayakawa, Arthur Conan Doyle, Alfred Dreyfus, Gabriele d'Annunzio, Marguerite Duras, Philippe Bouvard, Barbara Lewis, Buck Owens, Chet Baker, Fabian Forte, Gary Wright, George Harrison, Janis Joplin, Johnny Rivers, Mary Wells, Michael Bolton, Paul Butterfield, Toni Tennille.

CHIRON CONJUNCT SOUTH NODE

As with the North Node conjunction, those who have Chiron conjunct South Node have difficult lessons to learn. Those who do not learn it tend to fall back upon their past. Problems they have today are ascribed to a strange or terrible childhood, and there is a reluctance to try working them out. When they are under stress, they tend to fall back on this excuse, or begin to act in an erratic manner, allowing Chiron's Maverick nature to come out in its most negative expression. The lesson seems to be that they should move on from the past—not let it rule them. They learned a lot from it—but now, it is time to go forward. Those who do learn begin to share their unique insights with others. They have integrated Chiron and it is so much a part of their nature that they can draw upon it whenever another is in need of being helped. They aim their sights at the North Node and seem to attract people who can be helped by their Chiron.

EXAMPLES of people with Chiron conjunct South Node: Merle Haggard, Dick Martin, George Sanders, Billy Carter, Clifford Odets, Arturo Toscanini,

John Anderson, Craig Breedlove, Kathryn Grayson, Robert Holley, Ursula LeGuin, Jules Massenet, Camille Flammarion, Paul Reynaud, Karl Ernst Krafft, Josephine Baker, Jerry Reed, Bill Wyman, Charlie Daniels, June Tabor, Kenny Loggins.

ANGLES

If Chiron is conjunct one of the four angles it is extremely powerful, even if it makes no other aspect. It then becomes extremely important for the individual to live his/her own life, no matter what others may think. The person often has a 'cause' that s/he takes up related to the natal sign of Chiron. In such a case, it is not necessarily the burning passion of a Mars or Pluto dedication—but is definitely a part of the everyday life. By having Chiron on an angle, the individual sees some aspect of life in a very original perspective. Should such a person become interested in helping others, this unique viewpoint makes for an excellent counselor, teacher, therapist or healer. It also seems to give the native an extra talent, or ability, that sets the native apart from the general population. Here are a few thoughts on each of the angles:

CHIRON CONJUNCT ASCENDANT

The general description for Chiron in the first house fits people who have Chiron conjunct Ascendant, but even more strongly and more noticeably. [See Interpreting Chiron, pg XX.]

The eyes of these people attract attention. It is said that 'the eyes are the windows to the soul', and if this be true, these people seem to have very old souls—their eyes look as though they could tell you a thousand stories. In the more evolved types the 'cause' is usually some group of people whom they feel needs help or support—some group that they perceive as being treated unfairly. It is extremely difficult to remain indifferent to those with Chiron conjunct Ascendant —they seem to almost force you to form some opinion about them.

CHIRON CONJUNCT IC

The earliest environment that can be remembered by those who have Chiron on the cusp of the 4th house is different from that of friends and neighbors. This difference may have been considered normal, while other people's homelife may have been looked upon as strange. Some individuals attempt to submerge their Chiron—to repress the knowledge of their unusual background, and strive in the direction of their 10th house, trying to fit in and be accepted by everyone. If they choose this path they are rarely happy. Others tend to go to the other extreme. They make Chiron's maverick nature a part of their everyday life, always living for today with no concern for tomorrow. The happiest individuals, however, are those who perceive the uniqueness of their early life as a Godsend, for it is this which gives them their unique perspective on life in general. This type is truly qualified to help others, especially with deep problems. They have insights which can only be achieved by being an outsider and thus truly objective.

CHIRON CONJUNCT DESCENDANT

One of the major lessons these people must learn is how to deal with other people. It seems that early in life they form some ideas or attitudes about their fellow human beings which make it difficult for them to relate properly to others. At the same time, they may have remarkable insight into other people and may really want to help other human beings. They go through some very heavy self-examinations, eventually, before they realize just how their own attitudes have kept them from truly relating to other people. For some, this occurs early—for others, not until the Chiron return. Once it does occur they then take a unique perspective on any relationship, for they have learned many things about what can go wrong, and many things about other people in general. They often become counselors, as they develop an excellent one-on-one manner in dealing with people.

CHIRON CONJUNCT MC

This, too, is like a concentrated form of the description given for Chiron in the 10th house. I have very little to add to Interpreting Chiron here, except that these people should choose careers that give them a great deal of freedom and that encourage them to experiment. If you can conceive of the MC as what a person is striving to become—the 'ego-ideal', so to speak, then you can understand why this person wants very much to become whole. It is an excellent position for a teacher as well as for any career which encourages people to 'see the light.'

CHIRON IN OTHER ASPECTS TO THE ANGLES

Space does not permit going into each aspect to all four angles. So let me say that ANY aspect of Chiron to an angle makes Chiron more important in your chart. A square makes you easily dissatisfied with the ordinary circumstances of life; a trine enables you to use that angle to go around the rules, if need be; a sextile gives you the need to pay a little more attention to that angle than other people do. Overall, keep in mind the basic imperative represented by Chiron's sign and house position, and then view the aspect to the angle as the framework within which to sort out the lessons to be learned.

CHIRON AND OTHER POINTS

You should also observe Chiron in relation to any other points you use in chart interpretation. Chiron conjunct an asteroid, for example, seems to make that asteroid more prominent in the chart, as though the person's life would be out of balance if s/he ignored it. It also seems to give the person a greater understanding of the principles of that asteroid than most people have. Chiron conjunct the Vertex and Eastpoint can be viewed as amplifying Chiron almost as much as putting Chiron upon the ascendant/descendant axis. Chiron located at the midpoint of two other planets can act as a channel enabling the person to tap the energies of those other bodies. While I have not worked with Chiron and Parts, or Solstice Points, I would expect it works there too.

CHIRON AND THE 165° ASPECT

Al H. Morrison has suggested that I explore Chiron in the 165° aspect. He wrote that 'It is in the affairs of the houses tenanted by the planets in this aspect that the native has this unending capability of carrying on, continuing, in total disregard of all practical reality. There is nothing like the nagging persistence of the 165° aspect, just never say die, never stop trying, never give up on negotiating the non-negotiable.'

I had not previously given this nameless aspect any thought, but I did investigate it, and was totally amazed by the results. Here follows a preliminary study. Please research it yourself, and send us your findings.

I went through several hundred charts looking for Chiron in the 165° aspect, and found an unusual pattern. In the charts of the famous and successful, some Chiron/165° aspects came up very often while some planets were hardly ever related to Chiron by this arc.

So far, I have found 23 famous people with Chiron 165° Mars, and 17 with Chiron 165° Saturn, but only 8 who have this aspect between Chiron and Venus, and only 1 who has Chiron 165° Pluto. I also took it to the angles, and while 9 have turned up with Chiron 165° the IC, only one has it to the MC.

These results may change as we look at many more charts, but they are quite intriguing.

The overall pattern I have found, when Chiron is 165° to any planet, supports Al's description of persistence. But even more, it seems that the planet in this aspect to Chiron becomes much more active and much more visible as part of the person's image. This planet is the one that is the vehicle for the persistence. The person pushes, unendingly, with the aspected planet, while Chiron acts to part or overcome the obstacle in the way of the planet. Sometimes Chiron seems to create additional, unusual problems first which the person must resolve—and in so doing, develop more and more persistence in many different kinds of environment. This must be the 'teacher' facet of Chiron showing up.

Interestingly, Chiron was 165° to Mercury at the time of its discovery. Perhaps this is one reason we have been pushing so hard, so fast, to find out everything we can about Chiron as quickly as possible. And Chiron is 165° the Sun in the chart for the Association for Studying Chiron—instilling the very purpose of the organization with this never-give-up attitude.

Here follows a brief tour of Chiron 165° to the planets as searched so far. Please apply what follows to your charts, to see if you come up with similar results.

SUN 165° CHIRON

Much enthusiasm, energy, and usually a great deal of optimism. Almost always described by others as being hard-working, with a tendency to experiment—to always look for alternative methods to accomplish their ends. But while they enjoy the new, they tend to resist, very strongly, any change imposed on them from outside!

EXAMPLES of people with Sun 165° Chiron: Chuck McKinley, William Rehnquist, Muhammad All, Wendell Willkie, Cornell MacNell, Arthur Schlesinger, Robert Smithson, Clifford Odets, O. Henry, Nikola Tesla, Guy Lombardo, Roger Moore, Norman Vincent Peale, Jimmy Carter, Michel Gauquelin. [Note: Francolse Gauquelin has Chiron 165° Saturn.]

MOON 165° CHIRON

A tendency to be very charming and witty, full of ideas. A need to communicate is amplified, and it seems, so is the intelligence. Most seem to have the ability to lead others. Negatively there can be a tendency toward arrogance, even abusiveness, which must be watched. Very versatile as long as they choose to try new things—but a bit resistant to new things suggested by others.

EXAMPLES of people with Moon 165° Chiron: Michael Tilson Thomas, Leo Guild, Jack Past, Bob Gunton, William Huffman Stewart, Bert Convy, Kurt Russell, Lyndon B. Johnson, Ethel Merman.

MERCURY 165° CHIRON

Here again there seems to be a great deal of intelligence, or at least the projection of being intelligent. Usually quite witty, with a powerful need to talk. Often described as quick thinking, or of 'having an answer for everything.' This type is hardworking, especially when involved in mental or communication pursuits.

EXAMPLES of people with Mercury 165° Chiron: Robert Bruce Mathlag, Robin Evan Roberts, Roger Staubach, Johnny Carson, Henry Cabot Lodge, David St. Clair, Bennet Cerf, George C. Scott, George Harrison, Rich Little.

VENUS 165° CHIRON

This aspect makes the person overly concerned with one or more aspects of Venus, pushing the planet right out in front of their list of priorities. For some this leads to an early love of money, possessions and pleasure. For others it is love, and the concept of love. There is a great vulnerability to pain quite early in life. Some react by learning from it, some by projecting it outward as a desire to 'get even', and some go under, relishing their suffering.

EXAMPLES of people with Venus 165° Chiron: Thomas Otten Paine, Tom Poston, Richard Speck, Janis Joplin, Harry Tracy, Shah Pahlavi of Iran, Ray Stevens, Neil Diamond.

MARS 165° CHIRON

Mars, in some form or another, seems to express the main thrust of the life. You can sense in most people who have this aspect a strong killer instinct, although it may be modified and channeled by other aspects. The basic tendency is to be unpretentious, straightforward, very active, firm and strong willed. These people always need challenges, always need to be active. While most seem to be aggressive, another type appears to hide aggressiveness to the point of elaborate, purposeful cover-up pretenses. This type presents self as very low-keyed, but the perceptive can sense within them the potential for attack.

EXAMPLES of people with Mars 165° Chiron: Louis Armstrong, Bill Mauldin, Yves Montand, Baron Manfred Von Richtofen, William Saroyan, Bela Lugosi, Jack Nicholson, Warren Beatty, Billy Carter, Roberta Cowell, Moses Gann, Ken Kesey, Bob Lilly, Otis Chandler, John Clifford, William Colby, Judy Collins, Wayne Embry, Kathryn Grayson, Craig Breedlove, Robert C. Byrd, Isaac Asimov, Princess Grace Kelly.

JUPITER 165° CHIRON

These people are always in need of 'something'—always looking for answers. They must always go further, further, further. The sense of freedom is very strong, and there an accompanying hatred of any limitations imposed from outside.

EXAMPLES of people with Jupiter 165° Chiron: Anthony Joseph Foyt, Rex Harrison, Conrad Moricand, Friedrich Nietzsche, Harry Tracy [see also Venus 165° Chiron for this convicted murderer], Jan Fleming, Miguel Hidalgo.

SATURN 165° CHIRON

These people initially have an unflagging curiosity, and as they get older, they either amplify it or repress it. Most are very tough under fire, down-to-earth people. Saturn for these individuals is a very powerful planet and they are always stressing it somehow. For some Saturn is externalized, and the person sees the world as a very miserable place or as a place full of enemies. For others Saturn is pursued as a goal, or chosen as a path, so that they become involved m uncovering the nature and structures of the larger environment. It is an excellent position for the researcher. Many personify the way most of us would like to be.

EXAMPLES of people with Saturn 165° Chiron: Yogi Berra, Joan Caulfield, Hugh Downs, Clay Felker, Robert Alan Good, Louis Groza, Robert Kastelmeier, Eleanor Parker, Garth Allen, Camille Flammarion, Alfred E. Housman, Dr. Sam Sheppard, Gore Vidal, Judy Garland, Norman Lear, Lee Marvin, Francoise Gauquelin [see note under Sun 165° Chiron].

CHIRON 165° URANUS

These people refuse to submit individuality to any outside control. They feel compelled to 'do their own thing' no matter what.

EXAMPLES of people with Chiron 165° Uranus: Steve Cauthen, Paul Gauguin, Jay Waverly North, Craig Russell.

CHIRON 165° NEPTUNE

There seems to be a concern with power here, but not in the Plutonian sense. The concern is with having enough power to change what something is to what they want it to be.

EXAMPLES of people with Chiron 165° Neptune: Mayor Richard J. Daley (Sr.), Estes Kefauver, Don Ameche, David O. Selznlck, Walter Slezak.

CHIRON 165° PLUTO

Here is where I need your help, dear reader. The only example I have found so far of this aspect is Richard DeMont, an athlete and champion swimmer, who has the dubious distinction of being the first Olympic participant ever to be disqualified from championship for the alleged use of drugs. Please send in the charts of other people who have this aspect, so we may find the positive expressions of it.

IC 165° CHIRON

This aspect surprised me by being so much more prevalent than the aspect to the MC. Perhaps it is because this aspect puts Chiron only 15° from the MC, thus making Chiron a very elevated planet? One common element seems to be a love of show, often manifested in a fondness for clothes. In any case, these people truly get into whatever role they are playing, and identify with it in a total sense. They always seem to make a big impression.

EXAMPLES of people with IC 165° Chiron: David Warren Brubeck, John Renaldo Ottina, Sam Peckinpah, Jane Russell, Gay Talese, Jim Bailey, Herman Goering, Morgana King, Rick Springfield.

MC 165° CHIRON

Since the only individual I have found so far with this aspect is General Frederick Carlton Weyand, who was Commander of American forces in South Vietnam, I will reserve judgement on the meaning of this aspect. Here is another plea for help from the reader.

ASCENDANT 165° CHIRON

The ascendant, whatever sign it may be, is emphasized. The person projects the qualities of the rising sign more strongly than is usual, and always seems to make an impression on anybody they meet.

EXAMPLES of people with Ascendant 165° Chiron: Sandy Duncan, Claude Roy Kirk, Eddie Albert, Maurice Ravel, Lana Turner.

DESCENDANT 165° CHIRON

These people are usually quite thorough in their activities. They refuse to let other people alter their course of action, whatever it may be. They are often deeply involved in their work, which is often specialized or unusual.

EXAMPLES of people with Descendant 165° Chiron: Bobby Stone, James Blish, Dr. Walter Koch, Vincent Price.

ONE FINAL THOUGHT ABOUT THE 165° ASPECT

Since it is rarely mentioned in astrological literature, it may be a good idea for us to investigate all other 165° aspects in our charts involving planets other than Chiron. In this way we can get a better feel for the aspect itself, and will then be more able to understand what Chiron means when it is involved. I myself have Jupiter 165° Saturn, and I am just beginning to fathom what that means for me.

Perhaps the biggest clue to its meaning will come from seeing it as a part of a whole aspect family: 165° — 11/24ths, 150° = 10/24ths, 135° = 9/24ths, 120° = 8/24ths, et cetera. What do you think?

Chapter IV: MOVING ALONG

Thus far I have stressed natal Chiron. But just like any of the major planets, Chiron is also of importance by both transits and progression.

As I stated in **Interpreting Chiron**, you can get a good idea of how Chiron acts in transit by reading up on its keywords. Experience has shown, also, that this will work in understanding it by progression, as well. There are a few points that I would like to add here.

TRANSITS

Before you can truly understand what Chiron will do in a transit, you must first study its natal position and look to its natal aspects. While I have seen Chiron produce some type of effect no matter what planet it is transiting, I have found that the most significant events seem to occur when Chiron is making a transiting aspect to a planet or point that was also in aspect to natal Chiron. I find that the most worthwhile course of study to understand Chiron in transit is to make a list as follows:

1. Transiting Chiron in every aspect to natal Chiron. This gives you your Chiron cycle which is uniquely your own. Include not just the hard aspects, but trines and sextiles as well. While the hard aspects may strike you as being the most significant in your life, the soft aspects will also be turning points and will enable you to get a much clearer picture of what your natal Chiron means to you.

2. Next, follow the same procedure for transits of Chiron to those planets that were in aspect to natal Chiron. While some of the dates in the above list will be the same as these, if the planets are natally in close aspect, other dates will now come up if you have any minor aspects to Chiron such as Septiles and Quintiles. Amazing as it may seem, a transit to one of the planets in natal minor aspect to Chiron tends to stimulate the natal minor aspect.

3. Now you can begin to look at transits to the remaining planets and

points in your natal chart. No doubt these will all be important. But it has been my experience that these transits are much more easily understood if you have first studied events found in steps 1 and 2.

Here follows a brief article on Chiron transits which was printed in **THE KEY**, and also in *Mercury Hour*.

For many months now the Association for Studying Chiron [ASC] has been handing out a questionnaire about what has occurred in people's lives under various Chiron transits. While many of these questionnaires have not yet been returned, we have received enough to report some of the preliminary results. We will still be sending them out for quite awhile now, so if you have not received one, or know of someone who would be happy to fill one out—let us know and we will be happy to mail out as many as you need. [And if you have not yet returned yours—PLEASE do so!]

The first thing that we observed is that there are certain events which seem to occur under almost any Chiron aspect, no matter which planet was being transited. On the other hand, certain events are so identified with a particular planet and only show up when Chiron transits that body. For this questionnaire we asked about the transiting conjunction of Chiron to each planet in the natal chart, to the MC, and the ASC. We also asked that people look for squares and oppositions of Chiron to all the personal planets. Finally we asked specifically for Chiron in square and opposition to its natal position. We had two big problems in the responses.

1. Many people who responded have not, as yet, experienced many of the Chiron transits, and so had to leave those sections blank. However, we had enough of each to tabulate.

2. Many people crossed out our questions, and filled in other planets, or other aspects, or progressed aspects. While we appreciated all the data, we ask you to please answer only the questions we have written—if you want to send any other data, please do so on a separate sheet!

These are events that occurred under most, or all, various Chiron transits: Major move or relocation, often very far away; Spouse leaving, or leaving the spouse; Meeting someone who later became the spouse; Mother or father remarrying; Birth of child; Birth of sibling; Death of someone close; Start attending school.

ALSO, health was a major issue under each type of Chiron transit, both one's own health, and an interest in other people's health. However the direction of this health focus varied from aspect to aspect. When it was about a particular health problem, or a particular part of the anatomy, over half of the cases had the focus tied into the aspecting planet, such as Chiron conjunct Venus focusing on tonsils, or Chiron conjunct Jupiter on the Liver.

Aside from the common threads running through all the aspects as mentioned above, each planet did have a number of events repeated among various respondents. Here follows [a report on] each area focused on in the questionnaire:

Chiron conjunct Sun: Many reported events which caused major change in their social life; Many reported lessons that came from asserting the self, and the resulting events, or of relying on what they felt were 'sure things', and then events bringing realizations that made them see that they were being quite self-centered; Frequent reports of events that brought feelings of alienation; Many felt that something occurred which really 'put me in my place'; A number of focuses on health and vitality, and health of the heart, both of the self, and of others. More events under this transit were traumatic than pleasant.

Chiron conjunct Moon: Many reported major issues of dealing with femininity in their lives—both their own, and the females in their lives; Major change in habits reported, either as a result of health problems, or what was learned in class or from books; Many changes of residency. Some events under this transit were traumatic, but less often than pleasant or just inconvenient.

Chiron conjunct Ascendant: Quite a few reported their first time in a foreign country, or far away from home; Often a time of many illnesses; Frequent mention of getting something one has wanted for a long time, or taking advantage of an opportunity in spite of opposition from others; Frequent description of an event or series of events which led to greater maturity. Those events which were traumatic were usually related to a death, or a major realization about the negative side of the world and its people.

Chiron conjunct Mercury: Most reported a great deal of focus on new ideas coming in, or having to deal with some sort of communications problems; Many referred to it as being mentally stimulating, or of a time of going to school or of returning to school after an absence; Health problems, often related to nerves or exhaustion; A number reported starting a business.

Chiron conjunct Venus: Many reported changes at their jobs, or change of jobs, or the direction of their career; Some reported traumatic events in their social lives which changed them; Often reported was a major change in attitude toward a loved one, some for the better, some leading to breaking away; Under this aspect more than any other, people reported failing in love, or meeting loves; Also more under this aspect was the reporting of discovery of previously unsuspected talents, or of trying some new artistic endeavor for the first time. Many focuses on the health problems of other people.

Chiron conjunct Mars: Many reported taking some major independent step for the first time; A number reported an event, or series of events, which led to a major change in their attitude toward sex, or their own sexuality; A number reported the beginning of major projects. Very few traumatic events reported.

Chiron conjunct Jupiter: Many reported either becoming more religious, becoming more concerned with spiritual matters, or of becoming disillusioned with the beliefs of their parents; Major events reported which changed attitudes toward life, and which influenced beliefs for whole rest of life; Most people reported positive events, such as increase of popularity or improvement at job or in grades at school.

Chiron conjunct Saturn: Frequent reporting of a change in relationships, or the final end of a relationship, or a relationship becoming a commitment for the first time; Many references to dental problems of various kinds; A number reported a major job change or commitment to permanent job. More problems came to a head under this aspect than under most others.

Chiron conjunct Chiron: Many reports of trips to foreign countries. A number of people reported taking interest in some new field, which soon dominated their lives from that point on; Much focus upon all the worthwhile things people had learned in their lives so far; A number told of having to focus on some crisis that a relative was having; A number focused on some major personal crisis that led to a major healing of some kind.

Chiron conjunct Uranus: A majority reported either a major trip, or a major move, or a major job change; Many reported it was a time of feeling very alone, or very "different."

Chiron conjunct Neptune: A number reported major changes in religion or in philosophy; Many told of a major disillusionment which brought them, eventually, more in touch with reality; A number reported first experiences with either the occult, psychic or spiritual. When health was mentioned its was almost always a change for the better.

Chiron conjunct Pluto: Most of the reports were about beginning something that entailed hard work, such as a job, or a new school, or going back to school after a long absence; A number reported incidents that showed them just how much power they really had in their life, or how little—and often, how much respect they really had from others; A number told of events that truly showed them how they were different from the opposite sex, or different from their peers.

Chiron conjunct MC: Many referred to some first in their public life, such as the first time giving a lecture, or the first job leading to a worthwhile career; A number reported major conflicts with authority, or with some person in a professional capacity, that led to said authority or professional being ousted from a position, or removed from having any influence over the respondent; A number reported major disappointments which led to rethinking their lifestyle and eventually improving their lives.

Chiron square Sun: A high number of health crises, often leading to exhaustion or depression; Many reported changes in status—getting married, or separation from mate, or no longer being an only child, or having the first child; Most reported becoming aware of something or someone that changed their lives, such as meeting a spiritual guide, or being informed by a doctor that they must change their lifestyle or their health would worsen.

Chiron square Moon: Most reported changes in their relationship with a woman, or with their own femininity, or having to fend for the self after being supported for awhile; A number of females reported health problems coming to a head in the areas of female anatomy. Overall, the biggest events reported, and most often mentioned, concerned things that drastically altered the daily routine, or that involved having to make a major adjustment to attitudes about everyday life.

Chiron square Mercury: A number reported strong needs to increase communicating, either by writing more letters, writing in general, teaching or lecturing; A surprising number referred to military re-assignment or transfer; A number found a first love at this time, or a love that was 'forbidden.'

Chiron square Venus: Over half the respondents reported events involving love, and usually a major lesson resulting from it, such as discovering they were in a rut, falling for the same type over and over, or that they were too limited in their definition of love; A number reported being more aware of sensory experiences, or getting more involved with art or music; A number told of entering into disciplines to change their lifestyles.

Chiron square Mars: Very few responses to this one. Those who did referred to one of three areas—conflict with authority, major medical work such as surgery, or some major promotion or improvement in status.

Chiron square ASC: A number reported clashes with authority, or major disputes with mates, or separations from mates; Many told of getting involved with people or groups that had entirely different lifestyles; A number reported a major move.

Chiron opposition Sun: Most reported a change in their social life, either by meeting a whole bunch of new people, or by beginning, or ending a major relationship; A number reported major changes in career.

Chiron opposition Moon: The two most common themes were becoming much more aware of their own bodies, either through a change, or a health crisis, and a major change in education in some way, such as entering a graduate degree program.

Chiron opposition ASC: Over half reported the end of a marriage or close relationship; a number reported a new level reached in existing relationships, or a change in attitude about the self as a result of a relationship.

Chiron opposition Mercury: Not enough respondents to get any clear picture.

Chiron square Chiron: There was no consistency as to type of experiences, but almost everyone reported events that changed their lives drastically—and most events were those which forced them to face either a new facet of life, or a larger concept of the world, or a change in how they fitted into life. A number did report feeling very out-of-place in whatever group or position they had at the time, and a strong need to make a change.

Chiron opposition Chiron: A number began school; Many broke a relationship, and/or began a new relationship; A number did a great deal of traveling, often for the first time; A number had a major change in their relationship to the other members or their family.

Chiron conjunct, square or opposition to the ASC/MC midpoint: Most reported a great deal of restlessness; Many told of economic or career crisis causing them to take some extreme action; A number reported changes in relationships; A number reported major crises in sex, either through such events as rape, or loss of virginity, or miscarriage; A number ended major relationships; Many told of deaths, or births.

Before I leave the subject of transits, there are two other points I wish to discuss. First, since the transit of Chiron brings a remarkable opportunity to exert true free will and bring about a major turning point—the more planets that are receiving the Chiron transit—the more parts of oneself that one can bring into the moment of Chiros—and thus the more parts of self one can bring into the decision-making process. Thus the more far-reaching the possibilities, the more doors one can open, and the greater potential for personal evolution toward wholeness. And if three or more bodies are being aspected within a very short span of time, the effect often seems to influence the entire chart with a kind of 'ripple' effect—influencing even planets that are not being aspected by the transit.

Second, when Chiron makes a transit at the same time as the transit of another planet, Chiron frequently opens up situations where the other transit becomes more powerful—as though restrictions that might normally keep such a transit in check are removed. This becomes most noticeable with such transits as Mars and Pluto, which can be quite devastating if unchecked.

PROGRESSIONS

When I work with progressions, I use the 'day- for-year' method, because I seem to get the best results from it. I am not criticizing any other procedure for moving the planets through time—you are welcome to use whatever works best for you. But, because of my experiences with this method, the following section refers only to this type of progressions.

Because of the location of Chiron's orbit between Saturn and Uranus, it does not move very much by progression each year. In fact, the most I have seen it travel in any one year is nine minutes of arc—and this is not the normal rate. Even at this extreme speed, it would take over six years to move but one degree, while at the more typical rate of only a few minutes it might be fifteen or more years for that degree. [Obviously, it is extremely important to get precise positions for one's natal Chiron.]

Using the orbs given in the chapter on aspects, one can see that if Chiron were five degrees away from a conjunction to the Sun, for example, a whole lifetime would be spent before the exact aspect would be reached. And this lifetime would see the influence of Chiron growing stronger and stronger with each passing year. This would be the basic situation with Chiron in any progression if the aspect was applying at birth; getting stronger until it reaches exact culmination.

On the other hand if the Chiron aspect were separating at birth, one would NOT see any gradual tapering off of Chiron's influence. On the contrary, one would see a gradual acceptance and integration of the early influence so that it becomes more and more aligned with the whole self.

When a natal aspect progresses to become exact [culminates], the events represented by the aspect truly become manifest about 15' before the exact event. At its fastest rate, around two years worth of Chiron circumstances. Then the MOST dramatic circumstances seem to occur when it is applying by 5', on until 5' past exact culmination. Again, at its greatest speed, a period of a little over a year.

At the exact progression—there will almost always be one or more events dramatically fitting the nature of the aspected planet—but they will be in context of the entire set of events that have been going on all during the application of Chiron to the event. [Scenario].

Remember, utilize Chiron's keywords to get the best handle on the progressions. Plus, I have found that the concept, STEPPING STONE, seems to fit most progressions of Chiron to natal positions.

Now, as to the influence of a progressed planet reaching natal Chiron, I do not have much more to contribute than what was said in **Interpreting Chiron**. The progressing planet becomes changed—opened up—experiments, trying new things. It seems to remove inhibitions from the progressing body. Also there seems to be a great deal more freedom of choice in the area represented by that planet.

157

Chapter V: RELATIONSHIPS

Chiron is extremely important in the study of relationships. I am going to divide this chapter into two parts: Synastry, and Composite charts. I have found both of these to be extremely revealing in understanding of how individuals interact.

First I want to discuss briefly the concept of relationships themselves.

What seems to define a relationship is the particular connection that the people share—the common element between them. This is true whether it is a love relationship, teacher/pupil, parent/child or any other possible connection. And one word that pops up often as a key for Chiron is the phrase 'common ground.' In fact, when a chart is set up for the moment two people really meet for the first time, the Chiron aspects in the chart go into great detail to describe the common elements in the relationship, the reasons for getting together, as well as what the people 'think' they have in common. Then applying these aspects to the two natal charts will serve further to define the common ground, and add the insight of where the people differ from the expectations of each other. Very often, two people who feel 'fated' to meet will come together under a major Chiron transit to their respective natal charts.

SYNASTRY

When I first began to compare charts, looking for aspects from one person's Chiron to the chart of the other individual, I expected to find this only occasionally. I also expected that, when I did find it, the relationship would have something extreme or unique about it—something to set it far apart from other relationships. Well research has proven me very wrong on the first count—and almost as far off on the second.

I have been amazed at how common Chiron aspects appear in Synastry. In fact it seems to appear more often than not. I have a theory about why but will go into that later.

As for the nature of such [Chiron-marked] relationships—they usually seem to have no initial differences from other relationships, at least superficially. However, when you look deeper you begin to see that there is a difference, and the difference is in how open the people are to each other. Let us look at a few different aspects in order to make this clearer.

CONJUNCTION

If you have your natal Chiron in conjunction to a planet in another's chart, there is automatically some type of attraction, usually mutual. And the area of attraction fits the nature of the other planet. The attraction is not of sexual nature, unless the other planet is something like Mars or Venus. Rather, it is the attraction toward someone who seems to be traveling along the same path—a kindred spirit in some fashion. And, [here is a crucial point], what happens next depends a great deal upon the type of relationship, but even more, on the person's self-image. IF each individual is fairly well-balanced, an excellent relationship can develop here with a feeling of being true equals in whatever area the planet represents. This is truly a good thing in romance, as you can imagine. It can be very positive in teacher/pupil and parent/child relationships because both feel free to learn from the other. BUT, if one of the individuals feels severely lacking in this area, or in need of help, that person turns to the other as a teacher, or guide, and seeks the other's 'superior wisdom.' As you can imagine, this would be of benefit in counseling, or parent/child—but can be a possible hazard in such relationships as marriage. Given enough time the Chiron aspect tends to equalize differences, and so the two people have a chance to grow eventually to feel equal here. But, until then, it is possible to build up resentment against the very person from whom you are seeking help. No matter which type of relationship this is, one thing seems especially to be true—the planet that is aspecting Chiron from one chart to the other seems unable to keep up defenses to keep the Chiron person out. It is as if, for the Chiron person, the walls around the other come tumbling down—or at least the Chiron person has little trouble getting inside the walls the other person has built around self. And depending on how thick those walls were initially, and how dependent the person was on the security provided by the walls—such openness can be felt as truly fantastic, or extremely frightening. Especially since the person being aspected by the other's Chiron cannot develop any other way to erect walls around his/her planet.

SQUARE

Here we have something similar to the conjunction, but with a twist. There seems to be an attraction, yet a repulsion at the same time. This mixed feeling seems to be much stronger in the Chiron person than in the other individual. The Chiron person also seems to have the initial effect of getting past the other's defenses—but frequently causes resentment in so doing. The person being aspected by another's Chiron becomes capable of developing new defenses to keep the Chiron person out—but then the Chiron person becomes able to get through these new defenses, as well. Therefore, if the people are insecure, this aspect turns their relationship into a battlefield. Yet even so, both people grow because of it. Positively an awareness dawns about what is going on—and the two develop a relationship with great growth potential. They perceive the process of throwing up new walls as attempts to focus on insecurities. They do not feel threatened by them, but see them as a way of clearing out the rubbish. The result—mutual growth and increasing closeness.

OPPOSITION

Between any two planets, an opposition is an exchange. It can become a war, or a partnership. When Chiron in one person's chart opposes a planet in the chart of another person, the word 'exchange' takes on a very specific meaning: each person tends to take on qualities of the other. For example, let us say that one person's Chiron opposes the other person's Mars. The Chiron person will become more aggressive, more active, and tend to be somewhat physically attracted to the other person. The Mars person will become more individual, more of a Maverick, and more willing to open up and try new things. This can be a very positive thing, especially if each needs to grow in the area ruled by the opposing planet. If the Mars person needs to get out of ruts, or the Chiron person needs more self-assertion, the relationship can be really fantastic. However, if a person is afraid of the qualities s/he gets from the other—or is already active enough in those areas, the relationship can become extremely uncomfortable for one or both parties.

OTHER ASPECTS

Trines and sextiles from Chiron in one chart to planets in another chart also denote some of the same attraction, but the intensity is much less than with the hard aspects. There is also somewhat of a lowering of the defenses, but also not to such a drastic extent. These are good aspects to have between charts if there are other positive aspects, but alone they are not dramatically significant. Much more study is needed here.

As for other aspects between Chiron in one chart to bodies in another's chart, I have done relatively little research, so am unable to report anything at this time. [December, 1985.]

COMPOSITE CHARTS

To quote Robert Hand: 'The composite horoscope is created by finding the midpoint between pairs of planets and other sensitive points in the two natal horoscopes, that is, the Sun of one and the Sun of the other . . . and so forth. The composite Sun is the midpoint of the two Suns . . . '

I have found this type of chart to be extremely explicit about the nature of a relationship, describing how two people get along as a couple, rather than as two individuals. I have even seen two people with difficult synastry but a great composite get along for years and years.

It was quite a while, however, before I started to insert Chiron into composite charts. I have only been doing so, in fact, for the past two years. But the results have been so startling, that I feel that I must share them with you.

First, the house position of the composite Chiron represents an area of life where the two people have an unbelievable amount in common. It is also an area where, the longer they stay together, the more they find they have to share. For example, with Chiron in the 11th of the composite chart, they may have a number of good friends that they have in common. As they grow deeper into the relationship, it may be certain friends whom they share are main sources of great joy they share together. Another thing the house position represents is a point of release for tension—an area the two people can enter to rise above their problems, and seek relief from frustration. There is almost always at least one person the couple can go to, in this house, to seek advice and help. For example, Chiron in the 8th house in a composite chart may give the couple a good friend who is a psychiatrist, or perhaps a witch, whom they both trust for advice. If the relationship begins to fall apart, the house position of composite Chiron usually represents one area that seems to hold together longer than any other. That couple with composite Chiron in the 8th may find everything else breaking up, but still find their sexual relationship to be extremely fulfilling. The house where composite Chiron resides will also denote an area where the couple is not afraid to do things differently—to experiment. It is also an area where both individuals have a great influence on shaping the direction of each other. Composite Chiron in the 10th, for example, may denote a couple who help each other figure out exactly what each one wants to do for a career, and then help to open doors to enter the chosen profession[s]. They may even decide to take a major step—and together enter a new field, that neither gave much thought prior to the relationship.

The aspects the composite planets make to composite Chiron represent things in the relationship that are always changing—things that seem unable to find a nice, balanced secure way of expressing themselves. By being in the relationship in the first place, these people open themselves up to opportunities for growth—and the Chiron aspects are things that need to grow, and will not remain unchanging. They can be very positive—if the couple is aware of the need for growth, and if the love or friendship between the two people is real and strong. Or they could be cause for break-up—if the two people cannot deal with change, or cannot accept that growth is necessary in these areas. The hard aspects, of course, denote the most noticeable need for change. Take, for example, composite Chiron square composite Neptune. Here we have a couple who have dreams which must be changed in order to bring them more in line with reality. If they can recognize this, they can go on to realize many of their dreams. If not, they will find one event after another spoiling their search

161

for happiness. The soft aspects are less dramatic, but nevertheless denote areas where the couple needs to grow. Another thing that composite Chiron aspects represent is a feature of the relationship that differs from the 'norm' in some way, yet not simply for the sake of being different. Rather, it is some area in which the couple has just found their own particular way of doing things. Others may not approve, but the couple doesn't care. If the composite aspect is a conjunction, the couple almost always seem to have that feeling of having known each other for years, even in the first meeting.

To sum up, the best procedure to use in studying Chiron in relationships, is:

1. If the time is known, study the chart of the first meeting. It will tell you a great deal about why the two started a relationship.

2. Study the aspects between Chiron in one chart and points in the other chart. You will see a great deal about how open the two people are to each other.

3. Study the composite Chiron to find out just where the couple needs to grow the most.

Chapter VI: ODDS AND ENDS

There are a number of other areas in which I have found Chiron to have significance, but have not done in-depth research upon which to report. In this chapter I would like to mention a few of these areas, and comment upon them briefly.

CHIRON AND RELOCATION

Jim Lewis pioneered a service called ASTRO*CARTO*GRAPHY [TM], in which a person's birthchart is plotted by computer on a world map, to show the areas where each natal planet is on one of the four angles. His research has shown that a person's experiences in these parts of the world tie in directly to the planetary line that crosses the area.

When the opportunity came up for me to view maps that included Chiron, I jumped at the chance. A number of factors came up. First the Chiron lines seemed to pass through many of the countries that the individuals have always wanted to visit. Second, there were frequent events in the lives of the individuals that were somehow related to these countries—even though the persons had never visited those places. These were significant events which changed the lives of the persons. In my own case, my first real love told me that although she was born in the U.S.A., she spent the first ten years of her life in France. Not only did she open me up to much of life, but I also studied the French language just to communicate more deeply with her. My Chiron line passes through France—even through the town in which she lived! Her ascendant is exactly opposition my natal Chiron. Another instance: my Chiron line also passes through the Philippine Islands. In my youth I was given the opportunity to apply for a pen-pal, and did so. The computer selected someone in those Islands, and we became such good friends that I wrote to her for many years, and eventually met her when she moved to the U.S.A. Also, because of the positive experience with her, I applied for many other pen-pals, and at one time was writing to 12 different people. Prior to the first one, however, I had never even known anyone from another country well enough to write to them.

In an actual relocation chart—a chart adjusted to a new place of residence—Chiron denotes an area full of new experiences, and always represents things that bring major changes to your life if you reside there long. The further the new Chiron house is from the natal Chiron house, the more unique and interesting the changes will be. To give your life a real overhaul—either move to where the relocation Chiron is in the opposite house from the natal, or to where relocation Chiron is on one of the angles.

SOLAR RETURNS

In looking back over years of solar returns, I have come to this conclusion: every year of my life has had at least two significant events in it by which to remember the year. And one of these two significant events is always something that fits the house position of Chiron in the solar return chart. There is always something new in one's life, and that is one thing Chiron's position will show. Looking ahead to future solar return charts, I would say that wherever Chiron fails, you can expect new opportunities to arrive, as well as new lessons to learn. Of course, there is a little matter of free will. You can mess up the new opportunity, and you can refuse to learn the new lesson. An especially interesting year seems to be one in which Chiron is just outside of a house—that is, just about to enter that house. The new circumstances that arrive that year seem directly related to the house that Chiron is just about to move into.

HORARY

I only use Horary occasionally, so there is a great deal of work to be done here. If you have something to report on this expression of Chiron, PLEASE send us your data. What I have seen in Horary charts is that, in the house where Chiron resides, there is something beyond the immediate question that is important to the querent. Many times a door will open for the querent that will make the question irrelevant, or that will resolve the problem. This is especially true if Chiron occupies a house that is related to the question. Other times it points to something that is related to the question, but on some other level—to tell you that you have to go a bit beyond your question; you are on the right track, but you need to expand your question a little. And if Chiron appears in the chart just about to enter the house concerning the question— you can be sure that something is about to break very soon. For example—let us say the querent asks a question about whether a pet dog will come home— since s/he has been missing for awhile. I view the sixth house as having to do with pets, like dogs. Anyway, if you see Chiron in the fifth, but near the sixth cusp, you can be sure that something will occur very soon—either the dog's return, or information about why s/he has not come back.

ELECTIONS

By this, I don't mean charts set up for voting, I mean a chart set up before a planned event—a chart planned to make use of astrological influences. Preliminary observations indicate that, wherever you put Chiron in an election chart, take into account its position, you are able to spot possibilities for totally new situations to come into the picture.

♀ Chapter VII: CHIRON IN THE THIRD

In 1983, when I wrote **Interpreting Chiron**, something that I had observed in people with Chiron in the third house bothered me. The third house, by tradition, is the house of the logical mind. And yet, I had observed, 'In fact, their logical minds are not confined to logic—they are very closely linked to their emotions, their instincts, and other areas, and their emotions are very easily aroused.' I could not understand WHY this is the case.

Then, in the Aries issue of *The Networker* Rick Klimczak had an article entitled, **Revaluing the Third House**, which made everything clear. I want to reprint parts of it here [with Rick's permission], in hopes it will become clear to you as well.

"Let me just propose the addition of two new words to the third house keyword list: Dualities and Dilemma. Dualities, I think, should be on the list because divisions/dualities are a necessary prerequisite component to all perception . . . The idea of Dilemma should be included here for two reasons. First of all, astrologers have often spoken of the third house as being a problem solving house, since it is our first learning how to cope with the environment. On the external level then, the third house should also represent the dilemmas as well as the 'minor skills, instruments and conveniences' we evolve to deal with our dilemmas. . . . The other reason for adding dilemma to the third house list, the other part of the dilemma, you might say, is the internal intra-psychic issue of how one lives with one's perceptual categories. We may learn to make certain distinctions between inner and outer and this may become a workable duality in most situations, but all of our basic dualities are always subject to further challenge from the environment . . . In reality, all our basic definitions, particularly of what is inner and what is outer, are in constant flux and in a constant process of redefinition." He then finds connections between the third house as defined

166

by Dane Rudhyar, and some ideas from Fritz Peris and Gestalt psychology. Then he goes on to say, "This concept of the contact boundary is a particularly fruitful one in terms of getting at what the third house is actually about . . . [The third house] is the area where we either contact or withdraw from the environment... planets in the third (or planets ruling the signs there) have a lot to do with the style and the extent to which we contact the environment. These planets could also represent what and how we hold back from the environment, how we withdraw or avoid contact on some level . . . the contact/withdrawal rhythm may not coincide with our real requirements in the environment. This is quite evident in the behavior patterns of the neurotic. Let us quote Fritz Perls on the subject: 'All neurotic disturbances arise from the individual's inability to find and maintain the proper balance between himself and the rest of the world, and all of them have in common the fact that in neurosis the social and environmental boundary is felt as extending too far over into the individual.' Thus, all the neurotic defense mechanisms have in common some sort of problematic imbalance of what is perceived as inner and outer at the contact boundary of an individual. Gestalt psychology recognizes four basic defense mechanisms: Introjection (taking something which is 'outer' as being 'inner'); Projection (putting something which is 'inner' onto something or someone who is 'outer'); Confluence (a complete fusion and confusion about what is 'inner' and 'outer'); and Retroflection (redirecting something which is originally intended for the 'outer' and aiming it at the 'inner')." He then goes on to say that these defense mechanisms do not only belong to the third house, but "the third house represents the basic environmental adaptation patterns, the basic perceptual assumptions out of which one can evolve either a more or less healthy relationship to the environment or a neurotic imbalance represented by a defense mechanism. . . the tendency to use projection as a safety valve . . . has a great deal to do with the third house. A planet in the third house may operate 'like' the defense mechanisms of the neurotics) by constantly checking out the environment to see if there is some potential danger to the perspectives and/or prospective self-concepts the person is evolving there."

It has been observed before that the very division of the circle into house cusps is a form of Saturnian structuring of reality. Chiron represents the going beyond Saturn—sometimes as though the structure does not even exist. Thus Chiron in the third goes beyond even the boundaries of the house itself. Rick refers to the third as having the quality of learning to distinguish between an inner and an outer—self and environment. Chiron goes beyond even this boundary, making the person's judgement over this division extremely dependent on the moment; s/he may decide, at this moment, that there is no division; in the next moment s/he may decide that the division is very real. And as for the concept of defense mechanisms—if you have grown up with a totally Maverick view of the relationship between self and environment, your method of adapting to the latter would naturally be Maverick as well. Rather than a clear, distinct view of inner versus outer, or the neurotic versions listed by Perls, you would develop your own unique style, that would only include the inner/outer division when it suited you. Thus, logical minds not confined to logic—they are closely linked to their emotions.

Chapter VIII:

ANOTHER SIDE TO CHIRON: COMPUTERS, CAREERS

A number of basic themes come up often when Chiron is prominent in career-related houses. Some of the ones that are frequent are what you may expect: healer, therapist, herbal specialist, teacher, and even religious leader. One that surprised me, however, was computer-related careers. It seems to come up often.

That started me thinking, and so I began to trace down the specific dates in the history of computers. Amazingly, either a major Chiron aspect, or notable orbital position was prominent at every event in the development of computers. This led me to talk to a Dr. John G. Brainerd, Professor at the University of Pennsylvania, who was supervisor in charge of the ENIAC project—the work that built the world's first large-scale digital electronic general-purpose computer. Not only did he let me interview him over the phone, but he was kind enough to send me some printed material on the project. With this data, I was able to set up a computer/Chiron history. Here are a few of the more significant dates:

1895, Chiron reaches perihelion. Ancestor of computer born enabling the U.S. government to process ten years worth of data in a matter of months. Inventor starts a company, which later becomes IBM, incorporated 15 June 1911, upstate New York. Chiron at station, going Retrograde in Pisces, quincunx Venus, quincunx Mean Lunar North Node. Yod-like pattern.

Company is re-incorporated under the name International Business Machines, Inc. 15 February 1924, upstate New York. Chiron 17°34' Aries. Chiron trine midpoint Jupiter/Neptune, exact. Possibly sextile Moon, [aspect would be exact if time of Incorporation were circa 2:30 PM EST.]

2 April 1943. Chiron conjunct North Lunar Node. Dr. Brainerd prepares report which leads to ENIAC project. [World War II..

31 May 1943. Chiron conjunct Venus and Jupiter, trine Uranus. Actual

work on project begun.

November 1945. Chiron square Saturn, and only a few months after Chiron's perihelion. ENIAC in working order. [Formal announcement by War Department, 14 February 1946.]

1970. Chiron reaches aphelion. Shortly afterward, the first microprocessor chip is produced; leads the way to shrinking the size of computers.

1977. Chiron is discovered. Tandy Corporation launches the TRS-80 computer, which led to mass merchandising, and the explosive growth of the market for home computers.

But, why Chiron and computers? I had been taught that Uranus was the ruler of computers. This is what I concluded: I feel Chiron's connection with computers is at least two-fold. For one thing, it seems to be active at moments of major break-through, which change the pace, and even the direction, of the industry. Also, I perceive a connection because of the keyword QUALIFIER [See Chapter 1 in section 1.] To explain this second idea better let me digress a little. Roentgen, who discovered X-rays, had a very prominent Chiron. He discovered X-rays around the time of his Chiron return—and in the year of a Chiron perihelion. These little rays were the smallest ever discovered, thus redefining our idea of rays, as well as our concept of how short in wavelength they can be. His discovery led to great technological advancements, as well. X-rays, and the electric current necessary to operate a computer, are both extremely minute, yet super-powerful. Heretofore, both had been given to the rulership of Uranus. Perhaps that is correct. I feel that Chiron rules the interaction of these rays [energies] with matter, and the resulting power. X-rays enable us to see through walls [Saturn] without destroying them. [In fact, the only thing they do not go through is lead and the heavier-than-lead metals, which is like super-concentrated Saturn!] Electricity pushes a little tiny switch —now so small you need a microscope to see it—and this enables us to process vast volumes of data in no time at all—defeating Saturn. Uranus may rule the rays, but Chiron rules the meeting of the micro with the macro, and the meeting of the energy with the matter.

Now, this is information that could have gone into the first section of the book. But I put it here for a reason, which I hope will be clear to you shortly.

In natal charts I find Chiron representing all types of careers based on the use of something minute to bring about major changes. Of course it is involved in the charts of both computer operators and X-ray specialists. But in addition, it is also active in the charts of physicians who heal using such things as small quantities of herbal remedies [or synthetic versions of the active principles of herbs], vitamins, and trace elements. It is active in the charts of those who follow careers in psychology, where a few chosen words [in appropriate context] can bring about therapeutic changes. It is active in the charts of religious leaders who demonstrate incredibly intense faith.

I guess what it all comes down to is this—when you use Chiron in your analysis of possible careers, look at any field where the person deals with the power of something extremely small to bring about changes in the world around. I am reminded of something Christ said; something about having faith, the size of a mustard seed, and you could move mountains. Perhaps Chiron rules mustard seeds ?

Chapter IX: FISH IN THE NET

Faith the size of a mustard seed—

I introduced this book with some parallels between Chiron and Christ, and think I will close it with some more.

Christ was described as being in this world, but not of it. Chiron is in our solar system, but most likely came from some other far-away part of the universe.

Christ said to love God with your whole heart, soul-and mind. Chiron was said to have said, in the myths, to love Zeus above all else.

Perhaps both came from beyond our world, to give us the same message? If so, then I raise a question—could the Chiron myths have been a prophecy of the coming of Christ? If so, what does it mean for us now, since we are conscious of the planet Chiron?

The early Christians made a monogram of the first two Greek letters of Christ's name. These letters, CHI and RHO, when pronounced in an anglicized manner, sound almost like Chiron's name.

Some other aspects of Chiron's myths resemble figures in other religions. Since Chiron seems determined to guide us toward becoming whole—could its discovery now, as we move into Aquarius, be a sign of the unification of all religions into one truth?

These are the questions I raise, as a Christian and as a Chironic astrologer. Anyone out there have any answers?

♀ Afterword: THE KEY TO THE WORLD

Here is a brief look at how Chiron influences global states.

A significant problem in dealing with the horoscope of a nation is how to decide which founding data to use. Many countries have two, three or even more charts, each with its own advocates. Some nations are so long-established there is no possibility of determining any founding chart. Some countries are not really nations, but merely places recently set apart by arbitrary political actions by colonial powers. The chart of a government is not the same as the chart of a nation. There are many references to many dissenting views in this field. [A general round-up from the British point of view is included in the bibliography.]

I have elected to use those charts which I have found work the best in my research. You are welcome to disagree with my choices, and I would enjoy hearing from you if you propose an alternative to any of the following charts.

To begin with, let us look at the chart for the united States of America. I have long stood by the Gemini-rising chart: July 4, 1776, 2:14:45 AM LMT, Philadelphia, Pennsylvania, 75°08' West Longitude, 39°57' North Latitude.

Chiron's position has only strengthened my support of this chart over others.

Chiron occupies the eleventh house, at 20°09' Aries, sextile Mars [20°58' Gemini], square Mercury [24°28' Cancer], and sextile Moon [18°11' Aquarius].

First Chiron's house position says a great deal about the hopes and wishes of the USA—the need to follow its own path; the need to become a country composed of all different types. The square to Mercury emphasizes a tendency toward speaking its mind, no matter who gets irritated by it. It also adds further to the general restlessness of the population. The sextile to Mars emphasizes the pioneer [aggressive] spirit, and the desire to try methods nobody else has chosen. The sextile from the Moon (which does not exist in some other charts proposed for USA) serves to amplify the Uranus/Aquarian nature, making the country secure only when it feels it is following some higher destiny.

NOW, let us turn to the chart for the Union of Soviet Socialist Republics, (USSR.) For this, I prefer November 7, 1917, 12:59 PM LMT, Leningrad, 30°15' East Longitude, 59°55' North Latitude.

In this chart Chiron falls in the second house at 25°48' Pisces, retrograde, with the only close aspect being a close quincunx from the Moon at 22°36' Leo. Individuals with Chiron in the second often have a fascination with power [as such], and have major lessons to learn about money and possessions. They have their own totally unique value systems. In relationships, the unevolved types feel insecure unless they can control the direction of the relationship. The quincunx from the Moon here brings this emphasis to the People, and to major lessons the USSR must continually learn about basic human needs. In my opinion, it also tends to increase the government's tendency to be defensive and conscious of an always tightening need for security, as well as a need to keep distance between itself and others.

Burma is a much less well-known country. You can find it on a map of Asia, next to Thailand. What I like about this country's chart is that the exact time for independence from British rule was selected by Burmese astrologers. They use their own system of astrology which does not take into account the outer planets (not just Chiron)—so the Chiron aspects are all the more intriguing. The chart thus selected is for January 4, 1948, 4:20 AM LMT, Rangoon, 16° 45' North Latitude, 96° 20' East Longitude.

Chiron is at 21° Scorpio, not only conjunct South Lunar Node at 20°40' Scorpio, but closely square Saturn at 2¼° Leo, retrograde.

Ever since it was 'born', independent modern Burma has had a chronic problem—desire to continue using the old ways, yet having events force them to restructure, and change. They have also had a constant state of conflict within and from the outside. They now have a Socialist government, have driven Indians and Chinese from holding important positions, and have recently begun an effort to come to terms with other countries. For awhile Burma closed itself off, emphasizing isolationist philosophies—but this created more problems than it solved.

For South Africa I use two charts. First, the Union of South Africa occurred May 30, 1910, at 0 hours local time, Capetown, 33°55' South Latitude, 18°22' East Longitude.

Chiron is at 2°42' Pisces, sextile Saturn [at 1° 35' Taurus], quincunx Jupiter [at 4°37' Libra], and square Mercury [at 0°50' Gemini.] As in the USA, the square with Mercury emphasizes the tendency to speak its mind, and gives the population so much restlessness. The quincunx to Jupiter gives major lessons to learn about the basic philosophy of the country, as well as difficulties in penetrating belief systems well enough to alter it. The sextile to Saturn focuses upon the untapped potential of the country if the authorities could only work with the common people.

Chart two, for the Republic of South Africa, is for May 30, 1961, 0 hours local time, Pretoria, 26° 44' South Latitude, 28°12' East Longitude.

Chiron is at 6° 38' Pisces, square Sun [at 9°13' Gemini], opposition Pluto [at 5°35' Virgo], and trine Neptune [at 9°10' Scorpio].

Interestingly, although this chart came second, superseding the earlier chart, the earlier chart still responds to transits and progressions. Anyway, note that this second chart is not only on the anniversary of the first chart, but also just after the country's Chiron return. Chiron, as you can see, creates a T-square here, and a very unstable one at that. This T-square is responsible for the increasing disruption and violence, especially since transiting Uranus in Sagittarius, followed by Saturn, completed the mutable grand square in recent times. It is also the reason for the attempt of the government to solve the problems by fragmentation—giving 'independence' to 'homelands' such as Transkei in 1976, Bophutswana in 1977, and Venda in 1979.

The chart for Saudi Arabia is set for the capture of Riyadh by Ibn Saud, January 15, 1902, 2:47 AM GMT, 24°51' North Latitude, 46°42' East Longitude.

Chiron falls at 8°54' Capricorn, while the Ascendant is 9°54' Capricorn—a nice conjunction.

Ibn Saud was the founder of the ruling dynasty. His country has held a somewhat moderate position on crude oil prices, a major influence on other oil-producing countries. Saudi Arabia holds a unique position in the Arab community, not quite the same as any other Arab nation. Its outlook is colored by the circumstance that the holy cities of ISLAM, Medina and Mecca, are located in Saudi Arabia. One thing we must not forget: even though Chiron is conjunct the national Ascendant, it still falls in the country's 12th house. This gives a deep belief in the higher powers in the universe. It also makes it very difficult for the country to make conscious use of the higher qualities of Chiron.

Although it is not a country, The European Economic Community [EEC] has global importance, so I would like to look at its chart too. The data: January 1, 1958, 0 hours Central Europe Time, Bruxelles, 50°50' North Latitude, 4°21' East Longitude. Chiron is at 14°51' Aquarius, conjunct Venus at 15°17' Aquarius], sesquiquadrate the MC [at 29°30' Gemini].

The aim of the EEC (which has since merged with European Coal and Steel Community and the European Atomic Energy Community) is to integrate economies, coordinate social developments, and eventually bring about a political union in Europe among democratic states.

Australia has always interested me, ever since I had a pen-pal in Perth in the 60's. Two charts will be mentioned here.

The Australian Federation came into force on January 1, 1901, 0 hours local time, Melbourne, Vic, 145°00' East Longitude, 145°00' East Longitude,

175

37°50' South Latitude.

Chiron is at 28°40' Sagittarius, in conjunction with Mercury [at 27°04' Sagittarius] and Jupiter at [25°52' Sagittarius]. All are opposing Neptune [at 27°32' Gemini, retrograde.]

Australia has always had a maverick way of thinking. Long before this chart, Australia was populated by individuals and independent thinkers who did not let rules and structures inhibit their actions. There was a British Penal Colony in Australia until immigration from other sources increased in the 1850's.

Communication and education are stressed and viewed as basic free-doms. (There are said to be approximately one newspaper circulating for every two citizens, and an equal use of televisions and telephones.)

The other chart I like is for the opening of Canberra Parliament on May 9, 1927, 1:00 AM GMT, 149°08' East Longitude, 35°18 South Latitude.

Chiron is at 2°43', conjunct the MC [at 2°10' Taurus], and Mercury [at 4°55' Taurus] and quincunx Saturn [at 5°39' Sagittarius].

Here the Chiron/Mercury emphasis is even stronger and focused on the world image of the country. One geographic reflection of the maverick quality: Australia is the only country that can be called a continent, and the only continent that can also be looked upon as an island.

Leaving most other countries for consideration in future books, I want to mention, briefly, the positions of Chiron in a few more countries. I leave it to the reader to explore the meanings of Chiron in those charts.

We cannot be sure of the position of Chiron in 1066, but we have two later charts for Great Britain. The Union of Scotland and England, May 1, 1707 (Old Style, or Julian Calendar), 0 hours LMT, Westminster, 51° 30' North Latitude, 0°07.5' West Longitude.

Chiron here is as 9°32' Capricorn, retrograde, quincunx Uranus [at 9°21' Leo], and in square with Venus [at 6°54' Aries].

The United Kingdom, January 1, 1801, 0 hours LMT, same location.

Here, Chiron falls at 3°53' Sagittarius, square Pluto [at 2°36' Pisces], trine Jupiter [at 1°52' Leo, retrograde] and sextile Uranus [at 1°54' Libra, retrograde].

Note the Chiron/Uranus link in both charts.

The Kingdom of Italy, July 2, 1871, 11:40 AM LMT, Roma, 41°55' North Latitude, 12°28' East Longitude.

Chiron is around 11° Aries, completing a grand cardinal square involving Sun [at 10° Cancer], Mars [at 7° Libra], Saturn [at 6° Capricorn] and Moon [at 8° Capricorn].

The Republic of Italy: June 10, 1946, 18:00 MET, same location.

Chiron is about 16° Libra, conjunct Jupiter [at about 17° Libra].

Many charts are given for Japan. I feel that the one most usable of current events is for the restoration of sovereignty, April 28, 1952, 0 hours local time, Tokyo, 35°45' North Latitude, 139°45' East Longitude.

Chiron is at 12°27' Capricorn, retrograde.

The Republic of Turkey was proclaimed October 29, 1923, 20:30 local time, Ankara, 39°57' North Latitude, 32°50' East Longitude.

Chiron is around 18° Aries, retrograde, trine Neptune [at 20° Leo], quincunx Venus [at 18° Scorpio].

The Palestine Liberation Organization (PLO) is not a country, but it does participate in global affairs and conditions. May 22, 1964, 12:01 PM Standard Time, Jerusalem, Israel, 35°10' East Longitude, 31°47' North Latitude.

Chiron is at 18°24' Pisces, in the seventh house, trine Neptune [at 16°03' Scorpio, retrograde] and quincunx Moon [at 17°18' Libra]. Watch the news as Chiron squares its founding position in July and December of 1986, and again in April 1987.

Before I close this chapter, I want to explore global charts from another angle. I would like to present a few of the many charts that can be used to understand World War II, and explore the Chiron aspects.

On January 18, 1871, at 13:00 LMT in Versailles, France, Wilhelm I was proclaimed German Emperor.

Seeds of war were set with Chiron at 3°45' Aries, opposition Mars [at 5°34' Libra], with both square Saturn [at 4°01' Capricorn].

Adolf Hitler entered this world on April 20, 1889, 18:30 LMT (5:38 PM GMT), Braunau, Austria.

Chiron at 6°55' Cancer, opposing both the Moon [at 6°38' Capricorn] and Jupiter [at 8°15' Capricorn]. Note how Hitler's natal Chiron completes the Grand Cardinal Cross in the chart of the proclamation of the German Empire in 1871.

The chart for the Third Reich can be viewed as the chart for the inauguration of Hitler as Chancellor, 11:00 MET (some say 11:07), in Berlin, on January 30, 1933.

Chiron was 23°34' Taurus, conjunct the ascendant [at 19°26' – or 22°23' – Taurus], sextile Pluto [at 22°59' Cancer] and trine Jupiter [at 22°29' Virgo]. Please note this Chiron position is semisquare to the Chiron positions in the chart of the German Empire and Hitler's natal chart, and conjunct their midpoint!

Hitler gave the order to invade Poland on August 31, 1939, at 12:30 MET, Berlin.

Chiron was at 8°22' Cancer, square Jupiter [at 7°07' Aries] and sextile the Sun [at 7°10' Virgo].

The first shot of World War II was fired the following day. This occurred at the time of Hitler's Chiron return, thus setting off all the above noted aspects.

The chart I use for Poland at this critical period in history is set for November 14, 1918, 9:30 GMT, Warsaw. Pluto was at 6°23' Cancer, opposition Mars [at

2°14' Capricorn] and out-of-sign square to Chiron [at 29°17' Pisces, retrograde]. The Moon was at 26°32' Pisces, conjunct Chiron. Notice how closely Pluto aspects Hitler's Chiron!

Chiron appears in both positive and negative expressions in the charts of world affairs. When negative, it seems to remove obstacles, allowing such planets as Mars and Pluto to erupt without checks.

Ideally, future politicians would take this into account, before organizing governments or founding nations.

A NEW TYPE OF RULERSHIP

Most astrologers use the traditional system of rulership in their work. In this system the Sun rules Leo, the Moon rules Cancer, and the planets Mercury through Saturn rule two signs each. In addition, most astrologers have also added the planets Uranus, Neptune and Pluto to the system, giving each one co-rulership over one sign. [There is some dispute, however, about which signs they rule, especially in the case of Pluto.]

In the early 1970's, the asteroids Ceres, Pallas, Juno and Vesta were brought to the attention of astrologers thanks to the pioneering effort of Eleanor Bach. While these four bodies add a great deal of insight in the interpretation of charts, they have also added a bit of confusion to the whole idea of rulerships. Initially it was speculated that all four of them (and possibly the whole asteroid belt) had rulership over the sign of Virgo. This would help explain why Virgo has such an interest in the smallest of details, and also why Virgo is so different from the other Mercury-ruled sign, Gemini. But then, the hypothesis changed, giving Ceres and Vesta to Virgo, and Juno and Pallas to Libra.

These bodies are very small; much smaller than any planet. Can one or two bodies, as small as they are, co-rule a sign in the same way as giant Neptune co-rules Pisces? It was possible for me to accept the whole mass of asteroids ruling one sign. But if we start assigning different asteroids to different signs, the very concept of rulership much change.

This was made even more clear by two events: in 1977 the mini-planet Chiron was discovered. Even though it is only as large as one of the bigger asteroids, it appears to have an influence as potent as a major planet.

In 1980 *CAO TIMES* issued ephemerides of six previously unstudied asteroids, all of which have a noticeable influence in astrology.

Where, as far as rulership is concerned, do we put Chiron? And where do we put Hidalgo, Toro, Eros, Icarus, Sappho and Lilith? (Since then, more such ephemerides have been published for still more asteroids, with more promised.)

So what do we do? Assign each asteroid to a sign? There are literally thousands of asteroids, which means that each sign could end up with hundreds of rulers. Or, if all the asteroids are connected to Virgo and Libra, how do we interpret a chart where a person's ascendant can have over 1,000 rulers? I would like to propose a new category of rulerships, which would include Chiron and any asteroid that one decides to work with.

But first we must deal with the term "Rulership."

To rule is to exert control, direction, influence or authority over something. This is, for the most part, what the planets do to their respective signs. For example, Gemini is thinking and Mercury is the logical mind. Naturally the state of one's mind will exert considerable influence over what someone is thinking. I have no problems with the planets "RULING" signs, in this way.

It is my experience that the influence of Chiron, as well as that of the asteroids, is something entirely different. Yet I have found definite connections of each body to specific signs.

I have found that an asteroid relates to a specific facet of a sign, and has a great deal of influence in this narrow area. But other areas of the sign seem to be unaffected by said asteroid.

Take for example Ceres. I have seen it affect such things as the Virgo's concern over being useful and productive, as well as Virgo's concern for the sufferings of others. Yet when it comes to such concerns as Virgo's high concern with details and purity, Ceres seems to have no influence. But in that area Vesta shows its nature.

My hypothesis is that the asteroids represent very specific meanings, covering important, yet specialized areas, while the planets have to do with much larger, more generalized archetypes with a multitude of shades of meanings.

Essential to this hypothesis is the idea that those asteroids do not 'rule' those areas of a sign—rather, they act as filters.

To clarify, let us say that in order to deal with a certain area of a sign, you must go through the asteroid that has a connection to it. The asteroid filters out all energies and urges unrelated to its particular theme.

Thus we have a great deal of free will in each sign, making the decision as to which aspect of that sign (in other words, which asteroid) we choose to work through. In a way the asteroid belt even resembles a filter between the planets Mars and Jupiter!

As for Chiron, there is a modification of the above. For this I want to refer you to the mythology of Chiron. In the myth, he had a cave (called 'The Chironian') in a mountain. When a potential hero was entrusted to his care, he would take the pupil deep within his cave, and instruct him there. The pupil would not emerge until he had been transformed by Chiron into one prepared to fulfill his personal destiny.

Chiron, I feel, is where certain specific planets go, when they have gone as far as they can go on their own, to work for some higher purpose. That is, when a person has gone as far as he can in an area ruled by the sign, but wishes to go much further beyond, the energy of that sign's ruler turns to Chiron and Chiron takes over, bringing the person to the necessary state of evolvement in which to further pursue personal destiny. This is the "turning point", when the planet turns to Chiron and says, 'You take over.'

Notice that I said "certain specific planets go" to Chiron, not just one. I feel that Chiron helps out more than just one. Sagittarius is definitely one; Jupiter often sends to Chiron for help. Libra also seems to have this connection with Chiron, but I am unsure whether it is Venus which sends things to Chiron, or some as-yet-undiscovered ruler. (Trans-Pluto, or as Edith Wangemann names it, Isis, is said by many to be Libra's true ruler.)

It is possible that one or more other signs also do this. Indeed it is possible that all twelve do so. But I don't think so. I feel that when other signs send "pupils" to Chiron's cave, they do it sort of hopscotch, from their ruler to Libra or Sagittarius, then to Chiron. Perhaps it even bounces off their asteroid which then filters to Chiron.

 **Bibliography**

I. On Chiron:

CAO NEWSLETTER, various editions, Congress of Astrological Organizations, 1977-1978.

EPHEMERIS OF CHIRON, 1887-2000, computed by Daniel Green [Minor Planet Center, Smithsonian Institution Astrophysical Observatory, CAO TIMES, 1982.

DAILY POSITION EPHEMERIS OF CHIRON, 1891-2000, computed by Eve S. Gregory, CAO TIMES, 18 November 1985.

THE CONTINUING DISCOVERY OF CHIRON, by Erminie Lantero, Samuel Weiser, Inc., York Harbor ME, 1983.

WOMEN PRIESTS, THE ASTEROIDS & CHIRON, by Erminie Lantero, in CAO TIMES, Vol. 6, No. I, 1984

CHIRON INTERFACE, by Esther Moldauer, in CAO TIMES, Vol. 6, No. 3, 1985.

CHIRON, THE NEW PLANET IN YOUR HOROSCOPE, by Richard Nolle, AFA, Tempe AZ, 1983.

CHIRON, Monthly Positions, with stations, 1686-1889, computed by Mark Pottenger, distributed by CAO TIMES since 1980.

INTERPRETING CHIRON, by Zane B. Stein, Association for Studying Chiron, Lansdale PA, 1983. [Definitive text, since translated and republished in German and French].

THE KEY, edited by Zane B. Stein, The Association for Studying Chiron. [Monthly newsletter].

THE MEANING OF CHIRON, by Zane B. Stein, In The Astrological Review, Astrologers Guild of America, Inc., New York, 1980.

CHIRON - NEW PLANET - Mythology, Meaning, Practical Uses, by Dr. Hans Jorg Waiter, in CAO TIMES, Vol. 6, No. 2. (Definitive article, presented at 36 Arbeitstagung fuer kosmobiologische Forschung, 26 Okt. 1984. Translated from the German by Al H. Morrison)

MONTY PYTHON & CHIRON'S TOUCH OF HUMOR, by Dr. Hans Jorg Waiter, in CAO TIMES, Vol. 6, No. 3, 1985.

PEDESTRIANS WATCH AS CRANE LIFTS ANOTHER PLANET OVER N.Y.C., painting by Ranelle Wolfe, 29 August 1977, in CAO TIMES, Vol. 3, No. I.

II. Astrology:

MUNDANE ASTROLOGY, by Baigent, Harvey & Campion, The Aquarian Press, 1984.

IS THIS A CLIMACTERIC YEAR FOR YOU? by Manley Palmer Hall, re-published in The Best of The Illustrated National Astrological Journal, Editor, Edward L.A. Wagner, 1978.

PLANETS IN COMPOSITE, by Robert Hand, Pars Research, Inc., Mass., 1975.

SECRETS FROM A STARGAZER'S NOTEBOOK, by Debbi Kempton-Smith, Bantam Books, 1982.

RE-VALUING THE THIRD HOUSE, by Rick Klimczak, in The Networker Arachni Press, 816 Easley Street, #1531, Silver Spring MD 20910.

AN ASTROLOGICAL MANDALA, by Dane Rudhyar, Vintage Books, Random House, New York, 1973.

THE ASTROLOGY OF PERSONALITY, by Dane Rudhyar, Doubleday, New York, circa 1950.

III. Other:

THE ENIAC, by J.G. Brainerd & T.K. Sharpless, in Electrical Engineering Litho February 1948.

GENESIS OF THE ENIAC, by John G. Brainerd, in Technology & Culture, July 1976.

THE HOLY BIBLE [King James Version].

THE COMPLETE BOOK OF NATURAL MEDICINES, by David Carroll, Summit Books, 1980.

THE OMNI BOOK OF MEDICINE, Edited by Owen Davies, Zebra Books, Kensington Publishing Corp., New York.

A ZOO OF CENTAURS & OTHER STRANGE ANIMALS CONVERSE WITH A DRAGON.* A folio of drawings by Mrs. Lyne Kohlhoff, 21025 Lassen Street #205, Chatsworth CA 91311.

COMMON AND UNCOMMON USES OF HERBS FOR HEALTHFUL LIVING, by Richard Lucas, Arco Publishing Co., New York. 1969.

BODY TIME, by Guy Gaer Luce, Bantam Books Inc. [reprint] 1971.

A QUESTION OF IDENTITY, by Joelie K.D. Mahoney, [Interview with Charles Kowal, with photos, in CAO TIMES, Vol. 3, No. 3. 1977.

THE WORLD ALMANAC & BOOK OF FACTS, Newspaper Enterprise Association, Inc., 1985.

PSYCHOTHERAPY EAST & WEST, by Alan W. Watts, Pantheon Books, Ballantine Books Inc., New York, 1961.

WEBSTER'S NEW WORLD DICTIONARY OF THE AMERICAN LANGUAGE, College Edition, The World Publishing Co., New York, 1968.

THE REFLEXIVE UNIVERSE, by Arthur M. Young, Delacorte Press, 1976.

Ephemeris of Chiron, 1900–2050

Every ten days. Midnight GMT

da-mo	°	′	da-mo	°	′	da-mo	°	′	da-mo	°	′
—1900—			02-15	03♑	03	04-11	14♑	34	06-05	22♑	03℞
01-01	18↗	54	02-25	03	46	04-21	14	40	06-15	21	35
01-11	19	59	03-07	04	23	05-01	14	37℞	06-25	21	04
01-21	21	01	03-17	04	52	05-11	14	27	07-05	20	29
01-31	21	57	03-27	05	13	05-21	14	08	07-15	19	53
02-10	22	48	04-06	05	24	05-31	13	44	07-25	19	17
02-20	23	31	04-16	05	27℞	06-10	13	13	08-04	18	43
03-02	24	06	04-26	05	22	06-20	12	39	08-14	18	13
03-12	24	33	05-06	05	07	06-30	12	02	08-24	17	48
03-22	24	51	05-16	04	45	07-10	11	24	09-03	17	28
04-01	24	59	05-26	04	17	07-20	10	48	09-13	17	16
04-11	24	58℞	06-05	03	43	07-30	10	14	09-23	17	11
04-21	24	47	06-15	03	06	08-09	09	45	10-03	17	13D
05-01	24	28	06-25	02	27	08-19	09	21	10-13	17	24
05-11	24	01	07-05	01	48	08-29	09	04	10-23	17	41
05-21	23	28	07-15	01	11	09-08	08	54	11-02	18	06
05-31	22	50	07-25	00	38	09-18	08	53D	11-12	18	38
06-10	22	10	08-04	00	11	09-28	08	59	11-22	19	15
06-20	21	29	08-14	29↗	50	10-08	09	14	12-02	19	58
06-30	20	50	08-24	29	36	10-18	09	36	12-12	20	44
07-10	20	14	09-03	29	31	10-28	10	06	12-22	21	34
07-20	19	43	09-13	29	35D	11-07	10	42	**—1904—**		
07-30	19	19	09-23	29	47	11-17	11	24	01-01	22	26
08-09	19	03	10-03	00♑	07	11-27	12	11	01-11	23	20
08-19	18	55	10-13	00	35	12-07	13	02	01-21	24	14
08-29	18	57D	10-23	01	10	12-17	13	56	01-31	25	07
09-08	19	07	11-02	01	52	12-27	14	52	02-10	25	58
09-18	19	26	11-12	02	40	**—1903—**			02-20	26	47
09-28	19	54	11-22	03	32	01-06	15	49	03-01	27	32
10-08	20	29	12-02	04	28	01-16	16	46	03-11	28	13
10-18	21	12	12-12	05	27	01-26	17	42	03-21	28	49
10-28	22	00	12-22	06	28	02-05	18	36	03-31	29	18
11-07	22	55	**—1902—**			02-15	19	27	04-10	29	41
11-17	23	53	01-01	07	29	02-25	20	14	04-20	29	57
11-27	24	55	01-11	08	30	03-07	20	56	04-30	00≈	06
12-07	26	00	01-21	09	29	03-17	21	33	05-10	00	07℞
12-17	27	05	01-31	10	26	03-27	22	03	05-20	00	01
12-27	28	11	02-10	11	19	04-06	22	26	05-30	29♑	47
—1901—			02-20	12	08	04-16	22	41	06-09	29	28
01-06	29	16	03-02	12	51	04-26	22	49	06-19	29	02
01-16	00♑	18	03-12	13	28	05-06	22	48℞	06-29	28	33
01-26	01	18	03-22	13	58	05-16	22	40	07-09	28	00
02-05	02♑	13	04-01	14♑	20	05-26	22♑	25℞	07-19	27♑	25℞

183

da-mo	°	′	da-mo	°	′	da-mo	°	′	da-mo	°	′
07-29	26♑	51℞	12-21	04♒	07	05-05	18♒	03	09-26	18♒	54℞
08-08	26	17	12-31	04	51	05-15	18	12	10-06	18	37
08-18	25	47	—1906—			05-25	18	15℞	10-16	18	26
08-28	25	21	01-10	05	37	06-04	18	11	10-26	18	21
09-07	25	00	01-20	06	25	06-14	18	01	11-05	18	22D
09-17	24	45	01-30	07	13	06-24	17	45	11-15	18	30
09-27	24	38	02-09	08	01	07-04	17	24	11-25	18	44
10-07	24	38 D	02-19	08	48	07-14	16	58	12-05	19	04
10-17	24	45	03-01	09	33	07-24	16	30	12-15	19	29
10-27	24	59	03-11	10	14	08-03	15	59	12-25	20	00
11-06	25	20	03-21	10	52	08-13	15	27	—1909—		
11-16	25	48	03-31	11	25	08-23	14	56	01-04	20	34
11-26	26	22	04-10	11	53	09-02	14	26	01-14	21	12
12-06	27	01	04-20	12	15	09-12	14	00	01-24	21	52
12-16	27	44	04-30	12	31	09-22	13	38	02-03	22	34
12-26	28	30	05-10	12	41	10-02	13	22	02-13	23	16
—1905—			05-20	12	43℞	10-12	13	11	02-23	23	59
01-05	29	19	05-30	12	39	10-22	13	06	03-05	24	40
01-15	00♒	10	06-09	12	28	11-01	13	08D	03-15	25	20
01-25	01	01	06-19	12	11	11-11	13	17	03-25	25	57
02-04	01	51	06-29	11	49	11-21	13	32	04-04	26	31
02-14	02	40	07-09	11	23	12-01	13	54	04-14	27	01
02-24	03	27	07-19	10	53	12-11	14	20	04-24	27	26
03-06	04	10	07-29	10	21	12-21	14	52	05-04	27	46
03-16	04	49	08-08	09	48	12-31	15	28	05-14	28	00
03-26	05	24	08-18	09	16	—1908—			05-24	28	09
04-05	05	53	08-28	08	46	01-10	16	07	06-03	28	11℞
04-15	06	15	09-07	08	20	01-20	16	49	06-13	28	08
04-25	06	31	09-17	07	58	01-30	17	32	06-23	27	58
05-05	06	41	09-27	07	42	02-09	18	17	07-03	27	43
05-15	06	43℞	10-07	07	31	02-19	19	01	07-13	27	23
05-25	06	38	10-17	07	28	02-29	19	44	07-23	26	59
06-04	06	26	10-27	07	31 D	03-10	20	25	08-02	26	32
06-14	06	08	11-06	07	41	03-20	21	04	08-12	26	03
06-24	05	44	11-16	07	58	03-30	21	39	08-22	25	32
07-04	05	16	11-26	08	21	04-09	22	09	09-01	25	03
07-14	04	45	12-06	08	49	04-19	22	36	09-11	24	35
07-24	04	12	12-16	09	23	04-29	22	56	09-21	24	09
08-03	03	38	12-26	10	00	05-09	23	11	10-01	23	48
08-13	03	05	—1907—			05-19	23	20	10-11	23	31
08-23	02	35	01-05	10	42	05-29	23	23℞	10-21	23	20
09-02	02	09	01-15	11	25	06-08	23	19	10-31	23	15
09-12	01	47	01-25	12	11	06-18	23	10	11-10	23	16D
09-22	01	32	02-04	12	57	06-28	22	54	11-20	23	23
10-02	01	22	02-14	13	43	07-08	22	34	11-30	23	36
10-12	01	20D	02-24	14	28	07-18	22	09	12-10	23	55
10-22	01	25	03-06	15	10	07-28	21	41	12-20	24	20
11-01	01	37	03-16	15	51	08-07	21	11	12-30	24	49
11-11	01	56	03-26	16	27	08-17	20	40	—1910—		
11-21	02	21	04-05	16	59	08-27	20	10	01-09	25	22
12-01	02	51	04-15	17	26	09-06	19	41	01-19	25	59
12-11	03♒	27	04-25	17♒	48	09-16	19♒	15℞	01-29	26♒	37

Ephemeris, 1900–2050

da-mo	°	′	da-mo	°	′	da-mo	°	′	da-mo	°	′
1910 02-08	27≈	18	07-03	06✶	48℞	11-24	06✶	27D	04-08	16✶	37
02-18	27	59	07-13	06	33	12-04	06	34	04-18	17	09
02-28	28	40	07-23	06	14	12-14	06	46	04-28	17	38
03-10	29	20	08-02	05	51	12-24	07	04	05-08	18	03
03-20	29	59	08-12	05	24	—**1913**—			05-18	18	24
03-30	00✶	35	08-22	04	56	01-03	07	27	05-28	18	40
04-09	01	07	09-01	04	27	01-13	07	55	06-07	18	51
04-19	01	36	09-11	03	59	01-23	08	26	06-17	18	57
04-29	02	00	09-21	03	32	02-02	08	59	06-27	18	57℞
05-09	02	19	10-01	03	07	02-12	09	36	07-07	18	52
05-19	02	33	10-11	02	47	02-22	10	13	07-17	18	41
05-29	02	41	10-21	02	31	03-04	10	51	07-27	18	26
06-08	02	43℞	10-31	02	20	03-14	11	29	08-06	18	07
06-18	02	39	11-10	02	15	03-24	12	06	08-16	17	44
06-28	02	30	11-20	02	16D	04-03	12	41	08-26	17	18
07-08	02	15	11-30	02	22	04-13	13	14	09-05	16	51
07-18	01	56	12-10	02	35	04-23	13	44	09-15	16	23
07-28	01	32	12-20	02	53	05-03	14	09	09-25	15	56
08-07	01	05	12-30	03	16	05-13	14	31	10-05	15	31
08-17	00	37	—**1912**—			05-23	14	48	10-15	15	08
08-27	00	07	01-09	03	44	06-02	15	00	10-25	14	49
09-06	29≈	38	01-19	04	16	06-12	15	06	11-04	14	34
09-16	29	10	01-29	04	50	06-22	15	07℞	11-14	14	24
09-26	28	46	02-08	05	27	07-02	15	02	11-24	14	20
10-06	28	24	02-18	06	05	07-12	14	52	12-04	14	22D
10-16	28	08	02-28	06	44	07-22	14	37	12-14	14	29
10-26	27	57	03-09	07	23	08-01	14	18	12-24	14	42
11-05	27	52	03-19	08	01	08-11	13	55	—**1915**—		
11-15	27	53D	03-29	08	37	08-21	13	29	01-03	15	00
11-25	28	00	04-08	09	11	08-31	13	02	01-13	15	23
12-05	28	12	04-18	09	41	09-10	12	33	01-23	15	50
12-15	28	31	04-28	10	08	09-20	12	06	02-02	16	20
12-25	28	55	05-08	10	31	09-30	11	40	02-12	16	53
—**1911**—			05-18	10	48	10-10	11	16	02-22	17	28
01-04	29	23	05-28	11	01	10-20	10	57	03-04	18	05
01-14	29	55	06-07	11	07	10-30	10	42	03-14	18	42
01-24	00✶	31	06-17	11	09℞	11-09	10	32	03-24	19	18
02-03	01	08	06-27	11	04	11-19	10	27	04-03	19	53
02-13	01	48	07-07	10	55	11-29	10	29D	04-13	20	27
02-23	02	28	07-17	10	40	12-09	10	36	04-23	20	58
03-05	03	07	07-27	10	21	12-19	10	48	05-03	21	26
03-15	03	46	08-06	09	58	12-29	11	06	05-13	21	50
03-25	04	24	08-16	09	32	—**1914**—			05-23	22	10
04-04	04	58	08-26	09	04	01-08	11	29	06-02	22	26
04-14	05	30	09-05	08	35	01-18	11	56	06-12	22	36
04-24	05	58	09-15	08	07	01-28	12	27	06-22	22	41
05-04	06	21	09-25	07	41	02-07	13	00	07-02	22	41℞
05-14	06	39	10-05	07	17	02-17	13	36	07-12	22	35
05-24	06	52	10-15	06	57	02-27	14	12	07-22	22	25
06-03	07	00	10-25	06	41	03-09	14	50	08-01	22	09
06-13	07	02℞	11-04	06	31	03-19	15	27	08-11	21	50
06-23	06✶	58℞	11-14	06✶	26℞	03-29	16✶	03	08-21	21✶	27℞

da-mo	°	'	da-mo	°	'	da-mo	°	'	da-mo	°	'
08-31	21♓	01℞	01-12	22♓	31	06-06	03♈	04	10-29	03♈	25℞
09-10	20	34	01-22	22	54	06-16	03	17	11-08	03	05
09-20	20	06	02-01	23	21	06-26	03	25	11-18	02	48
09-30	19	40	02-11	23	51	07-06	03	29	11-28	02	36
10-10	19	14	02-21	24	24	07-16	03	27℞	12-08	02	30
10-20	18	52	03-03	24	58	07-26	03	19	12-18	02	29 D
10-30	18	33	03-13	25	34	08-05	03	07	12-28	02	33
11-09	18	19	03-23	26	10	08-15	02	51	—1920—		
11-19	18	10	04-02	26	45	08-25	02	30	01-07	02	43
11-29	18	07	04-12	27	19	09-04	02	07	01-17	02	58
12-09	18	09D	04-22	27	52	09-14	01	41	01-27	03	18
12-19	18	17	05-02	28	21	09-24	01	14	02-06	03	42
12-29	18	30	05-12	28	48	10-04	00	47	02-16	04	10
—1916—			05-22	29	11	10-14	00	21	02-26	04	40
01-08	18	48	06-01	29	29	10-24	29♓	57	03-07	05	13
01-18	19	11	06-11	29	43	11-03	29	36	03-17	05	48
01-28	19	38	06-21	29	52	11-13	29	19	03-27	06	23
02-07	20	08	07-01	29	56	11-23	29	07	04-06	06	58
02-17	20	41	07-11	29	55℞	12-03	28	59	04-16	07	32
02-27	21	16	07-21	29	48	12-13	28	58 D	04-26	08	05
03-08	21	52	07-31	29	36	12-23	29	02	05-06	08	36
03-18	22	28	08-10	29	20	—1919—			05-16	09	05
03-28	23	04	08-20	29	00	01-02	29	11	05-26	09	30
04-07	23	39	08-30	28	37	01-12	29	25	06-05	09	51
04-17	24	11	09-09	28	11	01-22	29	44	06-15	10	08
04-27	24	42	09-19	27	44	02-01	00♈	08	06-25	10	20
05-07	25	09	09-29	27	17	02-11	00	35	07-05	10	27
05-17	25	33	10-09	26	51	02-21	01	06	07-15	10	29℞
05-27	25	52	10-19	26	27	03-03	01	39	07-25	10	26
06-06	26	06	10-29	26	05	03-13	02	13	08-04	10	17
06-16	26	16	11-08	25	48	03-23	02	48	08-14	10	04
06-26	26	21	11-18	25	35	04-02	03	24	08-24	09	47
07-06	26	20℞	11-28	25	27	04-12	03	58	09-03	09	25
07-16	26	14	12-08	25	24D	04-22	04	32	09-13	09	01
07-26	26	03	12-18	25	28	05-02	05	03	09-23	08	35
08-05	25	47	12-28	25	36	05-12	05	32	10-03	08	08
08-15	25	27	—1918—			05-22	05	57	10-13	07	41
08-25	25	04	01-07	25	50	06-01	06	19	10-23	07	16
09-04	24	38	01-17	26	09	06-11	06	36	11-02	06	52
09-14	24	11	01-27	26	32	06-21	06	49	11-12	06	32
09-24	23	44	02-06	26	59	07-01	06	57	11-22	06	16
10-04	23	17	02-16	27	30	07-11	06	59℞	12-02	06	05
10-14	22	53	02-26	28	02	07-21	06	56	12-12	05	59
10-24	22	31	03-08	28	37	07-31	06	49	12-22	05	59D
11-03	22	13	03-18	29	12	08-10	06	36	—1921—		
11-13	21	59	03-28	29	48	08-20	06	19	01-01	06	04
11-23	21	51	04-07	00♈	23	08-30	05	58	01-11	06	14
12-03	21	48	04-17	00	57	09-09	05	35	01-21	06	30
12-13	21	50D	04-27	01	28	09-19	05	09	01-31	06	50
12-23	21	59	05-07	01	58	09-29	04	42	02-10	07	15
—1917—			05-17	02	24	10-09	04	15	02-20	07	43
01-02	22♓	12	05-27	02♈	46	10-19	03♈	49℞	03-02	08♈	14

1915

186

da-mo	°	'	da-mo	°	'	da-mo	°	'	da-mo	°	'
1921 03-12	08♈	47	08-04	17♈	25℞	12-27	16♈	31℞	05-10	25♈	38
03-22	09	21	08-14	17	16	—**1924**—			05-20	26	11
04-01	09	57	08-24	17	01	01-06	16	32 D	05-30	26	42
04-11	10	32	09-03	16	43	01-16	16	40	06-09	27	09
04-21	11	06	09-13	16	21	01-26	16	52	06-19	27	33
05-01	11	39	09-23	15	56	02-05	17	10	06-29	27	52
05-11	12	10	10-03	15	29	02-15	17	32	07-09	28	07
05-21	12	38	10-13	15	02	02-25	17	59	07-19	28	17
05-31	13	02	10-23	14	35	03-06	18	28	07-29	28	22
06-10	13	23	11-02	14	10	03-16	19	00	08-08	28	21℞
06-20	13	39	11-12	13	47	03-26	19	34	08-18	28	15
06-30	13	51	11-22	13	28	04-05	20	10	08-28	28	04
07-10	13	57	12-02	13	13	04-15	20	46	09-07	27	48
07-20	13	59℞	12-12	13	03	04-25	21	21	09-17	27	28
07-30	13	55	12-22	12	58	05-05	21	55	09-27	27	05
08-09	13	46	—**1923**—			05-15	22	28	10-07	26	39
08-19	13	32	01-01	12	59D	05-25	22	59	10-17	26	11
08-29	13	14	01-11	13	06	06-04	23	26	10-27	25	43
09-08	12	53	01-21	13	18	06-14	23	50	11-06	25	16
09-18	12	28	01-31	13	35	06-24	24	09	11-16	24	51
09-28	12	02	02-10	13	56	07-04	24	25	11-26	24	28
10-08	11	35	02-20	14	22	07-14	24	35	12-06	24	10
10-18	11	08	03-02	14	51	07-24	24	40	12-16	23	57
10-28	10	42	03-12	15	23	08-03	24	40℞	12-26	23	49
11-07	10	19	03-22	15	56	08-13	24	34	—**1926**—		
11-17	09	59	04-01	16	31	08-23	24	24	01-05	23	46D
11-27	09	44	04-11	17	07	09-02	24	08	01-15	23	49
12-07	09	34	04-21	17	42	09-12	23	49	01-25	23	58
12-17	09	28	05-01	18	17	09-22	23	26	02-04	24	12
12-27	09	29D	05-11	18	49	10-02	23	00	02-14	24	31
—**1922**—			05-21	19	20	10-12	22	33	02-24	24	55
01-06	09	34	05-31	19	47	10-22	22	05	03-06	25	23
01-16	09	46	06-10	20	11	11-01	21	38	03-16	25	54
01-26	10	02	06-20	20	31	11-11	21	13	03-26	26	27
02-05	10	23	06-30	20	46	11-21	20	50	04-05	27	03
02-15	10	48	07-10	20	57	12-01	20	32	04-15	27	39
02-25	11	16	07-20	21	03	12-11	20	18	04-25	28	15
03-07	11	48	07-30	21	03℞	12-21	20	09	05-05	28	52
03-17	12	21	08-09	20	58	12-31	20	06	05-15	29	27
03-27	12	56	08-19	20	48	—**1925**—			05-25	30	00
04-06	13	31	08-29	20	33	01-10	20	08D	06-04	00♉	30
04-16	14	06	09-08	20	14	01-20	20	17	06-14	00	58
04-26	14	40	09-18	19	52	01-30	20	30	06-24	01	22
05-06	15	13	09-28	19	26	02-09	20	48	07-04	01	41
05-16	15	44	10-08	18	59	02-19	21	11	07-14	01	56
05-26	16	11	10-18	18	32	03-01	21	38	07-24	02	06
06-05	16	36	10-28	18	05	03-11	22	09	08-03	02	10
06-15	16	56	11-07	17	40	03-21	22	41	08-13	02	09℞
06-25	17	12	11-17	17	17	03-31	23	16	08-23	02	03
07-05	17	23	11-27	16	58	04-10	23	52	09-02	01	51
07-15	17	29	12-07	16	44	04-20	24	28	09-12	01	35
07-25	17♈	30℞	12-17	16♈	34℞	04-30	25♈	04	09-22	01♉	14℞

da-mo	°	'	da-mo	°	'	da-mo	°	'	da-mo	°	'
1926 10-02	00♉	50℞	02-14	01♉	55	07-08	13♉	37	11-30	15♉	26℞
10-12	00	23	02-24	02	16	07-18	13	57	12-10	14	59
10-22	29♈	55	03-05	02	41	07-28	14	12	12-20	14	37
11-01	29	27	03-15	03	11	08-07	14	22	12-30	14	19
11-11	29	00	03-25	03	43	08-17	14	26	—**1931**—		
11-21	28	34	04-04	04	18	08-27	14	24℞	01-09	14	07
12-01	28	12	04-14	04	55	09-06	14	17	01-19	14	01
12-11	27	54	04-24	05	33	09-16	14	04	01-29	14	01D
12-21	27	41	05-04	06	11	09-26	13	46	02-08	14	07
12-31	27	34	05-14	06	48	10-06	13	24	02-18	14	20
—**1927**—			05-24	07	24	10-16	12	58	02-28	14	38
01-10	27	32 D	06-03	07	58	10-26	12	30	03-10	15	02
01-20	27	35	06-13	08	30	11-05	12	00	03-20	15	30
01-30	27	45	06-23	08	58	11-15	11	30	03-30	16	02
02-09	28	00	07-03	09	22	11-25	11	02	04-09	16	38
02-19	28	20	07-13	09	42	12-05	10	36	04-19	17	16
03-01	28	45	07-23	09	57	12-15	10	14	04-29	17	56
03-11	29	13	08-02	10	06	12-25	09	56	05-09	18	37
03-21	29	45	08-12	10	11	—**1930**—			05-19	19	18
03-31	00♉	19	08-22	10	09℞	01-04	09	44	05-29	19	58
04-10	00	55	09-01	10	02	01-14	09	37	06-08	20	37
04-20	01	32	09-11	09	49	01-24	09	37D	06-18	21	14
04-30	02	09	09-21	09	32	02-03	09	43	06-28	21	48
05-10	02	46	10-01	09	10	02-13	09	55	07-08	22	18
05-20	03	21	10-11	08	45	02-23	10	12	07-18	22	45
05-30	03	55	10-21	08	17	03-05	10	35	07-28	23	06
06-09	04	26	10-31	07	48	03-15	11	02	08-07	23	23
06-19	04	54	11-10	07	19	03-25	11	33	08-17	23	33
06-29	05	18	11-20	06	51	04-04	12	08	08-27	23	38
07-09	05	37	11-30	06	25	04-14	12	45	09-06	23	37℞
07-19	05	52	12-10	06	03	04-24	13	24	09-16	23	30
07-29	06	02	12-20	05	46	05-04	14	03	09-26	23	16
08-08	06	06	12-30	05	33	05-14	14	43	10-06	22	58
08-18	06	04℞	—**1929**—			05-24	15	22	10-16	22	34
08-28	05	58	01-09	05	26	06-03	16	00	10-26	22	07
09-07	05	46	01-19	05	26D	06-13	16	36	11-05	21	37
09-17	05	29	01-29	05	31	06-23	17	08	11-15	21	06
09-27	05	07	02-08	05	42	07-03	17	38	11-25	20	35
10-07	04	43	02-18	05	59	07-13	18	03	12-05	20	05
10-17	04	16	02-28	06	20	07-23	18	24	12-15	19	38
10-27	03	47	03-10	06	47	08-02	18	40	12-25	19	15
11-06	03	18	03-20	07	17	08-12	18	50	—**1932**—		
11-16	02	51	03-30	07	50	08-22	18	55	01-04	18	57
11-26	02	25	04-09	08	26	09-01	18	53℞	01-14	18	45
12-06	02	03	04-19	09	04	09-11	18	45	01-24	18	39
12-16	01	46	04-29	09	43	09-21	18	32	02-03	18	39D
12-26	01	33	05-09	10	21	10-01	18	14	02-13	18	46
—**1928**—			05-19	10	59	10-11	17	51	02-23	18	59
01-05	01	26	05-29	11	36	10-21	17	25	03-04	19	18
01-15	01	24D	06-08	12	11	10-31	16	56	03-14	19	43
01-25	01	29	06-18	12	43	11-10	16	25	03-24	20	12
02-04	01♉	39	06-28	13♉	12	11-20	15♉	55℞	04-03	20♉	46

Ephemeris, 1900–2050

1932

da-mo	°	'	da-mo	°	'	da-mo	°	'	da-mo	°	'
04-13	21♉	23	09-05	04♊	04	01-18	04♊	56℞	06-11	17♊	12
04-23	22	02	09-15	04	04℞	01-28	04	43	06-21	18	03
05-03	22	43	09-25	03	58	02-07	04	36	07-01	18	53
05-13	23	25	10-05	03	45	02-17	04	36D	07-11	19	41
05-23	24	08	10-15	03	26	02-27	04	43	07-21	20	26
06-02	24	49	10-25	03	02	03-09	04	58	07-31	21	08
06-12	25	30	11-04	02	33	03-19	05	19	08-10	21	45
06-22	26	08	11-14	02	02	03-29	05	46	08-20	22	17
07-02	26	43	11-24	01	29	04-08	06	19	08-30	22	44
07-12	27	15	12-04	00	56	04-18	06	56	09-09	23	04
07-22	27	43	12-14	00	24	04-28	07	37	09-19	23	17
08-01	28	06	12-24	29♉	55	05-08	08	21	09-29	23	22
08-11	28	23	**—1934—**			05-18	09	08	10-09	23	20℞
08-21	28	35	01-03	29	31	05-28	09	55	10-19	23	10
08-31	28	40	01-13	29	12	06-07	10	44	10-29	22	53
09-10	28	39℞	01-23	28	58	06-17	11	32	11-08	22	30
09-20	28	32	02-02	28	52	06-27	12	18	11-18	22	01
09-30	28	19	02-12	28	53D	07-07	13	03	11-28	21	28
10-10	28	00	02-22	29	00	07-17	13	45	12-08	20	52
10-20	27	36	03-04	29	14	07-27	14	23	12-18	20	14
10-30	27	09	03-14	29	35	08-06	14	57	12-28	19	38
11-09	26	38	03-24	00♊	01	08-16	15	26	**—1937—**		
11-19	26	06	04-03	00	33	08-26	15	50	01-07	19	05
11-29	25	34	04-13	01	09	09-05	16	06	01-17	18	35
12-09	25	03	04-23	01	48	09-15	16	17	01-27	18	12
12-19	24	36	05-03	02	31	09-25	16	19℞	02-06	17	55
12-29	24	12	05-13	03	15	10-05	16	15	02-16	17	45
—1933—			05-23	04	01	10-15	16	04	02-26	17	44D
01-08	23	53	06-02	04	47	10-25	15	46	03-08	17	50
01-18	23	41	06-12	05	32	11-04	15	22	03-18	18	04
01-28	23	35	06-22	06	16	11-14	14	53	03-28	18	26
02-07	23	35D	07-02	06	59	11-24	14	20	04-07	18	54
02-17	23	42	07-12	07	38	12-04	13	45	04-17	19	29
02-27	23	56	07-22	08	14	12-14	13	09	04-27	20	09
03-09	24	16	08-01	08	45	12-24	12	35	05-07	20	53
03-19	24	42	08-11	09	11	**—1936—**			05-17	21	41
03-29	25	12	08-21	09	32	01-03	12	03	05-27	22	32
04-08	25	47	08-31	09	47	01-13	11	36	06-06	23	25
04-18	26	25	09-10	09	55	01-23	11	14	06-16	24	19
04-28	27	06	09-20	09	56℞	02-02	10	59	06-26	25	13
05-08	27	48	09-30	09	50	02-12	10	51	07-06	26	06
05-18	28	32	10-10	09	38	02-22	10	50D	07-16	26	58
05-28	29	16	10-20	09	19	03-03	10	58	07-26	27	47
06-07	30	00	10-30	08	55	03-13	11	12	08-05	28	33
06-17	00♊	42	11-09	08	26	03-23	11	34	08-15	29	15
06-27	01	22	11-19	07	54	04-02	12	02	08-25	29	51
07-07	01	59	11-29	07	20	04-12	12	35	09-04	00♋	22
07-17	02	32	12-09	06	45	04-22	13	14	09-14	00	46
07-27	03	02	12-19	06	13	05-02	13	57	09-24	01	02
08-06	03	26	12-29	05	42	05-12	14	43	10-04	01	12
08-16	03	45	**—1935—**			05-22	15	31	10-14	01	13℞
08-26	03♊	58	01-08	05♊	17℞	06-01	16♊	21	10-24	01♋	06℞

da-mo	°	'	da-mo	°	'	da-mo	°	'	da-mo	°	'
1937 11-03	00♋	51 Rx	03-18	04♋	08D	08-09	25♋	18	**—1942—**		
11-13	00	29	03-28	04	19	08-19	26	21	01-01	13♌	34 Rx
11-23	00	00	04-07	04	39	08-29	27	21	01-11	12	58
12-03	29♊	27	04-17	05	07	09-08	28	17	01-21	12	16
12-13	28	50	04-27	05	43	09-18	29	07	01-31	11	31
12-23	28	11	05-07	06	24	09-28	29	51	02-10	10	46
—1938—			05-17	07	12	10-08	00♌	28	02-20	10	03
01-02	27	33	05-27	08	04	10-18	00	57	03-02	09	25
01-12	26	57	06-06	09	00	10-28	01	18	03-12	08	53
01-22	26	26	06-16	09	59	11-07	01	28	03-22	08	30
02-01	25	59	06-26	11	00	11-17	01	29 Rx	04-01	08	16
02-11	25	40	07-06	12	02	11-27	01	20	04-11	08	13D
02-21	25	28	07-16	13	03	12-07	01	02	04-21	08	20
03-03	25	25	07-26	14	05	12-17	00	35	05-01	08	37
03-13	25	30D	08-05	15	04	12-27	00	01	05-11	09	05
03-23	25	43	08-15	16	00	**—1941—**			05-21	09	41
04-02	26	04	08-25	16	53	01-06	29♋	21	05-31	10	26
04-12	26	33	09-04	17	41	01-16	28	38	06-10	11	19
04-22	27	08	09-14	18	24	01-26	27	55	06-20	12	18
05-02	27	49	09-24	19	00	02-05	27	12	06-30	13	23
05-12	28	35	10-04	19	29	02-15	26	34	07-10	14	33
05-22	29	25	10-14	19	49	02-25	26	02	07-20	15	46
06-01	00♋	19	10-24	20	01	03-07	25	37	07-30	17	01
06-11	01	15	11-03	20	04 Rx	03-17	25	21	08-09	18	18
06-21	02	12	11-13	19	57	03-27	25	15	08-19	19	36
07-01	03	10	11-23	19	42	04-06	25	19D	08-29	20	54
07-11	04	07	12-03	19	18	04-16	25	32	09-08	22	09
07-21	05	03	12-13	18	47	04-26	25	55	09-18	23	22
07-31	05	57	12-23	18	11	05-06	26	27	09-28	24	32
08-10	06	48	**—1940—**			05-16	27	08	10-08	25	36
08-20	07	34	01-02	17	30	05-26	27	55	10-18	26	35
08-30	08	16	01-12	16	48	06-05	28	49	10-28	27	26
09-09	08	52	01-22	16	07	06-15	29	49	11-07	28	09
09-19	09	21	02-01	15	29	06-25	00♌	53	11-17	28	43
09-29	09	43	02-11	14	55	07-05	02	01	11-27	29	07
10-09	09	57	02-21	14	28	07-15	03	11	12-07	29	20
10-19	10	03	03-02	14	09	07-25	04	22	12-17	29	22 Rx
10-29	10	00 Rx	03-12	13	59	08-04	05	35	12-27	29	13
11-08	09	48	03-22	13	58D	08-14	06	46	**—1943—**		
11-18	09	29	04-01	14	06	08-24	07	57	01-06	28	53
11-28	09	02	04-11	14	24	09-03	09	05	01-16	28	24
12-08	08	29	04-21	14	50	09-13	10	09	01-26	27	46
12-18	07	52	05-01	15	25	09-23	11	09	02-05	27	04
12-28	07	12	05-11	16	06	10-03	12	03	02-15	26	17
—1939—			05-21	16	54	10-13	12	50	02-25	25	31
01-07	06	32	05-31	17	48	10-23	13	30	03-07	24	47
01-17	05	53	06-10	18	46	11-02	14	00	03-17	24	08
01-27	05	18	06-20	19	48	11-12	14	21	03-27	23	36
02-06	04	49	06-30	20	52	11-22	14	32	04-06	23	13
02-16	04	26	07-10	21	59	12-02	14	33 Rx	04-16	23	00
02-26	04	11	07-20	23	05	12-12	14	23	04-26	22	58D
03-08	04♋	05 Rx	07-30	24♋	12	12-22	14♌	03 Rx	05-06	23♌	06

190

Ephemeris, 1900–2050

da-mo	°	'	da-mo	°	'	da-mo	°	'	da-mo	°	'
1943 05-16	23♌	26	10-07	24♍	43	02-19	21♎	07℞	07-14	02♏	26
05-26	23	56	10-17	26	05	03-01	20	45	07-24	02	45
06-05	24	35	10-27	27	24	03-11	20	13	08-03	03	14
06-15	25	23	11-06	28	38	03-21	19	34	08-13	03	52
06-25	26	20	11-16	29	46	03-31	18	50	08-23	04	40
07-05	27	23	11-26	00♎	47	04-10	18	03	09-02	05	36
07-15	28	31	12-06	01	39	04-20	17	16	09-12	06	38
07-25	29	45	12-16	02	22	04-30	16	33	09-22	07	47
08-04	01♍	03	12-26	02	54	05-10	15	55	10-02	09	01
08-14	02	23	**—1945—**			05-20	15	26	10-12	10	19
08-24	03	45	01-05	03	15	05-30	15	05	10-22	11	39
09-03	05	08	01-15	03	24	06-09	14	55	11-01	13	01
09-13	06	30	01-25	03	21℞	06-19	14	57D	11-11	14	24
09-23	07	51	02-04	03	06	06-29	15	09	11-21	15	46
10-03	09	09	02-14	02	40	07-09	15	32	12-01	17	07
10-13	10	24	02-24	02	06	07-19	16	06	12-11	18	25
10-23	11	34	03-06	01	25	07-29	16	49	12-21	19	38
11-02	12	37	03-16	00	39	08-08	17	42	12-31	20	46
11-12	13	34	03-26	29♍	51	08-18	18	42	**—1948—**		
11-22	14	21	04-05	29	05	08-28	19	49	01-10	21	47
12-02	15	00	04-15	28	23	09-07	21	02	01-20	22	41
12-12	15	27	04-25	27	47	09-17	22	20	01-30	23	26
12-22	15	44	05-05	27	20	09-27	23	42	02-09	24	02
—1944—			05-15	27	03	10-07	25	06	02-19	24	26
01-01	15	49℞	05-25	26	57	10-17	26	32	02-29	24	40
01-11	15	42	06-04	27	03D	10-27	27	58	03-10	24	43℞
01-21	15	24	06-14	27	19	11-06	29	24	03-20	24	35
01-31	14	56	06-24	27	47	11-16	00♏	47	03-30	24	17
02-10	14	19	07-04	28	24	11-26	02	08	04-09	23	49
02-20	13	37	07-14	29	12	12-06	03	24	04-19	23	14
03-01	12	50	07-24	00♎	08	12-16	04	35	04-29	22	34
03-11	12	03	08-03	01	11	12-26	05	38	05-09	21	50
03-21	11	18	08-13	02	22	**—1947—**			05-19	21	05
03-31	10	37	08-23	03	37	01-05	06	34	05-29	20	22
04-10	10	04	09-02	04	58	01-15	07	21	06-08	19	43
04-20	09	39	09-12	06	21	01-25	07	58	06-18	19	11
04-30	09	25	09-22	07	47	02-04	08	23	06-28	18	46
05-10	09	22D	10-02	09	15	02-14	08	38	07-08	18	30
05-20	09	30	10-12	10	42	02-24	08	40℞	07-18	18	24
05-30	09	49	10-22	12	09	03-06	08	32	07-28	18	29D
06-09	10	19	11-01	13	33	03-16	08	12	08-07	18	44
06-19	10	59	11-11	14	54	03-26	07	43	08-17	19	09
06-29	11	48	11-21	16	11	04-05	07	06	08-27	19	43
07-09	12	46	12-01	17	21	04-15	06	24	09-06	20	26
07-19	13	50	12-11	18	25	04-25	05	38	09-16	21	17
07-29	15	01	12-21	19	20	05-05	04	52	09-26	22	15
08-08	16	17	12-31	20	06	05-15	04	09	10-06	23	19
08-18	17	37	**—1946—**			05-25	03	30	10-16	24	28
08-28	19	01	01-10	20	41	06-04	02	58	10-26	25	41
09-07	20	26	01-20	21	06	06-14	02	35	11-05	26	57
09-17	21	52	01-30	21	18	06-24	02	21	11-15	28	14
09-27	23♍	18	02-09	21♎	18℞	07-04	02♏	18D	11-25	29♏	32

da-mo	o	'	da-mo	o	'	da-mo	o	'	da-mo	o	'
1948 12-05	00♐	50	04-19	21♐	30℞	09-11	26♐	52	01-23	15♑	44
12-15	02	06	04-29	21	10	09-21	27	05	02-02	16	40
12-25	03	18	05-09	20	42	10-01	27	27	02-12	17	32
—1949—			05-19	20	08	10-11	27	57	02-22	18	21
01-04	04	27	05-29	19	29	10-21	28	34	03-04	19	04
01-14	05	31	06-08	18	48	10-31	29	17	03-14	19	42
01-24	06	28	06-18	18	07	11-10	00♑	07	03-24	20	13
02-03	07	17	06-28	17	27	11-20	01	01	04-03	20	37
02-13	07	58	07-08	16	51	11-30	01	59	04-13	20	53
02-23	08	30	07-18	16	21	12-10	03	00	04-23	21	01
03-05	08	52	07-28	15	58	12-20	04	02	05-03	21	02℞
03-15	09	04	08-07	15	43	12-30	05	05	05-13	20	54
03-25	09	05℞	08-17	15	37	**—1952—**			05-23	20	39
04-04	08	56	08-27	15	40D	01-09	06	07	06-02	20	17
04-14	08	37	09-06	15	52	01-19	07	08	06-12	19	49
04-24	08	10	09-16	16	13	01-29	08	07	06-22	19	16
05-04	07	36	09-26	16	43	02-08	09	02	07-02	18	41
05-14	06	56	10-06	17	20	02-18	09	52	07-12	18	04
05-24	06	14	10-16	18	05	02-28	10	36	07-22	17	28
06-03	05	31	10-26	18	57	03-09	11	14	08-01	16	54
06-13	04	49	11-05	19	53	03-19	11	45	08-11	16	23
06-23	04	11	11-15	20	54	03-29	12	08	08-21	15	57
07-03	03	39	11-25	21	58	04-08	12	23	08-31	15	38
07-13	03	15	12-05	23	05	04-18	12	29	09-10	15	25
07-23	02	59	12-15	24	12	04-28	12	27℞	09-20	15	20
08-02	02	52	12-25	25	20	05-08	12	16	09-30	15	22D
08-12	02	55D	**—1951—**			05-18	11	58	10-10	15	33
08-22	03	07	01-04	26	26	05-28	11	32	10-20	15	51
09-01	03	29	01-14	27	31	06-07	11	01	10-30	16	17
09-11	04	01	01-24	28	32	06-17	10	26	11-09	16	49
09-21	04	40	02-03	29	28	06-27	09	49	11-19	17	27
10-01	05	28	02-13	00♑	19	07-07	09	11	11-29	18	11
10-11	06	22	02-23	01	04	07-17	08	33	12-09	18	59
10-21	07	21	03-05	01	42	07-27	07	59	12-19	19	50
10-31	08	26	03-15	02	12	08-06	07	30	12-29	20	43
11-10	09	34	03-25	02	33	08-16	07	06	**—1954—**		
11-20	10	45	04-04	02	45	08-26	06	49	01-08	21	38
11-30	11	58	04-14	02	47℞	09-05	06	39	01-18	22	33
12-10	13	11	04-24	02	41	09-15	06	38D	01-28	23	28
12-20	14	23	05-04	02	27	09-25	06	45	02-07	24	21
12-30	15	33	05-14	02	04	10-05	07	01	02-17	25	11
—1950—			05-24	01	35	10-15	07	24	02-27	25	57
01-09	16	40	06-03	01	00	10-25	07	55	03-09	26	39
01-19	17	43	06-13	00	22	11-04	08	32	03-19	27	16
01-29	18	41	06-23	29♐	42	11-14	09	15	03-29	27	47
02-08	19	32	07-03	29	03	11-24	10	04	04-08	28	11
02-18	20	16	07-13	28	26	12-04	10	56	04-18	28	28
02-28	20	52	07-23	27	53	12-14	11	51	04-28	28	37
03-10	21	19	08-02	27	25	12-24	12	49	05-08	28	39℞
03-20	21	36	08-12	27	05	**—1953—**			05-18	28	34
03-30	21	44	08-22	26	52	01-03	13	48	05-28	28	21
04-09	21♐	42℞	09-01	26♐	48D	01-13	14♑	47	06-07	28♑	01℞

192

Ephemeris, 1900–2050

da-mo	°	'	da-mo	°	'	da-mo	°	'	da-mo	°	'
06-17	27♑	36℞	11-09	00♒	39	03-23	15♒	32	08-15	20♒	04℞
06-27	27	06	11-19	01	05	04-02	16	05	08-25	19	33
07-07	26	33	11-29	01	36	04-12	16	33	09-04	19	04
07-17	25	58	12-09	02	12	04-22	16	56	09-14	18	37
07-27	25	22	12-19	02	52	05-02	17	13	09-24	18	15
08-06	24	48	12-29	03	37	05-12	17	23	10-04	17	57
08-16	24	17	**—1956—**			05-22	17	26	10-14	17	45
08-26	23	50	01-08	04	24	06-01	17	24℞	10-24	17	39
09-05	23	29	01-18	05	12	06-11	17	14	11-03	17	40D
09-15	23	14	01-28	06	01	06-21	16	59	11-13	17	47
09-25	23	06	02-07	06	50	07-01	16	38	11-23	18	01
10-05	23	06D	02-17	07	38	07-11	16	13	12-03	18	20
10-15	23	13	02-27	08	24	07-21	15	44	12-13	18	45
10-25	23	28	03-08	09	07	07-31	15	13	12-23	19	15
11-04	23	49	03-18	09	46	08-10	14	41	**—1959—**		
11-14	24	17	03-28	10	21	08-20	14	09	01-02	19	50
11-24	24	52	04-07	10	50	08-30	13	39	01-12	20	28
12-04	25	31	04-17	11	13	09-09	13	13	01-22	21	08
12-14	26	15	04-27	11	30	09-19	12	50	02-01	21	50
12-24	27	02	05-07	11	41	09-29	12	32	02-11	22	33
—1955—			05-17	11	44℞	10-09	12	21	02-21	23	16
01-03	27	52	05-27	11	41	10-19	12	16	03-03	23	59
01-13	28	44	06-06	11	30	10-29	12	17D	03-13	24	39
01-23	29	36	06-16	11	14	11-08	12	25	03-23	25	18
02-02	00♒	27	06-26	10	52	11-18	12	40	04-02	25	52
02-12	01	18	07-06	10	26	11-28	13	01	04-12	26	23
02-22	02	05	07-16	09	56	12-08	13	27	04-22	26	50
03-04	02	50	07-26	09	24	12-18	13	59	05-02	27	11
03-14	03	31	08-05	08	51	12-28	14	35	05-12	27	26
03-24	04	07	08-15	08	18	**—1958—**			05-22	27	36
04-03	04	37	08-25	07	48	01-07	15	15	06-01	27	39
04-13	05	00	09-04	07	21	01-17	15	57	06-11	27	37℞
04-23	05	18	09-14	06	58	01-27	16	41	06-21	27	28
05-03	05	28	09-24	06	41	02-06	17	26	07-01	27	14
05-13	05	31℞	10-04	06	30	02-16	18	10	07-11	26	55
05-23	05	26	10-14	06	26	02-26	18	54	07-21	26	31
06-02	05	15	10-24	06	28D	03-08	19	37	07-31	26	04
06-12	04	57	11-03	06	38	03-18	20	16	08-10	25	35
06-22	04	34	11-13	06	54	03-28	20	52	08-20	25	04
07-02	04	06	11-23	07	17	04-07	21	24	08-30	24	34
07-12	03	34	12-03	07	46	04-17	21	52	09-09	24	05
07-22	03	01	12-13	08	19	04-27	22	14	09-19	23	39
08-01	02	27	12-23	08	57	05-07	22	30	09-29	23	17
08-11	01	53	**—1957—**			05-17	22	40	10-09	23	00
08-21	01	23	01-02	09	39	05-27	22	43	10-19	22	48
08-31	00	55	01-12	10	23	06-06	22	41℞	10-29	22	42
09-10	00	33	01-22	11	09	06-16	22	32	11-08	22	42D
09-20	00	17	02-01	11	56	06-26	22	17	11-18	22	48
09-30	00	07	02-11	12	43	07-06	21	57	11-28	23	01
10-10	00	05D	02-21	13	29	07-16	21	33	12-08	23	19
10-20	00	09	03-03	14	13	07-26	21	05	12-18	23	43
10-30	00♒	21	03-13	14♒	54	08-05	20♒	35℞	12-28	24♒	12

1954

da-mo	o	'	da-mo	o	'	da-mo	o	'	da-mo	o	'
—1960—			05-21	06✶	30	10-13	06✶	43℞	02-25	13✶	54
01-07	24≈	45	05-31	06	39	10-23	06	27	03-06	14	31
01-17	25	22	06-10	06	42℞	11-02	06	15	03-16	15	09
01-27	26	01	06-20	06	39	11-12	06	10	03-26	15	45
02-06	26	41	06-30	06	30	11-22	06	10D	04-05	16	20
02-16	27	23	07-10	06	16	12-02	06	15	04-15	16	53
02-26	28	05	07-20	05	58	12-12	06	27	04-25	17	22
03-07	28	45	07-30	05	35	12-22	06	44	05-05	17	48
03-17	29	25	08-09	05	09	**—1963—**			05-15	18	10
03-27	00✶	01	08-19	04	41	01-01	07	07	05-25	18	27
04-06	00	35	08-29	04	12	01-11	07	33	06-04	18	39
04-16	01	05	09-08	03	43	01-21	08	04	06-14	18	46
04-26	01	30	09-18	03	15	01-31	08	38	06-24	18	48℞
05-06	01	51	09-28	02	50	02-10	09	14	07-04	18	44
05-16	02	05	10-08	02	29	02-20	09	51	07-14	18	34
05-26	02	15	10-18	02	12	03-02	10	30	07-24	18	20
06-05	02	18	10-28	02	00	03-12	11	08	08-03	18	01
06-15	02	15℞	11-07	01	54	03-22	11	45	08-13	17	39
06-25	02	07	11-17	01	54D	04-01	12	21	08-23	17	14
07-05	01	53	11-27	02	00	04-11	12	55	09-02	16	46
07-15	01	34	12-07	02	11	04-21	13	25	09-12	16	19
07-25	01	11	12-17	02	29	05-01	13	52	09-22	15	51
08-04	00	44	12-27	02	52	05-11	14	15	10-02	15	25
08-14	00	16	**—1962—**			05-21	14	33	10-12	15	01
08-24	29≈	46	01-06	03	19	05-31	14	45	10-22	14	41
09-03	29	16	01-16	03	50	06-10	14	53	11-01	14	26
09-13	28	48	01-26	04	24	06-20	14	55℞	11-11	14	15
09-23	28	23	02-05	05	01	06-30	14	51	11-21	14	10
10-03	28	01	02-15	05	40	07-10	14	42	12-01	14	11D
10-13	27	44	02-25	06	19	07-20	14	28	12-11	14	17
10-23	27	32	03-07	06	58	07-30	14	09	12-21	14	29
11-02	27	25	03-17	07	37	08-09	13	47	12-31	14	46
11-12	27	25D	03-27	08	13	08-19	13	22	**—1965—**		
11-22	27	31	04-06	08	48	08-29	12	54	01-10	15	08
12-02	27	44	04-16	09	19	09-08	12	26	01-20	15	34
12-12	28	01	04-26	09	47	09-18	11	58	01-30	16	04
12-22	28	25	05-06	10	11	09-28	11	32	02-09	16	37
—1961—			05-16	10	29	10-08	11	08	02-19	17	12
01-01	28	52	05-26	10	43	10-18	10	47	03-01	17	48
01-11	29	24	06-05	10	51	10-28	10	31	03-11	18	25
01-21	30	00	06-15	10	53℞	11-07	10	20	03-21	19	02
01-31	00✶	37	06-25	10	50	11-17	10	14	03-31	19	38
02-10	01	17	07-05	10	41	11-27	10	15D	04-10	20	12
02-20	01	57	07-15	10	27	12-07	10	21	04-20	20	44
03-02	02	38	07-25	10	09	12-17	10	32	04-30	21	13
03-12	03	17	08-04	09	46	12-27	10	50	05-10	21	38
03-22	03	55	08-14	09	21	**—1964—**			05-20	21	59
04-01	04	31	08-24	08	53	01-06	11	12	05-30	22	15
04-11	05	03	09-03	08	24	01-16	11	38	06-09	22	26
04-21	05	32	09-13	07	56	01-26	12	08	06-19	22	33
05-01	05	56	09-23	07	29	02-05	12	41	06-29	22	33℞
05-11	06✶	16	10-03	07✶	04℞	02-15	13✶	17	07-09	22✶	29℞

da-mo	°	'	da-mo	°	'	da-mo	°	'	da-mo	°	'
1965 07-19	22♓	19℞	12-11	21♓	42D	04-24	01♈	16	09-16	05♈	08℞
07-29	22	05	12-21	21	49	05-04	01	46	09-26	04	41
08-08	21	46	12-31	22	01	05-14	02	12	10-06	04	14
08-18	21	23	**—1967—**			05-24	02	35	10-16	03	48
08-28	20	58	01-10	22	19	06-03	02	54	10-26	03	23
09-07	20	31	01-20	22	41	06-13	03	08	11-05	03	02
09-17	20	03	01-30	23	08	06-23	03	18	11-15	02	45
09-27	19	36	02-09	23	37	07-03	03	22	11-25	02	32
10-07	19	11	02-19	24	10	07-13	03	21℞	12-05	02	25
10-17	18	48	03-01	24	44	07-23	03	15	12-15	02	22 D
10-27	18	28	03-11	25	19	08-02	03	04	12-25	02	26
11-06	18	13	03-21	25	55	08-12	02	48	**—1970—**		
11-16	18	03	03-31	26	31	08-22	02	28	01-04	02	34
11-26	17	58	04-10	27	06	09-01	02	05	01-14	02	48
12-06	17	59 D	04-20	27	39	09-11	01	40	01-24	03	07
12-16	18	06	04-30	28	09	09-21	01	13	02-03	03	30
12-26	18	18	05-10	28	36	10-01	00	46	02-13	03	57
—1966—			05-20	29	00	10-11	00	20	02-23	04	28
01-05	18	35	05-30	29	19	10-21	29♓	55	03-05	05	00
01-15	18	57	06-09	29	34	10-31	29	34	03-15	05	34
01-25	19	24	06-19	29	44	11-10	29	16	03-25	06	09
02-04	19	53	06-29	29	49	11-20	29	02	04-04	06	44
02-14	20	26	07-09	29	49℞	11-30	28	54	04-14	07	19
02-24	21	01	07-19	29	43	12-10	28	51	04-24	07	52
03-06	21	36	07-29	29	33	12-20	28	54 D	05-04	08	24
03-16	22	13	08-08	29	17	12-30	29	02	05-14	08	53
03-26	22	49	08-18	28	58	**—1969—**			05-24	09	18
04-05	23	24	08-28	28	35	01-09	29	15	06-03	09	40
04-15	23	58	09-07	28	10	01-19	29	34	06-13	09	58
04-25	24	29	09-17	27	43	01-29	29	57	06-23	10	11
05-05	24	57	09-27	27	16	02-08	00♈	23	07-03	10	19
05-15	25	21	10-07	26	49	02-18	00	53	07-13	10	22
05-25	25	41	10-17	26	24	02-28	01	25	07-23	10	20℞
06-04	25	57	10-27	26	02	03-10	02	00	08-02	10	13
06-14	26	08	11-06	25	44	03-20	02	35	08-12	10	00
06-24	26	13	11-16	25	30	03-30	03	10	08-22	09	44
07-04	26	13℞	11-26	25	21	04-09	03	45	09-01	09	23
07-14	26	08	12-06	25	18	04-19	04	19	09-11	09	00
07-24	25	58	12-16	25	20 D	04-29	04	51	09-21	08	34
08-03	25	43	12-26	25	27	05-09	05	20	10-01	08	07
08-13	25	24	**—1968—**			05-19	05	46	10-11	07	40
08-23	25	02	01-05	25	40	05-29	06	08	10-21	07	14
09-02	24	36	01-15	25	58	06-08	06	27	10-31	06	50
09-12	24	09	01-25	26	21	06-18	06	40	11-10	06	30
09-22	23	42	02-04	26	47	06-28	06	49	11-20	06	13
10-02	23	15	02-14	27	17	07-08	06	53	11-30	06	01
10-12	22	50	02-24	27	49	07-18	06	51℞	12-10	05	54
10-22	22	27	03-05	28	23	07-28	06	44	12-20	05	52D
11-01	22	08	03-15	28	59	08-07	06	33	12-30	05	56
11-11	21	54	03-25	29	34	08-17	06	16	**—1971—**		
11-21	21	44	04-04	00♈	09	08-27	05	56	01-09	06	06
12-01	21♓	40℞	04-14	00♈	44	09-06	05♈	33℞	01-19	06♈	20

195

da-mo	°	'	da-mo	°	'	da-mo	°	'	da-mo	°	'
1971 01-29	06♈	40	06-22	17♈	01	11-14	17♈	13Rx	03-29	22♈	59
02-08	07	03	07-02	17	13	11-24	16	54	04-08	23	34
02-18	07	31	07-12	17	20	12-04	16	39	04-18	24	10
02-28	08	01	07-22	17	22Rx	12-14	16	28	04-28	24	46
03-10	08	34	08-01	17	18	12-24	16	23	05-08	25	21
03-20	09	08	08-11	17	10	—1974—			05-18	25	54
03-30	09	43	08-21	16	57	01-03	16	24D	05-28	26	25
04-09	10	18	08-31	16	39	01-13	16	30	06-07	26	52
04-19	10	53	09-10	16	18	01-23	16	42	06-17	27	17
04-29	11	26	09-20	15	54	02-02	16	58	06-27	27	37
05-09	11	57	09-30	15	27	02-12	17	20	07-07	27	53
05-19	12	25	10-10	15	00	02-22	17	45	07-17	28	03
05-29	12	51	10-20	14	33	03-04	18	14	07-27	28	09
06-08	13	12	10-30	14	08	03-14	18	45	08-06	28	09Rx
06-18	13	29	11-09	13	44	03-24	19	19	08-16	28	04
06-28	13	42	11-19	13	24	04-03	19	54	08-26	27	54
07-08	13	49	11-29	13	09	04-13	20	30	09-05	27	39
07-18	13	51Rx	12-09	12	58	04-23	21	05	09-15	27	20
07-28	13	49	12-19	12	52	05-03	21	40	09-25	26	57
08-07	13	41	12-29	12	52D	05-13	22	12	10-05	26	32
08-17	13	28	—1973—			05-23	22	43	10-15	26	04
08-27	13	11	01-08	12	57	06-02	23	11	10-25	25	37
09-06	12	50	01-18	13	08	06-12	23	35	11-04	25	09
09-16	12	26	01-28	13	24	06-22	23	56	11-14	24	44
09-26	12	00	02-07	13	45	07-02	24	12	11-24	24	21
10-06	11	33	02-17	14	10	07-12	24	23	12-04	24	02
10-16	11	06	02-27	14	38	07-22	24	29	12-14	23	48
10-26	10	40	03-09	15	09	08-01	24	30Rx	12-24	23	39
11-05	10	17	03-19	15	42	08-11	24	25	—1976—		
11-15	09	57	03-29	16	17	08-21	24	16	01-03	23	35
11-25	09	40	04-08	16	52	08-31	24	01	01-13	23	37D
12-05	09	29	04-18	17	27	09-10	23	43	01-23	23	45
12-15	09	22	04-28	18	02	09-20	23	20	02-02	23	58
12-25	09	22D	05-08	18	35	09-30	22	55	02-12	24	16
—1972—			05-18	19	05	10-10	22	28	02-22	24	39
01-04	09	26	05-28	19	33	10-20	22	01	03-03	25	06
01-14	09	36	06-07	19	58	10-30	21	34	03-13	25	36
01-24	09	52	06-17	20	19	11-09	21	08	03-23	26	09
02-03	10	12	06-27	20	35	11-19	20	45	04-02	26	43
02-13	10	36	07-07	20	46	11-29	20	26	04-12	27	19
02-23	11	04	07-17	20	53	12-09	20	11	04-22	27	55
03-04	11	34	07-27	20	54Rx	12-19	20	02	05-02	28	31
03-14	12	07	08-06	20	50	12-29	19	57	05-12	29	06
03-24	12	42	08-16	20	41	—1975—			05-22	29	40
04-03	13	17	08-26	20	27	01-08	19	59D	06-01	00♉	11
04-13	13	52	09-05	20	09	01-18	20	06	06-11	00	38
04-23	14	26	09-15	19	48	01-28	20	18	06-21	01	03
05-03	14	59	09-25	19	23	02-07	20	35	07-01	01	23
05-13	15	30	10-05	18	56	02-17	20	57	07-11	01	38
05-23	15	59	10-15	18	29	02-27	21	23	07-21	01	49
06-02	16	23	10-25	18	02	03-09	21	53	07-31	01	54
06-12	16♈	44	11-04	17♈	36Rx	03-19	22♈	25	08-10	01♉	54Rx

196

Ephemeris, 1900–2050

da-mo	o	'	da-mo	o	'	da-mo	o	'	da-mo	o	'
1976 08-20	01♉	49℞	**—1978—**			05-17	10♉	26	10-08	17♉	17℞
08-30	01	38	01-02	01♉	09℞	05-27	11	03	10-18	16	51
09-09	01	23	01-12	01	06D	06-06	11	37	10-28	16	23
09-19	01	03	01-22	01	10	06-16	12	10	11-07	15	53
09-29	00	40	02-01	01	19	06-26	12	38	11-17	15	23
10-09	00	14	02-11	01	34	07-06	13	03	11-27	14	54
10-19	29♈	46	02-21	01	54	07-16	13	24	12-07	14	27
10-29	29	18	03-03	02	18	07-26	13	40	12-17	14	04
11-08	28	50	03-13	02	46	08-05	13	50	12-27	13	46
11-18	28	25	03-23	03	18	08-15	13	55	**—1981—**		
11-28	28	02	04-02	03	52	08-25	13	55℞	01-06	13	33
12-08	27	43	04-12	04	28	09-04	13	48	01-16	13	25
12-18	27	29	04-22	05	05	09-14	13	36	01-26	13	24D
12-28	27	21	05-02	05	43	09-24	13	19	02-05	13	30
—1977—			05-12	06	20	10-04	12	58	02-15	13	41
01-07	27	18	05-22	06	56	10-14	12	32	02-25	13	58
01-17	27	20D	06-01	07	30	10-24	12	05	03-07	14	21
01-27	27	29	06-11	08	02	11-03	11	35	03-17	14	48
02-06	27	43	06-21	08	30	11-13	11	06	03-27	15	19
02-16	28	02	07-01	08	55	11-23	10	37	04-06	15	54
02-26	28	25	07-11	09	15	12-03	10	11	04-16	16	31
03-08	28	53	07-21	09	31	12-13	09	48	04-26	17	10
03-18	29	24	07-31	09	41	12-23	09	30	05-06	17	50
03-28	29	57	08-10	09	46	**—1980—**			05-16	18	30
04-07	00♉	33	08-20	09	45℞	01-02	09	17	05-26	19	10
04-17	01	09	08-30	09	39	01-12	09	09	06-05	19	49
04-27	01	46	09-09	09	28	01-22	09	08D	06-15	20	25
05-07	02	22	09-19	09	11	02-01	09	13	06-25	20	59
05-17	02	58	09-29	08	50	02-11	09	23	07-05	21	30
05-27	03	31	10-09	08	25	02-21	09	40	07-15	21	56
06-06	04	03	10-19	07	58	03-02	10	01	07-25	22	18
06-16	04	31	10-29	07	30	03-12	10	27	08-04	22	35
06-26	04	55	11-08	07	01	03-22	10	58	08-14	22	46
07-06	05	15	11-18	06	33	04-01	11	31	08-24	22	51
07-16	05	31	11-28	06	07	04-11	12	07	09-03	22	51℞
07-26	05	41	12-08	05	44	04-21	12	45	09-13	22	44
08-05	05	46	12-18	05	26	05-01	13	24	09-23	22	31
08-15	05	46℞	12-28	05	12	05-11	14	03	10-03	22	14
08-25	05	40	**—1979—**			05-21	14	42	10-13	21	51
09-04	05	29	01-07	05	05	05-31	15	20	10-23	21	25
09-14	05	13	01-17	05	03D	06-10	15	55	11-02	20	55
09-24	04	52	01-27	05	07	06-20	16	28	11-12	20	25
10-04	04	28	02-06	05	17	06-30	16	58	11-22	19	54
10-14	04	02	02-16	05	32	07-10	17	23	12-02	19	24
10-24	03	34	02-26	05	53	07-20	17	44	12-12	18	57
11-03	03	05	03-08	06	18	07-30	18	00	12-22	18	34
11-13	02	37	03-18	06	47	08-09	18	11	**—1982—**		
11-23	02	12	03-28	07	20	08-19	18	16	01-01	18	15
12-03	01	49	04-07	07	55	08-29	18	15℞	01-11	18	02
12-13	01	31	04-17	08	32	09-08	18	09	01-21	17	55
12-23	01♉	17℞	04-27	09	10	09-18	17	57	01-31	17	54D
			05-07	09♉	48	09-28	17♉	39℞	02-10	18♉	00

197

1982

da-mo	°	'	da-mo	°	'	da-mo	°	'	da-mo	°	'
02-20	18♉	12	07-15	01♊	23	12-06	05♊	27℞	04-20	11♊	32
03-02	18	30	07-25	01	52	12-16	04	55	04-30	12	13
03-12	18	53	08-04	02	16	12-26	04	25	05-10	12	58
03-22	19	22	08-14	02	35	—1985—			05-20	13	45
04-01	19	54	08-24	02	48	01-05	03	59	05-30	14	34
04-11	20	30	09-03	02	55	01-15	03	39	06-09	15	24
04-21	21	08	09-13	02	55℞	01-25	03	24	06-19	16	13
05-01	21	48	09-23	02	49	02-04	03	17	06-29	17	01
05-11	22	30	10-03	02	37	02-14	03	16D	07-09	17	48
05-21	23	11	10-13	02	19	02-24	03	23	07-19	18	32
05-31	23	53	10-23	01	55	03-06	03	36	07-29	19	13
06-10	24	32	11-02	01	28	03-16	03	56	08-08	19	49
06-20	25	10	11-12	00	57	03-26	04	22	08-18	20	20
06-30	25	45	11-22	00	25	04-05	04	54	08-28	20	46
07-10	26	17	12-02	29♉	52	04-15	05	30	09-07	21	05
07-20	26	45	12-12	29	21	04-25	06	09	09-17	21	17
07-30	27	08	12-22	28	52	05-05	06	52	09-27	21	23
08-09	27	25	—1984—			05-15	07	38	10-07	21	20℞
08-19	27	37	01-01	28	27	05-25	08	24	10-17	21	11
08-29	27	43	01-11	28	08	06-04	09	11	10-27	20	54
09-08	27	43℞	01-21	27	54	06-14	09	58	11-06	20	31
09-18	27	36	01-31	27	47	06-24	10	44	11-16	20	03
09-28	27	24	02-10	27	46D	07-04	11	27	11-26	19	30
10-08	27	06	02-20	27	53	07-14	12	09	12-06	18	55
10-18	26	43	03-01	28	06	07-24	12	46	12-16	18	18
10-28	26	16	03-11	28	25	08-03	13	19	12-26	17	43
11-07	25	46	03-21	28	51	08-13	13	48	—1987—		
11-17	25	14	03-31	29	21	08-23	14	10	01-05	17	10
11-27	24	42	04-10	29	56	09-02	14	27	01-15	16	41
12-07	24	12	04-20	00♊	34	09-12	14	37	01-25	16	18
12-17	23	44	04-30	01	15	09-22	14	40℞	02-04	16	01
12-27	23	20	05-10	01	59	10-02	14	36	02-14	15	51
—1983—			05-20	02	43	10-12	14	25	02-24	15	49D
01-06	23	01	05-30	03	28	10-22	14	07	03-06	15	55
01-16	22	48	06-09	04	13	11-01	13	43	03-16	16	08
01-26	22	41	06-19	04	56	11-11	13	15	03-26	16	29
02-05	22	41D	06-29	05	38	11-21	12	43	04-05	16	56
02-15	22	47	07-09	06	16	12-01	12	09	04-15	17	30
02-25	22	59	07-19	06	51	12-11	11	34	04-25	18	08
03-07	23	18	07-29	07	22	12-21	11	00	05-05	18	51
03-17	23	42	08-08	07	48	12-31	10	29	05-15	19	38
03-27	24	12	08-18	08	09	—1986—			05-25	20	28
04-06	24	45	08-28	08	23	01-10	10	01	06-04	21	19
04-16	25	22	09-07	08	31	01-20	09	40	06-14	22	11
04-26	26	02	09-17	08	33℞	01-30	09	24	06-24	23	04
05-06	26	44	09-27	08	27	02-09	09	16	07-04	23	55
05-16	27	26	10-07	08	15	02-19	09	15D	07-14	24	45
05-26	28	10	10-17	07	57	03-01	09	21	07-24	25	33
06-05	28	52	10-27	07	34	03-11	09	35	08-03	26	17
06-15	29	34	11-06	07	06	03-21	09	55	08-13	26	57
06-25	00♊	13	11-16	06	34	03-31	10	22	08-23	27	32
07-05	00♊	50	11-26	06♊	01℞	04-10	10♊	54	09-02	28♊	02

Ephemeris, 1900–2050

da-mo	°	'	da-mo	°	'	da-mo	°	'	da-mo	°	'
1987											
09-12	28Ⅱ	24	01-24	02♋	28℞	06-18	16♋	19	11-10	09♌	29
09-22	28	40	02-03	02	00	06-28	17	21	11-20	09	36
10-02	28	48	02-13	01	38	07-08	18	25	11-30	09	33℞
10-12	28	49℞	02-23	01	24	07-18	19	30	12-10	09	20
10-22	28	42	03-05	01	18	07-28	20	34	12-20	08	57
11-01	28	27	03-15	01	21D	08-07	21	37	12-30	08	26
11-11	28	05	03-25	01	32	08-17	22	37	**—1992—**		
11-21	27	37	04-04	01	52	08-27	23	34	01-09	07	49
12-01	27	04	04-14	02	19	09-06	24	26	01-19	07	07
12-11	26	28	04-24	02	53	09-16	25	14	01-29	06	22
12-21	25	50	05-04	03	34	09-26	25	55	02-08	05	38
12-31	25	13	05-14	04	20	10-06	26	29	02-18	04	57
—1988—			05-24	05	11	10-16	26	55	02-28	04	21
01-10	24	38	06-03	06	05	10-26	27	12	03-09	03	51
01-20	24	06	06-13	07	02	11-05	27	19	03-19	03	31
01-30	23	41	06-23	08	01	11-15	27	18℞	03-29	03	20
02-09	23	22	07-03	09	01	11-25	27	07	04-08	03	18D
02-19	23	10	07-13	10	01	12-05	26	47	04-18	03	28
02-29	23	07D	07-23	10	59	12-15	26	18	04-28	03	47
03-10	23	11	08-02	11	56	12-25	25	44	05-08	04	16
03-20	23	24	08-12	12	50	**—1991—**			05-18	04	53
03-30	23	45	08-22	13	41	01-04	25	04	05-28	05	39
04-09	24	12	09-01	14	26	01-14	24	22	06-07	06	31
04-19	24	46	09-11	15	06	01-24	23	39	06-17	07	30
04-29	25	26	09-21	15	40	02-03	22	58	06-27	08	34
05-09	26	11	10-01	16	06	02-13	22	22	07-07	09	43
05-19	27	00	10-11	16	25	02-23	21	51	07-17	10	54
05-29	27	51	10-21	16	34	03-05	21	28	07-27	12	08
06-08	28	45	10-31	16	35℞	03-15	21	14	08-06	13	23
06-18	29	41	11-10	16	27	03-25	21	09D	08-16	14	38
06-28	00♋	37	11-20	16	11	04-04	21	14	08-26	15	52
07-08	01	32	11-30	15	46	04-14	21	29	09-05	17	05
07-18	02	26	12-10	15	15	04-24	21	52	09-15	18	14
07-28	03	18	12-20	14	39	05-04	22	25	09-25	19	20
08-07	04	07	12-30	13	59	05-14	23	05	10-05	20	20
08-17	04	52	**—1990—**			05-24	23	52	10-15	21	14
08-27	05	31	01-09	13	18	06-03	24	45	10-25	22	01
09-06	06	05	01-19	12	38	06-13	25	43	11-04	22	39
09-16	06	33	01-29	12	00	06-23	26	46	11-14	23	08
09-26	06	53	02-08	11	28	07-03	27	52	11-24	23	27
10-06	07	06	02-18	11	03	07-13	29	00	12-04	23	35
10-16	07	10	02-28	10	45	07-23	00♌	09	12-14	23	32℞
10-26	07	06℞	03-10	10	35	08-02	01	19	12-24	23	19
11-05	06	54	03-20	10	35D	08-12	02	28	**—1993—**		
11-15	06	34	03-30	10	44	08-22	03	35	01-03	22	55
11-25	06	07	04-09	11	02	09-01	04	40	01-13	22	23
12-05	05	35	04-19	11	28	09-11	05	40	01-23	21	44
12-15	04	58	04-29	12	02	09-21	06	36	02-02	21	00
12-25	04	19	05-09	12	43	10-01	07	26	02-12	20	14
—1989—			05-19	13	30	10-11	08	10	02-22	19	29
01-04	03	40	05-29	14	22	10-21	08	45	03-04	18	47
01-14	03♋	02℞	06-08	15♋	19	10-31	09♌	12	03-14	18♌	10℞

199

da-mo	o	'	da-mo	o	'	da-mo	o	'	da-mo	o	'
1993 03-24	17♌	41 Rx	08-16	11♍	33	**—1996—**			05-22	26♎	36 Rx
04-03	17	22	08-26	12	56	01-08	13♎	55	06-01	26	08
04-13	17	12	09-05	14	21	01-18	14	14	06-11	25	49
04-23	17	13D	09-15	15	46	01-28	14	21	06-21	25	41
05-03	17	25	09-25	17	10	02-07	14	16 Rx	07-01	25	43D
05-13	17	47	10-05	18	32	02-17	13	59	07-11	25	57
05-23	18	20	10-15	19	52	02-27	13	32	07-21	26	21
06-02	19	01	10-25	21	08	03-08	12	56	07-31	26	56
06-12	19	51	11-04	22	18	03-18	12	14	08-10	27	40
06-22	20	48	11-14	23	22	03-28	11	28	08-20	28	33
07-02	21	52	11-24	24	18	04-07	10	40	08-30	29	33
07-12	23	00	12-04	25	05	04-17	09	55	09-09	00♏	40
07-22	24	14	12-14	25	42	04-27	09	14	09-19	01	53
08-01	25	30	12-24	26	09	05-07	08	40	09-29	03	10
08-11	26	49	**—1995—**			05-17	08	14	10-09	04	31
08-21	28	10	01-03	26	23	05-27	07	59	10-19	05	54
08-31	29	30	01-13	26	26 Rx	06-06	07	55D	10-29	07	18
09-10	00♍	50	01-23	26	17	06-16	08	02	11-08	08	43
09-20	02	08	02-02	25	57	06-26	08	20	11-18	10	06
09-30	03	22	02-12	25	27	07-06	08	49	11-28	11	27
10-10	04	33	02-22	24	49	07-16	09	28	12-08	12	45
10-20	05	39	03-04	24	05	07-26	10	17	12-18	13	58
10-30	06	37	03-14	23	18	08-05	11	14	12-28	15	06
11-09	07	29	03-24	22	31	08-15	12	18	**—1998—**		
11-19	08	11	04-03	21	46	08-25	13	29	01-07	16	06
11-29	08	44	04-13	21	07	09-04	14	46	01-17	16	58
12-09	09	06	04-23	20	35	09-14	16	06	01-27	17	41
12-19	09	17	05-03	20	13	09-24	17	30	02-06	18	14
12-29	09	16 Rx	05-13	20	01	10-04	18	56	02-16	18	35
—1994—			05-23	20	00D	10-14	20	24	02-26	18	46
01-08	09	04	06-02	20	11	10-24	21	51	03-08	18	45 Rx
01-18	08	41	06-12	20	33	11-03	23	16	03-18	18	33
01-28	08	10	06-22	21	06	11-13	24	40	03-28	18	11
02-07	07	30	07-02	21	48	11-23	26	00	04-07	17	40
02-17	06	46	07-12	22	40	12-03	27	14	04-17	17	02
02-27	05	59	07-22	23	39	12-13	28	23	04-27	16	19
03-09	05	12	08-01	24	46	12-23	29	25	05-07	15	34
03-19	04	29	08-11	25	59	**—1997—**			05-17	14	49
03-29	03	51	08-21	27	17	01-02	00♏	18	05-27	14	06
04-08	03	22	08-31	28	39	01-12	01	01	06-06	13	29
04-18	03	02	09-10	00♎	03	01-22	01	34	06-16	12	59
04-28	02	52	09-20	01	30	02-01	01	55	06-26	12	38
05-08	02	53D	09-30	02	57	02-11	02	05	07-06	12	27
05-18	03	06	10-10	04	24	02-21	02	02 Rx	07-16	12	26D
05-28	03	29	10-20	05	50	03-03	01	49	07-26	12	35
06-07	04	03	10-30	07	13	03-13	01	25	08-05	12	55
06-17	04	46	11-09	08	32	03-23	00	52	08-15	13	25
06-27	05	38	11-19	09	46	04-02	00	12	08-25	14	04
07-07	06	38	11-29	10	53	04-12	29♎	27	09-04	14	52
07-17	07	44	12-09	11	53	04-22	28	40	09-14	15	47
07-27	08	56	12-19	12	44	05-02	27	55	09-24	16	50
08-06	10♍	13	12-29	13♎	25	05-12	27♎	12 Rx	10-04	17♏	58

Ephemeris, 1900–2050

da-mo	°	′	da-mo	°	′	da-mo	°	′	da-mo	°	′
1998 10-14	19♏	10	02-26	16♐	26	07-20	23♐	50℞	12-12	08♑	45
10-24	20	26	03-07	16	52	07-30	23	24	12-22	09	45
11-03	21	45	03-17	17	08	08-09	23	05	—**2003**—		
11-13	23	05	03-27	17	14	08-19	22	54	01-01	10	45
11-23	24	25	04-06	17	10℞	08-29	22	52D	01-11	11	46
12-03	25	45	04-16	16	56	09-08	22	58	01-21	12	45
12-13	27	02	04-26	16	34	09-18	23	14	01-31	13	42
12-23	28	15	05-06	16	04	09-28	23	38	02-10	14	36
—**1999**—			05-16	15	28	10-08	24	11	02-20	15	25
01-02	29	25	05-26	14	48	10-18	24	50	03-02	16	09
01-12	00♐	28	06-05	14	05	10-28	25	36	03-12	16	48
01-22	01	25	06-15	13	23	11-07	26	28	03-22	17	19
02-01	02	14	06-25	12	44	11-17	27	25	04-01	17	44
02-11	02	53	07-05	12	09	11-27	28	25	04-11	18	00
02-21	03	24	07-15	11	40	12-07	29	28	04-21	18	08
03-03	03	43	07-25	11	19	12-17	00♑	33	05-01	18	08℞
03-13	03	52	08-04	11	06	12-27	01	38	05-11	17	59
03-23	03	51℞	08-14	11	03D	—**2002**—			05-21	17	43
04-02	03	39	08-24	11	09	01-06	02	42	05-31	17	20
04-12	03	17	09-03	11	24	01-16	03	44	06-10	16	52
04-22	02	47	09-13	11	49	01-26	04	44	06-20	16	19
05-02	02	10	09-23	12	22	02-05	05	40	06-30	15	43
05-12	01	29	10-03	13	03	02-15	06	31	07-10	15	05
05-22	00	45	10-13	13	51	02-25	07	16	07-20	14	28
06-01	00	02	10-23	14	45	03-07	07	55	07-30	13	54
06-11	29♏	20	11-02	15	45	03-17	08	26	08-09	13	23
06-21	28	44	11-12	16	48	03-27	08	49	08-19	12	57
07-01	28	14	11-22	17	55	04-06	09	03	08-29	12	38
07-11	27	52	12-02	19	04	04-16	09	09	09-08	12	26
07-21	27	39	12-12	20	14	04-26	09	06℞	09-18	12	22
07-31	27	36D	12-22	21	24	05-06	08	54	09-28	12	26D
08-10	27	42	—**2001**—			05-16	08	34	10-08	12	38
08-20	27	59	01-01	22	32	05-26	08	08	10-18	12	57
08-30	28	26	01-11	23	38	06-05	07	36	10-28	13	25
09-09	29	01	01-21	24	40	06-15	07	00	11-07	13	58
09-19	29	45	01-31	25	38	06-25	06	21	11-17	14	38
09-29	00♐	36	02-10	26	29	07-05	05	42	11-27	15	23
10-09	01	34	02-20	27	15	07-15	05	05	12-07	16	13
10-19	02	37	03-02	27	52	07-25	04	31	12-17	17	05
10-29	03	45	03-12	28	22	08-04	04	01	12-27	18	00
11-08	04	56	03-22	28	42	08-14	03	38	—**2004**—		
11-18	06	10	04-01	28	53	08-24	03	22	01-06	18	57
11-28	07	25	04-11	28	55℞	09-03	03	14	01-16	19	53
12-08	08	40	04-21	28	47	09-13	03	15D	01-26	20	49
12-18	09	54	05-01	28	31	09-23	03	23	02-05	21	43
12-28	11	06	05-11	28	07	10-03	03	41	02-15	22	35
—**2000**—			05-21	27	36	10-13	04	06	02-25	23	22
01-07	12	14	05-31	27	00	10-23	04	39	03-06	24	05
01-17	13	18	06-10	26	20	11-02	05	18	03-16	24	43
01-27	14	16	06-20	25	40	11-12	06	03	03-26	25	15
02-06	15	07	06-30	25	00	11-22	06	54	04-05	25	39
02-16	15♐	51	07-10	24♐	23℞	12-02	07♑	48	04-15	25♑	56

da-mo	°	'	da-mo	°	'	da-mo	°	'	da-mo	°	'
2004 04-25	26vs	06	09-17	28vs	00Rx	01-30	10≈	02	06-23	20≈	44Rx
05-05	26	08Rx	09-27	27	51	02-09	10	50	07-03	20	24
05-15	26	02	10-07	27	48D	02-19	11	37	07-13	19	59
05-25	25	48	10-17	27	53	03-01	12	22	07-23	19	31
06-04	25	28	10-27	28	06	03-11	13	04	08-02	19	01
06-14	25	02	11-06	28	25	03-21	13	42	08-12	18	30
06-24	24	32	11-16	28	51	03-31	14	17	08-22	17	58
07-04	23	58	11-26	29	23	04-10	14	46	09-01	17	29
07-14	23	22	12-06	30	00	04-20	15	09	09-11	17	02
07-24	22	46	12-16	00≈	41	04-30	15	26	09-21	16	39
08-03	22	12	12-26	01	27	05-10	15	37	10-01	16	21
08-13	21	41	**—2006—**			05-20	15	41	10-11	16	09
08-23	21	14	01-05	02	15	05-30	15	39Rx	10-21	16	03
09-02	20	53	01-15	03	04	06-09	15	30	10-31	16	03D
09-12	20	38	01-25	03	55	06-19	15	14	11-10	16	10
09-22	20	31	02-04	04	45	06-29	14	53	11-20	16	24
10-02	20	31D	02-14	05	34	07-09	14	28	11-30	16	43
10-12	20	39	02-24	06	21	07-19	13	59	12-10	17	09
10-22	20	55	03-06	07	05	07-29	13	28	12-20	17	39
11-01	21	17	03-16	07	45	08-08	12	55	12-30	18	14
11-11	21	47	03-26	08	20	08-18	12	23	**—2009—**		
11-21	22	22	04-05	08	50	08-28	11	53	01-09	18	52
12-01	23	03	04-15	09	14	09-07	11	26	01-19	19	33
12-11	23	48	04-25	09	32	09-17	11	03	01-29	20	16
12-21	24	36	05-05	09	42	09-27	10	45	02-08	21	00
12-31	25	28	05-15	09	46	10-07	10	33	02-18	21	43
—2005—			05-25	09	43Rx	10-17	10	28	02-28	22	26
01-10	26	20	06-04	09	33	10-27	10	29D	03-10	23	08
01-20	27	14	06-14	09	16	11-06	10	38	03-20	23	47
01-30	28	07	06-24	08	54	11-16	10	53	03-30	24	22
02-09	28	58	07-04	08	28	11-26	11	14	04-09	24	54
02-19	29	47	07-14	07	57	12-06	11	41	04-19	25	21
03-01	00≈	33	07-24	07	25	12-16	12	13	04-29	25	43
03-11	01	14	08-03	06	51	12-26	12	49	05-09	25	59
03-21	01	51	08-13	06	18	**—2008—**			05-19	26	10
03-31	02	22	08-23	05	47	01-05	13	29	05-29	26	14
04-10	02	46	09-02	05	20	01-15	14	12	06-08	26	12Rx
04-20	03	04	09-12	04	57	01-25	14	57	06-18	26	03
04-30	03	14	09-22	04	40	02-04	15	43	06-28	25	49
05-10	03	17Rx	10-02	04	29	02-14	16	28	07-08	25	30
05-20	03	13	10-12	04	25	02-24	17	13	07-18	25	07
05-30	03	02	10-22	04	28D	03-05	17	56	07-28	24	39
06-09	02	44	11-01	04	38	03-15	18	37	08-07	24	10
06-19	02	20	11-11	04	55	03-25	19	14	08-17	23	39
06-29	01	51	11-21	05	18	04-04	19	47	08-27	23	09
07-09	01	19	12-01	05	47	04-14	20	15	09-06	22	40
07-19	00	45	12-11	06	21	04-24	20	37	09-16	22	13
07-29	00	11	12-21	07	00	05-04	20	54	09-26	21	51
08-08	29vs	37	12-31	07	42	05-14	21	05	10-06	21	33
08-18	29	06	**—2007—**			05-24	21	09	10-16	21	20
08-28	28	39	01-10	08	28	06-03	21	07Rx	10-26	21	14
09-07	28vs	16Rx	01-20	09≈	15	06-13	20≈	58Rx	11-05	21≈	14D

Ephemeris, 1900–2050

da-mo	°	'	da-mo	°	'	da-mo	°	'	da-mo	°	'
2009 11-15	21≈	20	03-30	03✶	13	08-21	07✶	47℞	—**2014**—		
11-25	21	33	04-09	03	47	08-31	07	18	01-03	10✶	03
12-05	21	51	04-19	04	16	09-10	06	49	01-13	10	29
12-15	22	15	04-29	04	41	09-20	06	22	01-23	10	59
12-25	22	44	05-09	05	01	09-30	05	57	02-02	11	33
—**2010**—			05-19	05	16	10-10	05	35	02-12	12	08
01-04	23	17	05-29	05	26	10-20	05	18	02-22	12	45
01-14	23	54	06-08	05	29	10-30	05	06	03-04	13	23
01-24	24	33	06-18	05	27℞	11-09	05	00	03-14	14	01
02-03	25	15	06-28	05	18	11-19	04	59D	03-24	14	38
02-13	25	57	07-08	05	05	11-29	05	05	04-03	15	13
02-23	26	39	07-18	04	46	12-09	05	16	04-13	15	46
03-05	27	21	07-28	04	24	12-19	05	33	04-23	16	17
03-15	28	01	08-07	03	58	12-29	05	55	05-03	16	43
03-25	28	38	08-17	03	30	—**2013**—			05-13	17	06
04-04	29	12	08-27	03	00	01-08	06	21	05-23	17	23
04-14	29	43	09-06	02	31	01-18	06	52	06-02	17	36
04-24	00✶	09	09-16	02	03	01-28	07	26	06-12	17	43
05-04	00	30	09-26	01	38	02-07	08	02	06-22	17	45℞
05-14	00	46	10-06	01	16	02-17	08	40	07-02	17	42
05-24	00	56	10-16	00	58	02-27	09	18	07-12	17	33
06-03	00	59	10-26	00	46	03-09	09	57	07-22	17	19
06-13	00	57℞	11-05	00	40	03-19	10	35	08-01	17	01
06-23	00	49	11-15	00	39D	03-29	11	12	08-11	16	39
07-03	00	35	11-25	00	44	04-08	11	46	08-21	16	13
07-13	00	17	12-05	00	56	04-18	12	17	08-31	15	46
07-23	29≈	54	12-15	01	13	04-28	12	44	09-10	15	18
08-02	29	27	12-25	01	36	05-08	13	07	09-20	14	50
08-12	28	58	—**2012**—			05-18	13	26	09-30	14	24
08-22	28	29	01-04	02	03	05-28	13	39	10-10	14	00
09-01	27	59	01-14	02	34	06-07	13	48	10-20	13	40
09-11	27	30	01-24	03	08	06-17	13	50℞	10-30	13	23
09-21	27	04	02-03	03	45	06-27	13	47	11-09	13	12
10-01	26	42	02-13	04	24	07-07	13	38	11-19	13	06
10-11	26	24	02-23	05	04	07-17	13	25	11-29	13	06D
10-21	26	12	03-04	05	44	07-27	13	06	12-09	13	12
10-31	26	05	03-14	06	23	08-06	12	44	12-19	13	24
11-10	26	05D	03-24	07	00	08-16	12	19	12-29	13	40
11-20	26	10	04-03	07	35	08-26	11	51	—**2015**—		
11-30	26	22	04-13	08	07	09-05	11	23	01-08	14	02
12-10	26	40	04-23	08	36	09-15	10	55	01-18	14	28
12-20	27	03	05-03	09	00	09-25	10	28	01-28	14	58
12-30	27	31	05-13	09	19	10-05	10	03	02-07	15	31
—**2011**—			05-23	09	34	10-15	09	42	02-17	16	06
01-09	28	03	06-02	09	42	10-25	09	26	02-27	16	42
01-19	28	39	06-12	09	45	11-04	09	14	03-09	17	19
01-29	29	17	06-22	09	42℞	11-14	09	08	03-19	17	56
02-08	29	57	07-02	09	34	11-24	09	08D	03-29	18	32
02-18	00✶	37	07-12	09	21	12-04	09	13	04-08	19	07
02-28	01	18	07-22	09	02	12-14	09	25	04-18	19	39
03-10	01	59	08-01	08	40	12-24	09✶	41	04-28	20	09
03-20	02✶	37	08-11	08✶	14℞				05-08	20✶	34

da-mo	°	′	da-mo	°	′	da-mo	°	′	da-mo	°	′
2015 05-18	20♓	56	10-09	21♓	53℞	02-21	26♓	47	07-16	05♈	55℞
05-28	21	13	10-19	21	30	03-03	27	21	07-26	05	49
06-07	21	25	10-29	21	10	03-13	27	57	08-05	05	38
06-17	21	32	11-08	20	55	03-23	28	32	08-15	05	22
06-27	21	33℞	11-18	20	45	04-02	29	08	08-25	05	03
07-07	21	29	11-28	20	41	04-12	29	42	09-04	04	40
07-17	21	20	12-08	20	41D	04-22	00♈	15	09-14	04	14
07-27	21	06	12-18	20	48	05-02	00	45	09-24	03	48
08-06	20	47	12-28	21	00	05-12	01	12	10-04	03	20
08-16	20	25	—2017—			05-22	01	36	10-14	02	54
08-26	20	00	01-07	21	17	06-01	01	55	10-24	02	30
09-05	19	33	01-17	21	39	06-11	02	10	11-03	02	08
09-15	19	05	01-27	22	05	06-21	02	20	11-13	01	50
09-25	18	38	02-06	22	34	07-01	02	25	11-23	01	37
10-05	18	12	02-16	23	07	07-11	02	24℞	12-03	01	29
10-15	17	48	02-26	23	41	07-21	02	19	12-13	01	26
10-25	17	28	03-08	24	16	07-31	02	08	12-23	01	29D
11-04	17	13	03-18	24	53	08-10	01	53	—2020—		
11-14	17	02	03-28	25	28	08-20	01	34	01-02	01	37
11-24	16	57	04-07	26	03	08-30	01	11	01-12	01	50
12-04	16	57D	04-17	26	37	09-09	00	46	01-22	02	09
12-14	17	03	04-27	27	07	09-19	00	19	02-01	02	31
12-24	17	15	05-07	27	35	09-29	29♓	52	02-11	02	58
—2016—			05-17	27	59	10-09	29	25	02-21	03	28
01-03	17	32	05-27	28	20	10-19	29	01	03-02	04	00
01-13	17	53	06-06	28	35	10-29	28	39	03-12	04	34
01-23	18	19	06-16	28	46	11-08	28	20	03-22	05	09
02-02	18	49	06-26	28	51	11-18	28	06	04-01	05	44
02-12	19	21	07-06	28	51℞	11-28	27	57	04-11	06	19
02-22	19	56	07-16	28	46	12-08	27	54	04-21	06	53
03-03	20	32	07-26	28	36	12-18	27	56D	05-01	07	24
03-13	21	09	08-05	28	21	12-28	28	03	05-11	07	54
03-23	21	45	08-15	28	02	—2019—			05-21	08	20
04-02	22	21	08-25	27	40	01-07	28	16	05-31	08	42
04-12	22	54	09-04	27	15	01-17	28	34	06-10	09	00
04-22	23	26	09-14	26	48	01-27	28	57	06-20	09	14
05-02	23	54	09-24	26	21	02-06	29	23	06-30	09	23
05-12	24	19	10-04	25	54	02-16	29	53	07-10	09	26
05-22	24	40	10-14	25	29	02-26	00♈	25	07-20	09	25℞
06-01	24	56	10-24	25	06	03-08	00	59	07-30	09	18
06-11	25	08	11-03	24	47	03-18	01	34	08-09	09	06
06-21	25	14	11-13	24	33	03-28	02	09	08-19	08	50
07-01	25	15℞	11-23	24	23	04-07	02	44	08-29	08	30
07-11	25	10	12-03	24	19	04-17	03	18	09-08	08	07
07-21	25	00	12-13	24	21D	04-27	03	51	09-18	07	41
07-31	24	46	12-23	24	28	05-07	04	20	09-28	07	14
08-10	24	27	—2018—			05-17	04	47	10-08	06	47
08-20	24	05	01-02	24	40	05-27	05	10	10-18	06	21
08-30	23	40	01-12	24	57	06-06	05	28	10-28	05	57
09-09	23	13	01-22	25	19	06-16	05	43	11-07	05	36
09-19	22	45	02-01	25	46	06-26	05	52	11-17	05	19
09-29	22♓	18℞	02-11	26♓	15	07-06	05♈	56	11-27	05♈	06℞

Ephemeris, 1900–2050

2020

da-mo	°	'	da-mo	°	'	da-mo	°	'	da-mo	°	'
12-07	04♈	59℞	04-21	13♈	27	09-13	18♈	54℞	01-25	19♈	19
12-17	04	56 D	05-01	14	00	09-23	18	29	02-04	19	36
12-27	05	00	05-11	14	31	10-03	18	03	02-14	19	57
—2021—			05-21	15	00	10-13	17	36	02-24	20	23
01-06	05	09	05-31	15	25	10-23	17	09	03-06	20	51
01-16	05	23	06-10	15	46	11-02	16	43	03-16	21	23
01-26	05	41	06-20	16	03	11-12	16	20	03-26	21	57
02-05	06	05	06-30	16	16	11-22	16	00	04-05	22	32
02-15	06	32	07-10	16	24	12-02	15	44	04-15	23	08
02-25	07	02	07-20	16	26℞	12-12	15	33	04-25	23	43
03-07	07	34	07-30	16	23	12-22	15	28	05-05	24	18
03-17	08	08	08-09	16	15	**—2024—**			05-15	24	51
03-27	08	43	08-19	16	03	01-01	15	28D	05-25	25	22
04-06	09	18	08-29	15	46	01-11	15	33	06-04	25	50
04-16	09	53	09-08	15	25	01-21	15	44	06-14	26	14
04-26	10	26	09-18	15	01	01-31	16	00	06-24	26	35
05-06	10	58	09-28	14	35	02-10	16	21	07-04	26	51
05-16	11	26	10-08	14	08	02-20	16	46	07-14	27	02
05-26	11	52	10-18	13	41	03-01	17	14	07-24	27	09
06-05	12	14	10-28	13	15	03-11	17	45	08-03	27	09℞
06-15	12	32	11-07	12	51	03-21	18	19	08-13	27	05
06-25	12	45	11-17	12	31	03-31	18	53	08-23	26	55
07-05	12	53	11-27	12	15	04-10	19	29	09-02	26	41
07-15	12	56	12-07	12	03	04-20	20	04	09-12	26	22
07-25	12	54℞	12-17	11	57	04-30	20	39	09-22	26	00
08-04	12	46	12-27	11	56D	05-10	21	12	10-02	25	35
08-14	12	34	**—2023—**			05-20	21	42	10-12	25	08
08-24	12	17	01-06	12	01	05-30	22	10	10-22	24	40
09-03	11	57	01-16	12	11	06-09	22	35	11-01	24	13
09-13	11	33	01-26	12	27	06-19	22	56	11-11	23	47
09-23	11	08	02-05	12	47	06-29	23	12	11-21	23	24
10-03	10	41	02-15	13	11	07-09	23	24	12-01	23	05
10-13	10	14	02-25	13	39	07-19	23	31	12-11	22	50
10-23	09	48	03-07	14	10	07-29	23	32℞	12-21	22	40
11-02	09	24	03-17	14	42	08-08	23	28	12-31	22	36
11-12	09	04	03-27	15	17	08-18	23	19	**—2026—**		
11-22	08	47	04-06	15	52	08-28	23	05	01-10	22	37D
12-02	08	35	04-16	16	27	09-07	22	47	01-20	22	44
12-12	08	28	04-26	17	02	09-17	22	25	01-30	22	57
12-22	08	26D	05-06	17	35	09-27	22	00	02-09	23	14
—2022—			05-16	18	06	10-07	21	34	02-19	23	36
01-01	08	30	05-26	18	34	10-17	21	06	03-01	24	03
01-11	08	40	06-05	18	59	10-27	20	39	03-11	24	32
01-21	08	54	06-15	19	20	11-06	20	14	03-21	25	05
01-31	09	14	06-25	19	37	11-16	19	51	03-31	25	39
02-10	09	38	07-05	19	49	11-26	19	31	04-10	26	14
02-20	10	05	07-15	19	56	12-06	19	16	04-20	26	50
03-02	10	35	07-25	19	58℞	12-16	19	05	04-30	27	26
03-12	11	08	08-04	19	54	12-26	19	00	05-10	28	01
03-22	11	42	08-14	19	46	**—2025—**			05-20	28	35
04-01	12	17	08-24	19	33	01-05	19	01D	05-30	29	05
04-11	12♈	52	09-03	19♈	15℞	01-15	19♈	07	06-09	29♈	33

205

2026

da-mo	°	'
06-19	29♈	58
06-29	00♉	18
07-09	00	34
07-19	00	45
07-29	00	51
08-08	00	52℞
08-18	00	47
08-28	00	37
09-07	00	22
09-17	00	02
09-27	29♈	39
10-07	29	14
10-17	28	46
10-27	28	18
11-06	27	51
11-16	27	25
11-26	27	02
12-06	26	43
12-16	26	29
12-26	26	20
—2027—		
01-05	26	16
01-15	26	18D
01-25	26	26
02-04	26	39
02-14	26	57
02-24	27	20
03-06	27	47
03-16	28	17
03-26	28	50
04-05	29	25
04-15	00♉	01
04-25	00	38
05-05	01	14
05-15	01	49
05-25	02	23
06-04	02	54
06-14	03	22
06-24	03	47
07-04	04	07
07-14	04	23
07-24	04	34
08-03	04	39
08-13	04	39℞
08-23	04	34
09-02	04	23
09-12	04	08
09-22	03	48
10-02	03	25
10-12	02	58
10-22	02	30
11-01	02♉	02℞

da-mo	°	'
11-11	01♉	34℞
11-21	01	09
12-01	00	46
12-11	00	27
12-21	00	13
12-31	00	04
—2028—		
01-10	00	01
01-20	00	04D
01-30	00	12
02-09	00	26
02-19	00	45
02-29	01	09
03-10	01	37
03-20	02	08
03-30	02	42
04-09	03	17
04-19	03	54
04-29	04	31
05-09	05	08
05-19	05	44
05-29	06	18
06-08	06	49
06-18	07	18
06-28	07	42
07-08	08	03
07-18	08	19
07-28	08	29
08-07	08	35
08-17	08	35℞
08-27	08	29
09-06	08	18
09-16	08	02
09-26	07	41
10-06	07	17
10-16	06	50
10-26	06	22
11-05	05	53
11-15	05	25
11-25	04	59
12-05	04	36
12-15	04	18
12-25	04	04
—2029—		
01-04	03	56
01-14	03	53D
01-24	03	57
02-03	04	06
02-13	04	21
02-23	04	41
03-05	05	05
03-15	05♉	34

da-mo	°	'
03-25	06♉	06
04-04	06	40
04-14	07	17
04-24	07	54
05-04	08	32
05-14	09	10
05-24	09	46
06-03	10	20
06-13	10	52
06-23	11	21
07-03	11	46
07-13	12	07
07-23	12	23
08-02	12	34
08-12	12	39
08-22	12	39℞
09-01	12	33
09-11	12	21
09-21	12	05
10-01	11	43
10-11	11	19
10-21	10	51
10-31	10	22
11-10	09	53
11-20	09	25
11-30	08	59
12-10	08	36
12-20	08	17
12-30	08	04
—2030—		
01-09	07	56
01-19	07	54D
01-29	07	58
02-08	08	08
02-18	08	23
02-28	08	44
03-10	09	10
03-20	09	39
03-30	10	12
04-09	10	48
04-19	11	25
04-29	12	03
05-09	12	42
05-19	13	20
05-29	13	58
06-08	14	33
06-18	15	05
06-28	15	35
07-08	16	00
07-18	16	22
07-28	16	38
08-07	16♉	49

da-mo	°	'
08-17	16♉	54
08-27	16	54℞
09-06	16	47
09-16	16	35
09-26	16	18
10-06	15	57
10-16	15	32
10-26	15	04
11-05	14	34
11-15	14	04
11-25	13	35
12-05	13	09
12-15	12	46
12-25	12	27
—2031—		
01-04	12	14
01-14	12	06
01-24	12	04D
02-03	12	09
02-13	12	20
02-23	12	36
03-05	12	58
03-15	13	24
03-25	13	55
04-04	14	29
04-14	15	05
04-24	15	44
05-04	16	23
05-14	17	03
05-24	17	42
06-03	18	20
06-13	18	57
06-23	19	30
07-03	20	00
07-13	20	27
07-23	20	49
08-02	21	05
08-12	21	17
08-22	21	22
09-01	21	22℞
09-11	21	15
09-21	21	03
10-01	20	46
10-11	20	24
10-21	19	58
10-31	19	29
11-10	18	59
11-20	18	28
11-30	17	59
12-10	17	32
12-20	17	09
12-30	16♉	50℞

Ephemeris, 1900–2050

da-mo	°	′	da-mo	°	′	da-mo	°	′	da-mo	°	′
—2032—			05-23	26♉	28	10-15	06♊	00℞	02-27	07♊	14
01-09	16♉	36℞	06-02	27	10	10-25	05	37	03-08	07	27
01-19	16	29	06-12	27	50	11-04	05	09	03-18	07	47
01-29	16	28D	06-22	28	29	11-14	04	38	03-28	08	13
02-08	16	33	07-02	29	05	11-24	04	06	04-07	08	45
02-18	16	44	07-12	29	38	12-04	03	33	04-17	09	21
02-28	17	02	07-22	00♊	07	12-14	03	01	04-27	10	02
03-09	17	24	08-01	00	30	12-24	02	31	05-07	10	45
03-19	17	52	08-11	00	49	**—2035—**			05-17	11	31
03-29	18	23	08-21	01	02	01-03	02	06	05-27	12	19
04-08	18	58	08-31	01	09	01-13	01	45	06-06	13	07
04-18	19	36	09-10	01	09℞	01-23	01	31	06-16	13	56
04-28	20	16	09-20	01	03	02-02	01	23	06-26	14	43
05-08	20	56	09-30	00	51	02-12	01	22D	07-06	15	28
05-18	21	37	10-10	00	33	02-22	01	28	07-16	16	11
05-28	22	18	10-20	00	10	03-04	01	41	07-26	16	50
06-07	22	57	10-30	29♉	43	03-14	02	01	08-05	17	25
06-17	23	35	11-09	29	13	03-24	02	26	08-15	17	56
06-27	24	09	11-19	28	41	04-03	02	57	08-25	18	20
07-07	24	41	11-29	28	09	04-13	03	32	09-04	18	38
07-17	25	08	12-09	27	38	04-23	04	11	09-14	18	50
07-27	25	30	12-19	27	10	05-03	04	53	09-24	18	55
08-06	25	48	12-29	26	45	05-13	05	37	10-04	18	52℞
08-16	26	00	**—2034—**			05-23	06	23	10-14	18	42
08-26	26	06	01-08	26	25	06-02	07	09	10-24	18	25
09-05	26	06℞	01-18	26	12	06-12	07	54	11-03	18	02
09-15	26	00	01-28	26	04	06-22	08	39	11-13	17	34
09-25	25	47	02-07	26	03D	07-02	09	22	11-23	17	02
10-05	25	30	02-17	26	09	07-12	10	02	12-03	16	27
10-15	25	07	02-27	26	22	07-22	10	38	12-13	15	52
10-25	24	41	03-09	26	41	08-01	11	11	12-23	15	17
11-04	24	11	03-19	27	05	08-11	11	38	**—2037—**		
11-14	23	40	03-29	27	35	08-21	12	00	01-02	14	45
11-24	23	09	04-08	28	09	08-31	12	16	01-12	14	16
12-04	22	39	04-18	28	46	09-10	12	26	01-22	13	54
12-14	22	11	04-28	29	27	09-20	12	28℞	02-01	13	37
12-24	21	47	05-08	00♊	09	09-30	12	24	02-11	13	28
—2033—			05-18	00	53	10-10	12	13	02-21	13	26D
01-03	21	28	05-28	01	37	10-20	11	56	03-03	13	31
01-13	21	15	06-07	02	20	10-30	11	32	03-13	13	44
01-23	21	07	06-17	03	03	11-09	11	04	03-23	14	04
02-02	21	06D	06-27	03	44	11-19	10	33	04-02	14	31
02-12	21	12	07-07	04	21	11-29	09	59	04-12	15	04
02-22	21	24	07-17	04	56	12-09	09	25	04-22	15	42
03-04	21	42	07-27	05	26	12-19	08	52	05-02	16	24
03-14	22	06	08-06	05	52	12-29	08	21	05-12	17	09
03-24	22	34	08-16	06	12	**—2036—**			05-22	17	58
04-03	23	07	08-26	06	26	01-08	07	54	06-01	18	48
04-13	23	43	09-05	06	34	01-18	07	33	06-11	19	38
04-23	24	22	09-15	06	35℞	01-28	07	17	06-21	20	30
05-03	25	03	09-25	06	30	02-07	07	09	07-01	21	20
05-13	25♉	45	10-05	06♊	18℞	02-17	07♊	08 D	07-11	22♊	08

207

da-mo	°	′	da-mo	°	′	da-mo	°	′	da-mo	°	′
2037 07-21	22♊	54	12-13	01♋	41℞	04-26	08♋	22	09-18	01♌	53
07-31	23	37	12-23	01	03	05-06	09	03	09-28	02	39
08-10	24	15	—2039—			05-16	09	49	10-08	03	18
08-20	24	49	01-02	00	25	05-26	10	41	10-18	03	49
08-30	25	17	01-12	29♊	48	06-05	11	36	10-28	04	12
09-09	25	38	01-22	29	15	06-15	12	35	11-07	04	25
09-19	25	53	02-01	28	48	06-25	13	35	11-17	04	28℞
09-29	26	00	02-11	28	27	07-05	14	37	11-27	04	22
10-09	26	00℞	02-21	28	14	07-15	15	39	12-07	04	06
10-19	25	52	03-03	28	08	07-25	16	41	12-17	03	41
10-29	25	36	03-13	28	12D	08-04	17	41	12-27	03	08
11-08	25	14	03-23	28	23	08-14	18	39	—2042—		
11-18	24	46	04-02	28	43	08-24	19	33	01-06	02	30
11-28	24	14	04-12	29	10	09-03	20	22	01-16	01	48
12-08	23	38	04-22	29	44	09-13	21	07	01-26	01	04
12-18	23	01	05-02	00♋	24	09-23	21	44	02-05	00	21
12-28	22	25	05-12	01	09	10-03	22	15	02-15	29♋	41
—2038—			05-22	01	58	10-13	22	38	02-25	29	07
01-07	21	51	06-01	02	51	10-23	22	52	03-07	28	41
01-17	21	20	06-11	03	47	11-02	22	57	03-17	28	23
01-27	20	55	06-21	04	44	11-12	22	53℞	03-27	28	14
02-06	20	37	07-01	05	42	11-22	22	39	04-06	28	15 D
02-16	20	26	07-11	06	40	12-02	22	17	04-16	28	26
02-26	20	23D	07-21	07	36	12-12	21	48	04-26	28	47
03-08	20	27	07-31	08	31	12-22	21	13	05-06	29	17
03-18	20	40	08-10	09	23	—2041—			05-16	29	56
03-28	21	00	08-20	10	11	01-01	20	33	05-26	00♌	42
04-07	21	27	08-30	10	54	01-11	19	51	06-05	01	35
04-17	22	01	09-09	11	31	01-21	19	10	06-15	02	33
04-27	22	40	09-19	12	02	01-31	18	30	06-25	03	37
05-07	23	23	09-29	12	26	02-10	17	55	07-05	04	44
05-17	24	11	10-09	12	42	02-20	17	27	07-15	05	53
05-27	25	02	10-19	12	50	03-02	17	05	07-25	07	05
06-06	25	54	10-29	12	49℞	03-12	16	53	08-04	08	18
06-16	26	48	11-08	12	39	03-22	16	50D	08-14	09	30
06-26	27	42	11-18	12	22	04-01	16	56	08-24	10	41
07-06	28	36	11-28	11	56	04-11	17	12	09-03	11	50
07-16	29	28	12-08	11	25	04-21	17	36	09-13	12	56
07-26	00♋	18	12-18	10	48	05-01	18	09	09-23	13	57
08-05	01	05	12-28	10	09	05-11	18	49	10-03	14	53
08-15	01	48	—2040—			05-21	19	36	10-13	15	42
08-25	02	26	01-07	09	29	05-31	20	29	10-23	16	24
09-04	02	58	01-17	08	50	06-10	21	26	11-02	16	57
09-14	03	24	01-27	08	14	06-20	22	27	11-12	17	21
09-24	03	42	02-06	07	43	06-30	23	32	11-22	17	35
10-04	03	53	02-16	07	19	07-10	24	38	12-02	17	38℞
10-14	03	56℞	02-26	07	02	07-20	25	45	12-12	17	31
10-24	03	51	03-07	06	54	07-30	26	52	12-22	17	13
11-03	03	38	03-17	06	55D	08-09	27	58	—2043—		
11-13	03	17	03-27	07	04	08-19	29	02	01-01	16	46
11-23	02	50	04-06	07	22	08-29	00♌	03	01-11	16	12
12-03	02♋	18℞	04-16	07♋	49	09-08	01♌	01	01-21	15♌	31℞

208

da-mo	°	′	da-mo	°	′	da-mo	°	′	da-mo	°	′
2043 01-31	14♌	47℞	06-24	29♌	13	11-16	02♎	42	03-31	22♎	12℞
02-10	14	01	07-04	00♍	15	11-26	03	45	04-10	21	25
02-20	13	17	07-14	01	22	12-06	04	40	04-20	20	38
03-02	12	38	07-24	02	35	12-16	05	25	04-30	19	54
03-12	12	04	08-03	03	52	12-26	06	00	05-10	19	15
03-22	11	38	08-13	05	12	—2046—			05-20	18	43
04-01	11	22	08-23	06	34	01-05	06	24	05-30	18	19
04-11	11	16	09-02	07	56	01-15	06	36	06-09	18	07
04-21	11	21D	09-12	09	19	01-25	06	36℞	06-19	18	05D
05-01	11	36	09-22	10	41	02-04	06	24	06-29	18	14
05-11	12	01	10-02	12	00	02-14	06	02	07-09	18	34
05-21	12	35	10-12	13	16	02-24	05	29	07-19	19	05
05-31	13	18	10-22	14	28	03-06	04	49	07-29	19	46
06-10	14	09	11-01	15	33	03-16	04	04	08-08	20	36
06-20	15	07	11-11	16	32	03-26	03	17	08-18	21	34
06-30	16	11	11-21	17	22	04-05	02	30	08-28	22	39
07-10	17	19	12-01	18	03	04-15	01	47	09-07	23	50
07-20	18	32	12-11	18	34	04-25	01	09	09-17	25	07
07-30	19	47	12-21	18	53	05-05	00	39	09-27	26	27
08-09	21	04	12-31	19	01	05-15	00	20	10-07	27	51
08-19	22	22	—2045—			05-25	00	11	10-17	29	16
08-29	23	40	01-10	18♍	58℞	06-04	00	13D	10-27	00♏	42
09-08	24	57	01-20	18	43	06-14	00	26	11-06	02	08
09-18	26	11	01-30	18	17	06-24	00	51	11-16	03	32
09-28	27	22	02-09	17	42	07-04	01	26	11-26	04	53
10-08	28	28	02-19	17	01	07-14	02	11	12-06	06	10
10-18	29	28	03-01	16	15	07-24	03	04	12-16	07	22
10-28	00♍	22	03-11	15	28	08-03	04	06	12-26	08	27
11-07	01	08	03-21	14	41	08-13	05	14	—2048—		
11-17	01	44	03-31	13	59	08-23	06	29	01-05	09	25
11-27	02	11	04-10	13	24	09-02	07	48	01-15	10	14
12-07	02	27	04-20	12	57	09-12	09	11	01-25	10	53
12-17	02	32℞	04-30	12	40	09-22	10	36	02-04	11	21
12-27	02	25	05-10	12	34	10-02	12	03	02-14	11	38
—2044—			05-20	12	39D	10-12	13	31	02-24	11	43℞
01-06	02	08	05-30	12	55	10-22	14	57	03-05	11	37
01-16	01	41	06-09	13	22	11-01	16	22	03-15	11	20
01-26	01	06	06-19	13	59	11-11	17	44	03-25	10	54
02-05	00	24	06-29	14	46	11-21	19	02	04-04	10	18
02-15	29♌	39	07-09	15	41	12-01	20	14	04-14	09	37
02-25	28	52	07-19	16	44	12-11	21	20	04-24	08	52
03-06	28	07	07-29	17	54	12-21	22	17	05-04	08	06
03-16	27	26	08-08	19	09	12-31	23	06	05-14	07	22
03-26	26	52	08-18	20	28	—2047—			05-24	06	41
04-05	26	26	08-28	21	50	01-10	23	44	06-03	06	08
04-15	26	11	09-07	23	15	01-20	24	11	06-13	05	42
04-25	26	06D	09-17	24	42	01-30	24	26	06-23	05	26
05-05	26	11	09-27	26	08	02-09	24	30℞	07-03	05	20
05-15	26	28	10-07	27	33	02-19	24	21	07-13	05	25D
05-25	26	56	10-17	28	57	03-01	24	02	07-23	05	41
06-04	27	33	10-27	00♎	17	03-11	23	33	08-02	06	07
06-14	28♌	19	11-06	01♎	32	03-21	22♎	55℞	08-12	06♏	43

da-mo	°	'	da-mo	°	'	da-mo	°	'	da-mo	°	'
08-22	07♏	28	03-30	27♏	14℞	11-15	00♐	43	06-23	06♐	59℞
09-01	08	21	04-09	26	48	11-25	02	00	07-03	06	26
09-11	09	22	04-19	26	15	12-05	03	18	07-13	06	00
09-21	10	29	04-29	25	35	12-15	04	33	07-23	05	41
10-01	11	41	05-09	24	52	12-25	05	46	08-02	05	32
10-11	12	58	05-19	24	07	—2050—			08-12	05	33D
10-21	14	17	05-29	23	24	01-04	06	55	08-22	05	43
10-31	15	39	06-08	22	44	01-14	08	00	09-01	06	03
11-10	17	01	06-18	22	09	01-24	08	58	09-11	06	32
11-20	18	23	06-28	21	43	02-03	09	49	09-21	07	10
11-30	19	44	07-08	21	25	02-13	10	31	10-01	07	55
12-10	21	01	07-18	21	16	02-23	11	05	10-11	08	47
12-20	22	15	07-28	21	18D	03-05	11	29	10-21	09	46
12-30	23	24	08-07	21	30	03-15	11	42	10-31	10	49
—2049—			08-17	21	53	03-25	11	46℞	11-10	11	56
01-09	24	27	08-27	22	24	04-04	11	38	11-20	13	06
01-19	25	22	09-06	23	05	04-14	11	22	11-30	14	18
01-29	26	09	09-16	23	54	04-24	10	56	12-10	15	30
02-08	26	47	09-26	24	50	05-04	10	23	12-20	16	42
02-18	27	14	10-06	25	52	05-14	09	45	12-30	17♐	52
02-28	27	30	10-16	27	00	05-24	09	03			
03-10	27	35℞	10-26	28	11	06-03	08	20			
03-20	27♏	30℞	11-05	29♏	26	06-13	07♐	38℞			

2048

About the Author,

Zane B. Stein

I have been involved with astrology since 1969, and what I love most is astrological research. In November 1977, I read a story in the *New York Times* telling of the discovery of a "Tenth Planet," and I was excited, to say the least. Immediately, I wrote to Dr. Brian Marsden at the Smithsonian Astrophysical Observatory, who was kind enough to send me an ephemeris for the new body covering several months. I contacted Al H. Morrison, who had an associate of his translate the positions into zodiacal ones, and we began to study Chiron's transits. Dr. Marsden sent more complete ephemerides shortly, and we published these as soon as we could. In 1978, I organized the Association for Studying Chiron (ASC) which began collecting data and information about Chiron research from astrologers the world over. Very early, Chiron proved itself to be a major astrological influence.

This information was then printed in a newsletter, *The Key* (first issue March 31, 1979.) The ASC continued in its purpose until 1986, and during its existence a great wealth of information on Chiron was collected. (Plans are in the works to reprint The Key.)

The January 1981 issue of *Dell Horoscope* magazine published an article they had purchased from me, "Chiron: What Does It Mean To You?" (Incidentally, this was the first article I had ever sold to a magazine.) It introduced Chiron to the general astrological public, and included descriptions of Chiron through the natal houses. Dell liked this article so much that they republished it in their October 1984 issue and called it a "Notable Reprint."

August 25, 1981, I published, through the A.S.C., the first "Chiron Aspectarian," listing the major aspects of Chiron to the Sun and planets for 1901-2000. Calculations were done by Neil Michelsen of Astro Computing Services.

In 1983, with the help of my friend and mentor, the late Al H. Morrison, I published a pamphlet entitled "Interpreting Chiron," exploring what had been discovered about Chiron so far. Among other things, this included a section on Chiron through the houses, and the signs. This pamphlet was in high demand, and went through several printings over the next two years, but the demand for more information was even greater than that for this pamphlet. (More on the pamphlet in a moment.)

In 1985, Al published my book, "*Essence and Application: A View From Chiron*," which covered Chiron from every angle I could think of, including a guide to Chiron in each major aspect to the most important points in a person's chart. This book has become a classic, and is still the most quoted Chiron reference book in the world today.

After several reprints, Al and I decided to include "*Interpreting Chiron*" in future editions, so that the reader would have everything in one volume.

In May 1994, Al was the publisher of my "*Ephemeris of Pholus*," the second Centaur (discovered 1992), and several weeks later, my "*Ephemeris of Damocles*," a very unusual body, different than anything astronomers had ever seen before. As far as I know, these were the first publications of symbols for the above two bodies.

Pholus and Damocles reached a wider audience with the publication of my article, "*Chiron's Not Alone Anymore*" in the Leo 1994 issue of *Planet Earth* magazine.

The Feb. 1995 issue of *The Mountain Astrologer* included "*Hercules Unchained*," where I talk about Pholus, and the asteroid Heracles.

In May 1995, dear Al passed away, and did not leave me with a stock of books to sell. In fact, I was at a loss as to how to handle requests for "*Essence*." Then, my girlfriend Sandy suggested that I republish it myself. So, with the help of a friend with a scanner, I put my book on disk, made a few updates, and printed a limited edition, which quickly sold out. After several further small editions, it occurred to me how expensive it was to publish a small quantity of a book!

The Aquarius/Pisces 1996 issue of *Planet Earth* magazine contained my article, "*Einstein & Chiros*." In this, I show how Einstein expressed quite powerfully the principles of both Chiron and Pholus.

In the May/June 1997 issue of *Planet Earth*, I ran a tribute to my friend Al. If you want to find out a little of who he was, read "*Remembering Al H. Morrison*."

In the Aquarius/Pisces 1997 issue of *Planet Earth*, in my article, "*President Clinton's Second Term: Another Perspective*," I put forth the astrologically-based opinion that the President would not complete his term. My last two sentences: "In my opinion, he will not be stepping down due to ill health. Rather, it will have something to do with enemies he has made, and while he may be the victim of violence, I think the more likely cause will be impeachment."

Zane met and fell in love with a woman named Lynette while travelling around Australia in 2010, while transiting Chiron was trine his Sun. His request for a Visa was approved under a Chiron station, and his plane left to take him to his new home in Perth on August 18, 2011, the day his progressed Moon was exactly sextile his progressed Chiron. Zane and Lynette were married 5 November 2011, with Chiron sextile Zane's natal Chiron and trine Lynette's natal Moon.

Here is a partial list of books and other writings which have quoted, or referenced, some of my Chiron writings:

SECRETS FROM A STARGAZER'S NOTEBOOK by Debbi Kempton-Smith, Copyright 1982 by the author, published by Bantam Books

CHIRON, THE NEW PLANET IN YOUR HOROSCOPE by Richard Nolle, Copyright 1983 by the author, published by the American Federation of Astrologers

THE CONTINUING DISCOVERY OF CHIRON by Erminie Lantero, Copyright 1983 by the author, published by Samuel Weiser, Inc. (includes a Forward written by Zane B. Stein)

BIO OF A SPACE TYRANT by Piers Anthony, Copyright 1984 by the author, published by Avon Books

HOW TO RECTIFY A BIRTHCHART by Laurie Efrein, Copyright 1987 by the author, published by The Aquarian Press

CHIRON: RAINBOW BRIDGE BETWEEN THE INNER AND OUTER PLANETS by Barbara Hand Clow, Copyright 1987 by the author, published by Llewellyn Publications

ASTROLOGY FOR YOURSELF by Douglas Bloch & Demetra George, Copyright 1987 by the author, published by Wingbow Press

MECHANICS OF THE FUTURE: ASTEROIDS by Martha Lang Wescott, Copyright 1988 by the author, published by Treehouse Mountain Publications

CHIRON AND THE HEALING JOURNEY by Melanie Reinhart, Copyright 1989 by the author, published by The Penguin Group

WHOLENESS AND THE INNER MARRIAGE: The Chiron Sector and Relationship by Joyce Mason, Copyright 1992 by the author

MIDPOINT KEYS TO CHIRON by Chris Brooks, Copyright 1992 by the American Federation of Astrologers, published by the AFA

NEW INSIGHTS INTO ASTROLOGY by Nona Gwynn Press, Copyright 1993 by the author, published by Astro Communication Services

MYTHIC ASTROLOGY by Ariel Guttman & Kenneth Johnson, Copyright 1993 by the authors, published by Llewellyn Publications

THE ASTROLOGY ENCYCLOPEDIA by James R. Lewis, Copyright 1994 by Visible Ink Press, published by Visible Ink Press

ASTEROID NAME ENCYCLOPEDIA by Jacob Schwartz Ph.D., Copyright 1995 by the author, published by Llewellyn Publications

PHOLUS by Robert von Heeren and Dieter Koch, Copyright 1995 by Chiron Verlag, published by Chiron Verlag

THE CENTAUR PHOLUS by Marianne Alexander, Copyright 1996 by Pandora Publishing, published by Pandora Publishing

CHIRON EPHEMERIS WITH KEYS TO INTERPRETATION by Helen Adams Garrett & Rudy Flack, Copyright 1996 by the authors, published by A is A Publishing

COSMOS AND AIDS by Guy de Penguern, Copyright 1996 by AFA

THE MOON IN YOUR LIFE: BEING A LUNAR TYPE IN A SOLAR WORLD by Donna Cunningham, Copyright 1996 by the author, published by Samuel Weiser, Inc.

A HISTORY OF HOROSCOPIC ASTROLOGY by James Herschel Holden, Copyright 1996 by the Author, published by AFA

PRZESLANIE CHIRONA - Astrologiczna droga wewnetrznego uzdrowienia (translation: Chiron's Message. The astrological way of inner cure) by Piotr Piotrowski, Copyright 1997 by Studio Astropsychologii, published by Studio Astropsychologii, Bialystok (Poland)

AN EPHEMERIS FOR 1996 TL66 compiled by Philip Sedgwick, Copyright 1998 by the author, published by the author

PATTERNS OF THE PAST; THE BIRTHCHART, KARMA AND REINCARNATION by Judy Hall, Copyright 2000 by the author

THE CHIRON WORKSHOP given by Robert P. Blaschke, April 22, 2000

PATTERNS OF THE PAST by Judy Hall, Copyright 2001, Wessex Astrologer Ltd

CHIRON at 50: Return To The Scene Of The Crime by Cathy H. Burroughs, Copyright 2003 by the author.

MUSINGS OF A ROGUE COMET: CHIRON, PLANET OF HEALING by Martin Lass, Copyright 2003 by the author.

SOUL REFLECTIONS: MANY LIVES, MANY JOURNEYS by Marilyn C. Barrick, Copyright 2003 by the author and Summit University Press, published by Summit University Press

BRITISH ENTERTAINERS: THE ASTROLOGICAL PROFILES, THIRD EDITION by Frank C. Clifford, Copyright 2003 by the author, published by Flare Publications

CHIRON AND THE CENTAURS by Karen Drye, Copyright by the author.

CHIRON, THE WOUNDED HEALER by Rob Tillett, Copyright by the author.

CHIRON by Freya Owlsdottir, Copyright 2004 by the author.

ZODIAC BY DEGREES: 360 NEW SYMBOLS by Martin Goldsmith, Copyright 2004, Weiser Books.

ASTROLOGY AND THE ART OF HEALING by A.T. Mann, Copyright 2004 by the author, published by Paraview Press

THE TRUE PHILOSOPHER'S STONE by Suzzan Babcock, Copyright 2004 by Paul Magdalene, publisher AuthorHouse

CHIRON: HEALING BODY AND SOUL by Martin Lass, Copyright 2005, Weiser Books.

CHIRON: THE WISDOM OF A DEEPLY OPEN HEART by Adam Gainsburg, Copyright 2006 by Soulsign, published by Soulsign

ARABIAN PARTS FOR THE 21ST CENTURY: NEW FORMULAS FOR TODAY'S MEDICAL, TECHNOLOGICAL, AND SOCIAL CHALLENGES by Peggy Schick, copyright 2008 by the author, published by iUniverse, Inc.

INDEX

Better books make better astrologers.
Here are some of our other titles:

AstroAmerica's Daily Ephemeris, 2010-2020
AstroAmerica's Daily Ephemeris, 2000-2020
  - both for Midnight. Compiled & formatted by David R. Roell

Al Biruni
The Book of Instructions in the Elements of the Art of Astrology,
  1029 AD, translated by R. Ramsay Wright

David Anrias
Man and the Zodiac

Derek Appleby
Horary Astrology: The Art of Astrological Divination

E.H. Bailey
The Prenatal Epoch

Joseph Blagrave
Astrological Practice of Physick

C.E.O. Carter
The Astrology of Accidents
An Encyclopaedia of Psychological Astrology
Essays on the Foundations of Astrology
The Principles of Astrology, *Intermediate no. 1*
Some Principles of Horoscopic Delineation, *Intermediate no. 2*
Symbolic Directions in Modern Astrology
The Zodiac and the Soul

Charubel & Sepharial
Degrees of the Zodiac Symbolized, *1898*

H.L. Cornell
Encyclopaedia of Medical Astrology

Nicholas Culpeper
Astrological Judgement of Diseases from the Decumbiture of the
  Sick, *1655, and,* **Urinalia**, *1658*

Dorotheus of Sidon
Carmen Astrologicum, *c. 50 AD, translated by David Pingree*

Nicholas deVore
Encyclopedia of Astrology

Firmicus Maternus
Ancient Astrology Theory & Practice: Matheseos Libri VIII,
  c. 350 AD, translated by Jean Rhys Bram

Margaret Hone
The Modern Text-Book of Astrology

Alan Leo
The Progressed Horoscope, *1905*
The Key to Your Own Nativity, *1910*
Dictionary of Astrology, *edited by Vivian Robson, 1929*

William Lilly
Christian Astrology, books 1 & 2, *1647*
  The Introduction to Astrology, Resolution of all manner of questions.
Christian Astrology, book 3, *1647*
  Easie and plaine method teaching how to judge upon nativities.

Jean-Baptiste Morin
The Cabal of the Twelve Houses Astrological
  translated by George Wharton, edited by D.R. Roell

Claudius Ptolemy
Tetrabiblos, *c. 140 AD, translated by J.M. Ashmand*

Vivian Robson
Astrology and Sex
Electional Astrology
Fixed Stars & Constellations in Astrology
A Beginner's Guide to Practical Astrology
A Student's Text-Book of Astrology,
  Vivian Robson Memorial Edition

Diana Roche
The Sabian Symbols, A Screen of Prophecy

David Roell
Skeet Shooting for Astrologers

Richard Saunders
The Astrological Judgement and Practice of Physick, *1677*

Sepharial
The Manual of Astrology, the Standard Work
Primary Directions, a definitive study
Sepharial On Money. *For the first time in one volume, complete texts:*
  • **Law of Values**
  • **Silver Key**
  • **Arcana, or Stock and Share Key** — *first time in print!*

James Wilson, Esq.
Dictionary of Astrology

H.S. Green, Raphael & C.E.O. Carter
Mundane Astrology: *3 Books, complete in one volume.*

If not available from your local bookseller, order directly from:
The Astrology Center of America
207 Victory Lane
Bel Air, MD 21014

on the web at:
http://www.astroamerica.com

K σ n. node 143

CPSIA information can be obtained at www.ICGtesting.com
Printed in the USA
LVOW11s0244140916

504534LV00001B/90/P